INSTITUTIONAL DESIGN AND PARTY GOVERNMENT IN POST-COMMUNIST EUROPE

COMPARATIVE POLITICS

Comparative Politics is a series for students, teachers, and researchers of political science that deals with contemporary government and politics. Global in scope, books in the series are characterized by a stress on comparative analysis and strong methodological rigour. The series is published in association with the European Consortium for Political Research. For more information visit www.ecprnet.eu

The Comparative Politics series is edited by Kenneth Carty, Professor of Political Science, University of British Columbia; Ferdinand Müller-Rommel, Director of the Center for the Study of Democracy, Leuphana University; and Emilie van Haute, Professor of Political Science, Université libre de Bruxelles.

OTHER TITLES IN THIS SERIES

Representing the People
A Survey Among Members of Statewide and Substate Parliaments
Edited by Kris Deschouwer and Sam Depauw

New Parties in Old Party Systems
Persistence and Decline in Seventeen Democracies
Nicole Bolleyer

The Limits of Electoral Reform
Shaun Bowler and Todd Donovan

The Challenges of Intra-Party Democracy
Edited by William P. Cross and Richard S. Katz

If Money Talks, What Does it Say?
Corruption and Business Financing of Political Parties
Iain McMenamin

The Gendered Effects of Electoral Institutions
Political Engagement and Participation
Miki Caul Kittilson and Leslie A. Schwindt-Bayer

The Strain of Representation
How Parties Represent Diverse Voters in Western and Eastern Europe
Robert Rohrschneider and Stephen Whitefield

Party Patronage and Party Government in European Democracies
Edited by Petr Kopecký, Peter Mair, and Maria Spirova

Organizing Democratic Choice
Party Representation Over Time
Ian Budge, Michael McDonald, Paul Pennings, and Hans Keman

Challenging the State
Devolution and the Battle for Partisan Credibility
A Comparison of Belgium, Italy, Spain, and the United Kingdom
Sonia Alonso

Institutional Design and Party Government in Post-Communist Europe

CSABA NIKOLENYI

ecpr

OXFORD
UNIVERSITY PRESS

OXFORD
UNIVERSITY PRESS

Great Clarendon Street, Oxford, OX2 6DP,
United Kingdom

Oxford University Press is a department of the University of Oxford. It furthers the University's objective of excellence in research, scholarship, and education by publishing worldwide. Oxford is a registered trade mark of Oxford University Press in the UK and in certain other countries

First Edition published in 2014

Impression: 1

Published in the United States of America by Oxford University Press
198 Madison Avenue, New York, NY 10016, United States of America

British Library Cataloguing in Publication Data
Data available

Library of Congress Control Number: 2013956533

ISBN 978–0–19–967530–2

Printed in Great Britain by
CPI Group (UK) Ltd, Croydon, CR0 4YY

To my Andrea,

שִׂימֵנִי כַחוֹתָם עַל לִבֶּךָ כַּחוֹתָם עַל זְרוֹעֶךָ כִּי עַזָּה כַמָּוֶת אַהֲבָה
(שיר השירים 8:6)

Acknowledgements

I owe a deep gratitude to my colleagues, friends, students, and my family whose encouragement and support has made this book possible. My very special thanks to Ken Carty, Reuven Hazan, Bernard Grofman, Steven B. Wolinetz, Keith Dowding, Shaul Shenhav, Ian McAllistar, Bjorn-Erik Rasch, Hanna Beck, and Patrick Dumont for their comments and feedback on earlier drafts in conferences, workshops, and seminars. The Department of Political Science at the Hebrew University, the Department of Political Science at Concordia University, and the Center for European Studies of the Australian National University provided me with opportunities to present and discuss the work at different stages. My research would not have been possible without the generous financial assistance provided by the Social Sciences and Humanities Research Council of Canada, Concordia University, and the Center for European Studies of the Australian National University. I was fortunate to have at my disposal the able and dedicated assistance of a number of graduate and undergraduate research assistants from the Department of Political Science at Concordia University. My very special thanks to Dr Marat Grebennikov, Nancy Yacoub, Randy Pinsky, and Brent Gerchicoff. I am indebted to Oxford University Press for the reviewers' helpful comments as well as the speed and efficiency of the editorial team. Any mistake, error of commission, or omission remains, of course, my own. Concordia University's Faculty of Arts of Science allowed me to spend time away from my teaching and service duties and accept a Visiting Fellowship from the Center for European Studies of the Australian National University during the critical final stage of finishing the manuscript in December 2012.

My wife, Andrea, was a constant source of support and encouragement in times of doubt. My work would never haven been completed without her help and questioning spirit. My father, Gabor, Zsuzsanna, and my in-laws, Drs Csilla and George Gondos have been supportive in many more ways than one can imagine to help my dreams come true. My interest in political life was inspired by my dear mother, Edit, who passed away much too young and early to see this work completed. I remain in her debt forever.

Contents

List of Figures

List of Tables

1

Introduction

1.1 MULTI-PARTY GOVERNMENT IN EAST CENTRAL EUROPE

In their seminal study on the politics of multi-party government, Laver and Schofield pointed out that "[f]or most of Western Europe, the politics of coalition lie at the heart of business of representative government" (1990: 1). Twenty years later Strom, Müller-Rommel and Bergman have reiterated the same point by noting that "[o]ver the course of the twentieth century, the proportional version of parliamentarism has become the most common form of democratic governance, and nowhere is it more dominant than in Western Europe. . . . Because proportional systems rarely reward any party with a parliamentary majority, this form of government depends on and is conducive to inter-party bargaining over high stakes" (2010: 403). Evidently, there is no denying of the importance of coalition politics in Western Europe. However, proportional parliamentarism has become an equally common and dominant form of organizing the new post-communist democracies of East and Central Europe (ECE), and yet a systematic study of post-communist party coalition is sorely lacking in the comparative literature (Müller-Rommel, Fettelschoss and Harfst 2004). Similarly to Western Europe, representative government in ECE is quintessentially *multi-party government*, meaning that major decisions, policies and personnel appointments are made and controlled by coalitions of political parties that support, and make up, the government (Katz 1986). The ability of political parties to wrest decisive control over governments in the new European democracies is especially impressive given the well-documented weakness of their organizational structures and lack of stable electoral following (Rose 1995; Epperly 2011).

This book fills a growing gap in the literature on party coalitions in parliamentary systems of government by providing a comparative study, in a single framework, on how parties form and maintain electoral, parliamentary and executive coalitions in the ten post-communist democracies: Bulgaria, Czech Republic, Estonia, Hungary, Latvia, Lithuania, Poland, Romania, Slovakia, and Slovenia. Although the specific processes and timing of democratic political reforms, including the development of competitive multi-party systems, varied across the ten cases in their minute details, they all experienced fundamentally similar transformations as they moved from a thereto closed political system, Leninist authoritarianism, to one where political power became contested at the ballot box through an organized electoral process. These changes started at the same point in time, in the early 1990s when the first multi-party elections took place in each of the ten states, and reached a moment of maturity a decade and a half later when eight states (Czech Republic, Estonia, Hungary, Latvia, Lithuania, Poland, Slovakia, and Slovenia) were admitted to the European Union in 2004 followed by the admission of Bulgaria and Romania in 2007. During the twenty-three years (1990–2013) that have passed since democratization started in ECE, a total of sixty-five parliamentary elections took place in the ten states and 103 Prime Ministers led party governments.[1] The data set that forms the empirical base of this study includes party coalitions that were formed in all ECE elections and legislatures that had completed their term by 2010; in other words the temporal scope of this study is the first two complete decades following the transition to multi-party democracy.

This set of ECE party coalitions constitutes an excellent laboratory of cases to examine the unfolding dynamics of coalition politics in newly democratizing states. Specifically, I am interested in examining how the fundamental constitutional and institutional choices that were made at the time of the regime change in the ten states shaped the politics of coalition formation and party government. As I demonstrate later on, no two among the ten states adopted the same institutional mix to govern their post-communist political processes. Yet, some patterns do emerge with regard to the basic institutional choices that constitutional engineers made at the time of the transition. I will argue that the ten states fall in three clearly distinguishable groups with regard to the degree to which their electoral, parliamentary and executive institutions concentrate political power in a coalition that controls a legislative majority. Four states (Bulgaria, Estonia, Hungary, and Slovenia) make up the group with the highest level of power concentration, followed by an intermediate category (consisting of Latvia and Slovakia), and then a group of four states (Czech Republic, Lithuania, Poland, and Romania) where the political institutions are designed to disperse and separate rather than concentrate political power. In turn, these basic institutional variations matter because they present very different sets of institutional constraints under which political parties form, maintain and terminate governments: the more the institutions concentrate political power the harder the constraints on political parties and the stronger the incentives for them to build and sustain majority cabinets in office.

The central claim of this book is that *differences in the arrangement of political institutions systematically explain variations in patterns of multi-party government across the post-communist democracies.* Specifically, I argue that the institutional dispersion of political power matters for the emerging practice of party government in these new democracies: electoral systems, parliamentary structures and the nature of the presidency create exogenous institutional constraints under which the dynamics of coalition politics and party government unfold. In other words, my argument is that variations in institutional design, and specifically, the level of power dispersion, help explain: (i) when political parties begin the coalition formation process (before or after the electoral process); (ii) how large the governing coalitions become (majority versus minority); (iii) how durable these coalitions prove to be; (iv) and how successful they are in securing the election of a coalition candidate to the presidency in those states (Czech Republic, Estonia, Hungary, and Latvia) where the constitution requires the legislature to choose the head of state.

To foreshadow the findings of the successive chapters that follow, I will show that institutional structures that concentrate political power in a parliamentary majority tend to lead to large electoral coalitions, majority governments, stable cabinet coalitions, and fewer instances of divided government. Conversely, states with institutions that disperse political power from a parliamentary majority tend to have smaller electoral coalitions; they tend to have more minority cabinets; they will have more frequently changing government coalitions; and more instances of divided government. The concept of institutionally designed power dispersion and power concentration builds on Lijphart's seminal distinction between majoritarian and consensus democracy. However, it also departs from it in two significant ways. First, while all ten post-communist democracies belong to Lijphart's consensus type, my analysis brings out important variations among the ten cases. Second, whereas Lijphart's catalogue of political institutions, on the basis of which he establishes the binary distinction between majoritarian and consensus regimes, is driven by empirical observation, my notion of institutional power concentration is rooted in a theoretical understanding of the lifecycle of parliamentary party government (Bergman 2010). Every stage of this lifecycle takes place in a specific institutional setting that is constrained by the institutions which defines its boundaries and operations. These settings are the electoral, the parliamentary and the executive arenas, the institutions of which I look at when I define the measurement of institutional power concentration.

The relative lack of scholarly output about coalition politics in the region stands in sharp contrast to the voluminous literatures covering other areas of party politics in these new democracies, specifically voting and electoral behavior (Tworzecki 2004, Tucker 2006), party organization (Biezen 2003; Kopecky 2006), and the role of social cleavages in the structuring of patterns of party competition (Kitschelt 1992; Evans and Whitefield 1993, 2000; Kitschelt et al 1999; Lawson et al 1999; Whitefield 2002; Zielinski 2002; Evans 2006; Rohrschnedier and Whitefield 2009). The central thrust of these literatures has been to show the substantively and qualitatively distinct nature of party politics in ECE compared to Western Europe. As such, scholars have tended to emphasize that political parties in the region are weak and poorly institutionalized; that voters are fickle and lack durable attachment and loyalty to political parties; and that programmatic competition among parties is often overshadowed by considerations and dimensions of conflict that are not, or not always, related to questions about policy and ideology.

Indeed, there are good reasons why party development in ECE was a process fraught with challenges and difficulties. Unresolved issues about the inherited legacies of the authoritarian past; the pressing need to institute and deal with the often difficult consequences of critical social, economic and political reforms; as well as the geo-political tensions arising from the location of the ECE region between competing regional powers, the Euro-Atlantic community to the West, and Russia to the East, imposed severe constraints both on the development of stable and efficient democratic political institutions as well as on the range of values choices to structure political behavior. Political parties were particularly hard-pressed by these challenges. Decades of communist rule not only effectively destroyed what may have remained of the bonds between the pre-war historic political parties and their social constituents but also created masses of de-politicized citizens. Similarly, communist authoritarianism also incapacitated autonomous social organizations that could provide an anchoring and a base for the development of political parties in the new democratic era (Evans and Whitefield 1993; Kitschelt 1995). Of course, there was neither a uniform Leninist legacy nor a single post-Lenininst path to democratization and democratic consolidation: democratic politics in the states of ECE after 1990 has remained no less diverse than either the practices of communist rule or the pre-communist experiments with representative government had been before (Chirot 1991; Kitshcelt et al 1992; Schopflin 1993; Rotschild and Wingfield 2008).

Although the euphoria of regime change initially encouraged voters to flock to the ballot box in large numbers during the immediate post-transition elections, rates of electoral participation dropped significantly and consistently across the region thereafter (Kostadinova 2003) as has citizens' professed trust in both political parties as well as the governments that they formed (Rose 1995). Wherever they resurfaced after the fall of communism, historic political parties, i.e. parties that claimed organizational continuity predating the communist era, all but disappeared after the first few initial electoral rounds (Geddes 1995: 243–7). The new political parties that came into being after the fall of communism have not performed much better either in terms of institutionalizing their organizational structures and stabilizing their electorates. As a result, high levels of electoral volatility, organizational instability and frequent turnover of parliamentary deputies have become the hallmark of the party systems of the new democracies of the region. Indeed, ECE remains cited as the region with one of the highest levels of electoral volatility and party system under-institutionalization in the democratic world (Olson 1998; Birch 2003; Juberias 2004; Tavits 2005; Epperly 2011).

These findings imply that party politics in the new European democracies is fundamentally different from party politics in the mature democracies of Western Europe. Yet, when it comes to the practice of party *qua* coalition government, political parties in ECE are actually very similar both in their motivation and behavior to parties in the West. In spite of their weaknesses, ECE parties maintain control over government in the new democracies no less than they do in the mature democracies of Western Europe: not only do they play a central role in structuring and organizing electoral competition but they also provide alternative government proposals before the voters, and, most importantly for the present volume, they fill and make the institutions of representative government work. In terms of party and coalition government, Eastern and Western Europe converge: much like in the West, the overwhelming majority of governments in ECE are formed by multi-party coalitions.

Katz (1987: 7–8) argues that there are three prior conditions which political parties themselves must meet in order for party government to be present in the first place: they must exhibit cohesive team-like behavior; they must attempt to win control over all political power; and they must base their claims to legitimacy on the results of competitive elections. The more that political parties meet these basic standards of "partyness" the more "partyness" they can lend to government in turn. Conversely, where political parties fail to act as a team, where factionalism and internal divisions severely inhibit party cohesion; where political parties abandon their claim to power to other bodies, such as a directly elected non-partisan president, the bureaucracy, or the social partners characteristic of neo-corporatist models of interest intermediation; where political parties replace electoral success with non-democratic and non-representative sources of legitimacy, such as charismatic leadership, government can be hardly seen to be under the control of parties. Political parties in ECE unequivocally meet these conditions. Their frequent internal disputes, dissent and even fission notwithstanding, political parties in the post-communist democracies are not a collection of uncoordinated individuals with "a well-rooted tradition of individualism and non-solidarity among parliamentarians" (Reif 1987: 21) of the kind that prevented Fourth Republic France from having a party government model in place. Quite the contrary, parties in the ECE have mass corporate membership, separate from the following of individual deputies and candidates for office, even though party membership has been on the decline all over Europe; they do have clearly identifiable extra-parliamentary organizational structures that are integrated with the parliamentary party groups; and their deputies in parliament and ministers in cabinet act in a concerted team-like fashion (Kopecky 2000; Malova and Krause 2000; Ilonszki 2000; Fettelschoss and Nikolenyi 2008).

This general pattern of convergence with the West European model of coalition government, however, conceals at least five important differences and variations *among* the new democracies: it is precisely these variations that form the foundation of this book. First, even though the average level of parliamentary fragmentation in ECE is not significantly higher than that in Western Europe, some ECE states have had considerably more fragmented parliaments than others. For example, while the effective number of parties in the post-communist Bulgarian and Hungarian parliaments has been around three for the 1990–2010 period, the level of fragmentation is almost twice as high in Latvia and Slovenia. Therefore, the contexts that the numeric format of the party system provides for the formation and operation of multi-party governments vary considerably across the region.

Second, in some states (e.g. Hungary and Bulgaria) political parties contest elections by forming pre-electoral alliances which, depending on the outcome of the elections, may form the basis of government formation talks after the polls are over. Elsewhere, such alliances are either explicitly forbidden (Estonia) or they are discouraged by the electoral rules (e.g. Czech Republic and Slovakia). In yet other cases, electoral coalitions may play a significant role in the electoral process but their members do not stay together for the purposes of forming the new post-election government. A case in point is the electoral alliance between the Humanist Party and the Social Democratic Party in Romania, which failed to agree to forming a coalition government in 2004 in spite of having won the largest number of seats in the newly elected parliament (Samuels and Shugart 2010:2).

Third, while most of the time political parties form majority governments, in four countries (Czech Republic, Latvia, Poland, and Romania), minority governments are formed just as or even more often. In the immediate aftermath of the transitions to democracy, minority governments were a frequent election outcome in the entire region. However, in these four states they have become a regularly recurring feature of coalition politics even after the initial post-transition period. As Strom (1990) notes in his seminal study, minority governments are problematic in a parliamentary democracy because the latter operates with the norms and institutions of majority rule. An undersized cabinet clearly violates both. Yet, in some states minority governments tend to occur as a matter of routine while elsewhere they are unheard of. In yet other states the formation of a minority government may indicate a temporary bargaining failure, crises or an ad hoc aberration. There is a lot of evidence, however, suggesting that regardless of their seemingly anomalous characters minority cabinets represent a rational solution to a government formation process in Western Europe (Strom 1984, 1990) as well as in the East (Nikolenyi 2003).

Fourth, the new ECE democracies also vary in terms of the stability of their governments. For instance, whereas Hungarian and Slovak cabinets often lasted nearly their full term for the past twenty years, those in Latvia and Lithuania have tended to stay just a little over a year in office. Countries also differ as to the type of instability that rocks the incumbent governments. In some cases, cabinet instability is limited to changes within the same coalition that came to power after the general election (e.g. Poland) while in other countries it is not uncommon to see alternative coalitions replace each other in quick succession with the same inter-election period (e.g. Latvia).

Finally, a fifth source of variation pertains to the politics of divided government. In five cases (Bulgaria, Lithuania, Poland, Romania, and Slovenia) the post-communist constitution provides for a direct election of the head of state while in four states (Czech Republic, Estonia, Hungary, Latvia) the head of state is chosen indirectly by members of parliament or a broader electoral college

(Estonia). Slovakia is the only state in the region where the manner of choosing the president changed, in 1999, from the indirect parliamentary to the direct electoral method.[2] These constitutional differences have direct bearing on the ability of the governing coalition to have its presidential candidate (s)elected to be head of state and thus avoid a split in executive control. Even though the post-communist democracies have instituted parliamentary or semi-presidential forms of government with relatively weak institutional powers attached to the office of the presidency, compared to what we find in many former Soviet republics and in Latin America, post-communist presidents have still succeeded to wield considerable political power and influence from time to time (Baylis 1996; Taras 1997; Tavits 2009). Therefore, incumbent governments always care a lot about the outcome of the presidential contest and seek to secure the (s)election of their preferred candidate.

1.2 AN INSTITUTIONAL APPROACH TO THE STUDY OF COALITION GOVERNMENTS

The central argument of this book is that differences in the practice of coalition government across the ten ECE democracies are the result of the different ways in which parliamentary government has been instituted and designed. In other words, *patterns of coalition government reflect patterns of the institutional design of parliamentary government* in the ten states. As stated earlier, all of these new democracies opted for a parliamentary or semi-presidential instead of a presidential model of government at the time of transition. However, the details of the design differ considerably across the states. As I shall argue, it is these institutional differences that drive the variation in the cross-national practices of coalition politics that we reviewed above.

1.2.1 Institutions and Party Government

There are two main compelling reasons in favor of the adoption of an institutional approach. The first is methodological: the ten new democracies have adopted a diverse range of constitutional structures and political institutions which provide the researcher with an excellent opportunity to test the relationship between alternative institutional variables on the one hand and different *degrees* and *types* of party government on the other. The importance of the relationship between national political institutions and party government has already been stressed in the literature on Western Europe; however, to date there has been no attempt at a systematic exploration of this relationship across the East/West divide on the continent (Katz 1986: 17; Blondel and Cotta 1996: 11–12). The singular exceptions to this are the studies by Schleiter and Morgan-Jones (2009a, 2010) who examine the specific impact of parliamentary and semi-presidential systems of government on one particular aspect of party government in 28 European democracies: the appointment of non-partisan cabinet ministers. They find that semi-presidential systems tend to have more non-partisan ministers than purely parliamentary systems, and as a result they have a weaker nexus between party and government. This resonates well with earlier arguments made by Fiorina (1987), who characterizes the United States, a presidential democracy, as extremely low in party government, and by Katz (1996) who notes that

> [i]n contrast to the strong parties and clear lines of authority in the party government model, the Madisonian model is hostile to cohesive parties and is founded on divided and overlapping authority. Most centrally, the independent election, fixed terms, and extensive powers of the American president mean that American governments do not require a stable supporting coalition of the kind assumed by the conventional parliamentary model. (202)

Whether or not semi-presidential constitutions promote party government is complicated by evidence from France where party government developed precisely at the same time and because of the adoption of a directly elected powerful presidency at the dawn of the Fifth Republic (Reif 1987). In contrast to what the findings of Schleiter and Morgan-Jones imply, Katz (1987: 21) actually argues that the French semi-presidential system does not weaken party government because the head of state ultimately must govern through a prime minister and a cabinet that are dependent on the support of the legislature where majorities are organized and coordinated by parties and the coalitions that they form. All of these studies are unequivocal in claiming that a parliamentary system of government provides the best foundation for the development of strong party government.

A related complication has to do with the lack of consensus on what exactly defines a semi-presidential constitution. On the one hand, Elgie (1999) proposes an extremely minimalist definition according to which the criterion of semi-presidentialism is met if "a popularly elected, fixed term president exists alongside a prime minister and cabinet who are responsible to parliament." The above quoted studies by Schleiter and Morgan-Jones rely on this definition, which leads them to lump together in the same category cases as widely different as Russia and Slovakia, both of which have directly elected presidents, albeit with an extremely different level of power and authority attached to them. In contrast, Duverger's classic (1980) definition of semi-presidentialism consists of the following "three elements: (1) the president of the republic is elected by universal suffrage, (2) he possesses quite considerable powers; (3) he has opposite him, however, a prime minister and ministers who possess executive and governmental power and can stay in office only if the parliament does not show its opposition to them" (166). In short, for Duverger presidential powers matter, while for Elgie the mode of selection is critical.

With regard to the type of party government Katz (1987) and Reif (1987) identify three basic models: the bipolar, the coalitional and the dominant party government. The first model can be found in states where parliamentary elections tend to produce a clear winner: either a single party or a coalition tends to win a majority or at least a substantial plurality of the seats to make sure that the outcome of the election is clear and decisive. The electoral contest involves two major parties or two major blocs of parties and the voters decide directly which one of them will form the next government. In the bipolar party government model the chain of delegation connecting the voter and the executive is direct and uninterrupted by inter-party negotiations and coalition formation following the elections. To the extent that parties engage in post-election bargaining they do so more with regard to the allocation of specific cabinet portfolios and less in order to decide which set of parties will form the next executive. In Western Europe the bipolar model can be found, for instance, in England, Germany, Spain and Portugal, while Hungary is the clearest example of this model among the post-communist states. A detailed discussion about the development of the Hungarian case is provided in Chapter Four.

The other two models of party government, coalitional and dominant party, can be found in states where elections fail to produce a clear winner and parties have to negotiate the formation of the new government based on their respective policy positions and the bargaining power that their parliamentary seats afford. The difference between the two models has to do with the absence or presence of a privileged political party that tends to be in all or most coalitions that are formed. Where such a party is absent, parties can and will form alternative coalitions often within the same inter-election period, however, the presence of a dominant party will limit the range of coalition options possible. Examples of the coalitional party government in Western Europe include Belgium, and Holland, while Italy prior to 1993 is perhaps the best example of the dominant party government model. In ECE, the coalitional party government model has clearly prevailed in the Czech Republic while the pivotal position of the Liberal Democratic Party kept Slovenia an example of the dominant party government model during the first post-transition decade. Political institutions exert an important and powerful effect on the *type* of party government. The most important role in this regard is played by the electoral system rather than executive–legislative relations: single member as well as high threshold proportional representation electoral systems promote the bipolar model whereas lower threshold PR systems push for either the coalitional or the dominant party government model (Katz 1987: 17).

The post-communist ECE democracies show remarkable variation in terms of the main national political institutions, which affect both the degree and type of party government. With regard to the electoral system, it is evident that proportional representation (PR) is by far the most popular choice of electoral system in the post-communist region. In fact, only two of the ten states (Hungary and Lithuania) have used mixed-member electoral systems for all of their post-transition elections, although Bulgaria also used a mixed system to elect members of the constituent assembly in 1991. Recent electoral reforms in two states (Romania and Bulgaria) have introduced majoritarian elements without altering the essentially PR character of the existing electoral systems (Nikolenyi 2011). Notwithstanding this overall convergence on PR, the ten new democracies show considerable variation with regard to the specific design of their electoral systems. These differences are manifested in the choice of rules on the electoral registration and recognition of political parties, assembly size, the treatment of electoral coalitions, district magnitude, the ability of voters to alter the list of candidates that parties run, and the use of the mathematical formulae that covert votes into seats (Lijphart 1994; Gallagher and Mitchell 2005; Farrel 2011).

Concerning the election and powers of the presidency, six of ten ECE democracies have a directly elected president (Bulgaria, Lithuania, Poland, Romania, Slovakia since 1999 and Slovenia) while in the other four states (Czech Republic until 2013, Estonia, Hungary, and Latvia) parliament or some other electoral college chooses the head of state. Among the countries that have a directly elected head of state, the principal variation is the electoral timetable, i.e. the relative temporal proximity of presidential and legislative elections. As a matter of institutional design, Romania was the only state where the two sets of elections were held concurrently until 2004. Thereafter, a constitutional amendment which extended the length of the presidents' term in office from four to five years effectively decoupled presidential from legislative polls. In all other cases the two elections are held separately, although due to unforeseen circumstances, such as an early legislative election or presidential impeachment (Lithuania 2004), the electoral timetable may be disturbed with the result that the elections are held closer to one another.

Among the four states that elect the head of state indirectly, there are differences with regard to the number of rounds and the number of votes that a winning candidate is required to have. The Czech Republic is the only state with a bicameral parliament that selects the head of state indirectly and Estonia is exceptional in that failure on the part of the legislature leaves the ultimate choice to a broader electoral college consisting of representatives of local governments. Interestingly, there is no variation with regard to the electoral system used in the states that elected the head of state directly: all six states use a two-round majority system.

Presidencies differ not only in terms of the method of their election but also in terms of the actual powers of their office. The literatures on comparative and post-communist presidencies have no shortage of indices to measure presidential powers (Shugart and Carey 1992; Lucky 1994; McGregor 1994; Siaroff 1995; Hellmann 1996; Fry 1997; Beliaev 2006). Although there is no consensus on the best way of scoring and quantifying them, these studies clearly show the differences across the states: whereas some presidents are merely ceremonial figure-heads (e.g. Slovakia, Estonia), others may be more powerful (e.g. Czech Republic, Poland) and these differences often do not coincide with the method of presidential selection.

In terms of these foundational institutional choices, the ECE democracies show both similarities to and differences from their West European counterparts. As for the electoral system, PR is clearly the dominant choice in both ECE and in Western Europe. However, three West European states have electoral systems that do not have an equivalent at all in ECE: England's first-past-the-post, France's majority-run-off; and Ireland's single transferable vote. Mixed electoral systems are a little more frequently used in ECE than in Western Europe, where the only stable mixed system has been Germany's. In contrast to the electoral system, the institutions of parliamentary government in ECE and Western Europe are very different with respect to the office of the head of state: while almost half of the West European members of the European Union are constitutional monarchies (Belgium, Denmark, Holland, Luxembourg, the United Kingdom, Spain, and Sweden), none of the new democracies in Eastern and Central Europe resurrected their pre-war monarchical institutions.[3] In five other West European countries (Austria, Finland, France, Ireland, Portugal) the head of state is the directly elected president although there are significant cross-national differences in terms of the power of the office. In only three states (Germany, Greece, and Italy) is the republican president chosen indirectly by members of parliament. The most popular method of choosing the president is the direct election among the ten post-communist democracies as well, although the number of states with a directly elected head of state is relatively higher (6/10) than in the West (5/15).

Other institutional sources of the degree and type of party government are the *structure* and *power* of parliament relative to the executive. As for the structure, what matters is the size and cameral division of the legislature. Smaller legislatures elected by PR systems tend to be more fragmented than larger assemblies creating very different conditions for the type of party government established. Moreover, executive dominance is also stronger over smaller than over larger legislatures (Lijphart 2012: 27), which therefore increases the degree of power concentration as well as the type of party government. Bicameral legislatures may weaken party control over government in two principal ways. First, the partisan composition of the two chambers may be different, due to the use of different electoral systems or non-concurrent electoral timetables, which may mean that the parties that control the governing coalition in the first chamber could find their legislative agenda delayed or sidetracked by countervailing forces in the second chamber. Second, even the parliamentary groups of the same party may differ across the two chambers in terms of their policy outlooks, preferences and emphases, which can further weaken the overall control of the party over government. Again, the employ of different electoral systems or non-concurrent elections to the two chambers is likely to accentuate these differences.

With regard to parliamentary powers, the key mechanism is the role of the legislature in the formation and the termination of the cabinet. Clearly, party control over government is greater if the constitution requires a mandatory investiture vote that the legislature must pass to invest the new government in office. By contrast, in negative models of parliamentarism, the appointment of the government is delegated to the head of state, who may or may not belong to the same party or parties that are trying to form a government or may not even be a partisan figure at all. Rules of government termination should also affect the degree of party government: where the constitution makes the defeat of the incumbent government dependent on a constructive vote of no confidence party control over government increases due to the heightened stability of the executive. Otherwise, if the cabinet can be brought down by a simple vote of no confidence party control over the government will be weaker since the executive can be terminated more easily which also reduces its inherent stability.

The ten democracies vary considerably with regard to both the structure and powers of parliament. The smallest assembly is the first chamber of the Slovenian parliament with 90 seats while the largest one is the Polish *Sejm* with 460. As for the number of parliamentary chambers, only a minority of the ECE states has a second chamber but most of these, with the exception of Slovenia, are elected. In Poland and Romania elections to the second chamber are concurrent with those to the first chamber of parliament while in the Czech Republic the elections to the Senate take place according to a staggered timetable that is not linked at all with the elections to the lower chamber. In Romania, the two chambers are essentially equal in terms of their legislative authority, while the second chamber is clearly inferior to the first in the other three states. In the case of the Czech Republic, the Senate plays an equally powerful role to the Chamber of Deputies only in the process of selecting the Republic president, while in all other matters the Chamber is more powerful. All three states with a directly elected second chamber use different electoral systems to choose members of the two houses of parliament. In contrast to ECE, a majority of West European states, nine out of fifteen, have bicameral parliaments, however, most of them are not elected directly. Among the West European states, there is only a small minority of cases (Belgium, Italy, and Spain) where the second chamber is elected directly by the voters while in the other six states the upper chamber consists of indirectly chosen delegates of subnational political units.

The post-communist democracies also vary on the rules of government formation and termination. All but one of the states, the exception being Latvia, have some kind of *constitutional* provisions that oblige the new government to pass a vote of investiture before it can officially start its term. However, there are significant cross-national differences in the details of these procedures in terms of the discretion that the head of state can exercise in designating the party that can try to form a government first (the *formateur*) and the margin of support that is required for the investiture vote to pass. For example, the constitution of Bulgaria makes it clear that the order in which parties can be invited to form a government must follow the descending order of the number of seats they have won in the election. Elsewhere the president may decide on his or her own whom to invite to form a government; however, while in some cases (e.g. Hungary) the president can only nominate a prime minister to parliament, in other cases (e.g. Czech Republic) the president actually appoints the prime minister who is then obliged to demonstrate parliamentary support for the new government within a specified period of time. The West European states are almost evenly split between negative and positive forms of government investiture: the former is used in the four Nordic states, Portugal and the UK, while the latter are adopted in in Belgium, Holland, Germany, Ireland, Italy and Spain (Bergman 1993: 59).

With regard to government termination, the key institutional difference among the ten states pertains to the use of constructive votes of no-confidence, i.e. the constitutional requirement that the legislature must designate the new prime minister simultaneously with the passage of the vote of no-confidence in the incumbent executive. Of the ten states only three have adopted this measure: Hungary, Poland, and Slovenia. Interestingly, the use of the constructive vote of no-confidence is just as rare in Western Europe: of the 15 West European EU member states only Germany and Spain have this rule in their constitutions.

Table 1.1 summarizes the key institutional differences among the fifteen established and the ten new European democracies on three dimensions: the electoral system, the number of parliamentary chambers and the constitutional system of government. The latter two are combined in order to facilitate the ease of presentation and reduce the number of variables on which the twenty-five states are compared. The term semi-presidentialism in this Figure is used in the same sense as proposed by Elgie (1999). Moving from the top left toward the bottom-right cell of the table we find institutional mixes that increasingly divide and disperse political power (Colomer 2001) amongst an increasing number of institutional veto players (Tsebelis 1995, 2000, 2002). The most power concentrating mix is the empty cell

TABLE 1.1 *The national political institutions of European democracies*

Electoral systems / Legislative and executive type	Single-member system	Mixed-member systems	PR
Unicameral parliamentary		*Hungary*	Estonia, *Latvia*, Denmark, Greece, Luxembourg, Portugal, Sweden
Unicameral semi-presidential		*Lithuania*	*Bulgaria*, *Slovakia*, Iceland, Finland
Bicameral parliamentary	England	Germany	*Czech Republic*, Netherlands, Spain, Italy
Bicameral semi-presidential	France		*Poland*, *Romania*, *Slovenia*, Austria, Ireland

in the top left that would feature a single parliamentary chamber elected by some sort of a plurality or majority electoral system either with a monarch or an indirectly elected president as the head of state. The polar opposite is an institutional design featuring a bicameral legislature with at least the first chamber elected by PR and a directly elected president. Over time, there have been important changes in the institutional structures of several states. For example, Finland switched to a direct election of the presidency in 1994 and Italy switched back and forth between PR and a mixed electoral system since the early 1990s. For the West European states, the Figure shows the institutional structure as it was in 2011; for ECE it shows the mix that was in place for the most part since the transition to democracy.

The Table underlines the point that was made earlier about the fundamental institutional similarities across East and West: while the overwhelming majority of both the established Western and the new ECE democracies elect their first parliamentary chambers by PR, they differ slightly in terms of their prevalent mode to further disperse political power either by bicameral or semi-presidential institutions. The Table also draws attention to three special cases in ECE, which are unique in the region in terms of their overall institutional mix: the Czech Republic, Hungary and Lithuania, of which the latter two have no comparable institutions in the West. Other than these two, however, the remaining eight states share identical combinations of institutional features with comparable West European counterparts.

1.2.2 Institutions and Coalition Theory

The second reason for adopting an institutionalist perspective is theoretical. Whereas the dominant approaches to the study of coalition politics used to be decidedly institution-free, stressing parties' office- (e.g. Riker 1962; Lieserson 1966) and policy-seeking motivations as the key driver of coalition politics (e.g. Axelrod 1970; de Swaan 1973; Strom and Müller-Rommel 1999), the recent scholarship in comparative coalition studies has explicitly stressed the importance of institutions (Strom, Budge and Laver 1994; Strom, Müller-Rommel and Bergman 2003, 2010; Diermeier, Eraslan and Merlo 2003, 2007; Diermeier and Krehbiel 2003; Schleiter and Morgan-Jones 2009a,b).

Based on the assumptions that political parties are driven by the pursuit of office or policy or both, the first and second generations of coalition theoretic models predicted that parties should form winning, i.e., majority, coalitions ofeither different types, such as the minimally winning coalitions (Riker 1962), minimally winning and ideologically connected coalitions (Axelrod 1970), coalitions that include the dominant and central parties, when such are present in the legislature (Roozendaal 1992). An important weakness of the classic office-seeking theories was their inability to predict the formation of minority governments, which by definition are not winning in terms of parliamentary voting arithmetic. Although policy-seeking models were able to account for the formation of such governments by stressing that the central location of the ideological space allows a party to form a minority government, the real breakthrough in understanding the formation of such governments was provided by Strom (1990) who explicitly stressed the role that parliamentary institutions play in making undersized cabinets and equilibrium choice. In the aftermath of Strom's work, the coalition theoretic literature has joined the wave of neo-institutionalism that shaped much of the broader comparative politics literature since the 1980s.

Laver and Schofield (1990: 7–10) aptly noted that until the 1990s the literature on comparative coalition governments developed in two distinct schools of scholarly traditions; the European and the American (Laver and Schofield 1990: 7–10). Whereas the former always emphasized the importance of institutional and contextual details in understanding coalition processes and outcomes, it never aspired to produce testable, falsifiable theories that can be the foundation of replicable empirical findings. The conventional European coalition literature was, and has largely remained, extremely rich in empirical detail but theoretically inductive. In stark contrast, inspired by the rational choice revolution in the social sciences, American scholars of coalition politics focused on deductive theory building and formal modeling of coalition politics subjected to increasingly more sophisticated ways of empirical testing. As of the early 1990s, however, the two traditions have been converging due to the mutual recognition that (i) institutions matter for the understanding of multi-party government and that (ii) deductive theory coupled with replicable empirical analysis contributes to the accumulation of wisdom and the general social scientific enterprise.

The starting point for this neo-institutional breakthrough in comparative coalition studies is the body of literature focusing on constraints of all types as the independent variables explaining government formation (Laver and Budge 1992; Strom, Budge and Laver 1994). Constraints were defined as "any restriction on the set of feasible cabinet coalitions that is beyond the short-term control of the players" (Strom, Budge and Laver 1994: 308). They were further broken down into two kinds: hard and soft constraints. Whereas hard constraints effectively rule out specific coalitions to be formed by particular parties, soft constraints make the formation of one coalition or another more or less likely. In other words, hard constraints are both specific, as they pertain to particular coalition combinations, and enforceable, meaning that they are "backed up by credible enforcement mechanisms," (Strom, Budge and Laver 1994: 308) while soft constraints may be such to a much lesser extent.

In the real political world, constraints on the coalition bargaining process are exerted by exogenously defined institutions, such as cabinet formation and operation rules, legislative decision-making rules, external veto players as well as specific commitments and rules that parties, the actors in the bargaining process, impose on themselves. At the same time, the actors, i.e. political parties themselves, can also create constraints endogenously. For example, a particular party may make a specific electoral pledge not to enter into coalition with a particular other party. This promise to the electorate raises the party's audience costs because breaking it would lead to the party's loss of credibility in the eyes of its voters which may well lead to electoral losses in the future (Kohno 1997).

Constraint theory was developed largely in response to the failure of institution-free game theoretic models, stressing the size and ideological-policy preferences of political parties as independent variables, to explain the formation of minority governments. Budge and Laver (1986) claimed that the reason why game theoretic models may fail to predict the formation of minority governments is the assumption that they make about the cabinet formation game being constant-sum. This implies that there has to be an absolute winner and a loser in the game. However, quite often, it will be parties other than those that are best positioned to win the game that end up forming the government. Budge and Laver suggested, therefore, changing both the assumption and the terminology: they offer to replace winning with viability, and the assumption of constant-sum with that of variable-sum. According to them, "[a] protocoalition V will form a viable government if there is no alternative coalition A which is supported by parties controlling more legislative votes than those supporting V, and which all parties supporting A prefer to form rather than V" (Budge and Laver 1986: 485–506). Also, they suggested that there were no absolute winners or losers in the game, and, therefore, the game was not necessarily finished once the government has been formed. Who gets to form the government is not necessarily the same as winning the game in an absolute sense. Rather it is better seen as the viable, as opposed to the winning, outcome under the existing constraints structuring the context of bargaining.

In spite of the consensus that institutions matter for coalition dynamics, the empirical reference point of much of this literature remains the pool of established West European democracies (Strom, Müller-Rommel and Bergman 2010). On the one hand, this makes sense given the long-term stability of institutions of parliamentary democracy and party government in that part of the world. The new ECE democracies, however, present a laboratory of cases where the short-term and immediate of effects of institutions can be examined. Furthermore, these new democracies constitute a set of hard cases for the test of institutional theories of coalition politics. Given the relatively weaker levels of party system institutionalization in the region, and that democracy was still in the process of consolidation for most of the past twenty years, one would expect that political institutions might not have the same bite as they do in the mature democracies of the West. Arguably, political institutions themselves are often too malleable and too unstable in new democracies with the result that they become the dependent variable of party politics rather than the other way around. However, this has not been the case. Although constitutional amendments have taken place over time (Roberts 2009), in some states more than others, and modifications have been made to the electoral rules, these changes have not altered the basic nature of the constitutional and institutional choices that politicians made at the time of the transitions to democracy. Therefore, the post-communist democracies of ECE provide an excellent set of cases where we can examine the effects of institutional diversity in new democracies while controlling for the stability of the fundamental characteristics of these institutions.

It is also important to point out that studying the ways in which political institutions shape the dynamics of coalition government fills an important lacuna in the literature on post-communist parliaments. This literature has extensively addressed questions on the level of parliamentary institutionalization and professionalization (Ostrow 2000; Remington 1994; Remington and Smith 1996; Ostrow; Agh 1997; Wiatr 1997; Olson 1998; Olson and Crowther 2002; Clark, Verseckatite and Lukosaitis 2006); the development of different national legislative institutions (Olson and Norton 2007); the new parliamentary elites (Ilonszki and Edinger 2007); and the representative functions that post-communist parliaments perform with regard to particular social groups and constituencies (Chiva 2007; Galligan and Clavero 2008; Rueschmeyer and Wolchik 2009). However, comparative studies on party coalitions in these parliaments are much more sparse. Moreover, scholars who look at the relationship between the party system and parliamentary development tend to consider the former as the independent rather than the dependent variable (Olson and Norton 2007; for an exception, see Schleiter and Morgan-Jones 2009a), which, as we know from the West European evidence is not always the case.

1.3 POLITICAL INSTITUTIONS, DEMOCRATIC TRANSITIONS AND SOCIAL CLEAVAGES

It is important to note that political institutions in ECE neither emerged in a vacuum nor have they shaped the development and behavior of political parties alone and in isolation from societal forces. The rich literature on the origins and the diversity of post-communist institutional design has shown that the balance of power between the communist government and the opposition as well as the extent and nature of divisions within each camp had a direct influence on the type of electoral system and constitution that would be adopted (Lijphart 1992; Elster 1993; Whitefield 1993; Geddes 1996; Elster et al 1998). In general, where communists were in a stronger bargaining position vis-à-vis the reformers, they would push for stronger presidential and weaker parliamentary authority as well as electoral systems that resembled the communist practice of majority- or plurality-based rules. In other words, the stronger the reformers were the greater the likelihood that stronger parliaments elected by proportional representation electoral systems would become the new the institutional choice.

The political arrangement that characterized communist rule affected the eventual balance of powers between communists and reformers in the late 1980s, which in turn determined both the mode of the democratic transition itself as well as the nature of the post-transition institutional. Specifically, three fundamental types of Leninist rule have been distinguished: the bureaucratic-authoritarian, the national accommodative and the patrimonial one (Kitschelt 1995; Kitschelt et al 1999). In places where communist rule was firmly entrenched and institutionalized via strict bureaucratic controls, e.g. Czechoslovakia or the former East Germany, the prospect for a consensual and negotiated transition was slim. Therefore, in those states democracy was arrived at through the overnight collapse and implosion of the communist power structure leaving the reformers a free hand in designing the new constitutional architectures. Elsewhere, communist rule itself had been negotiated and based on an implicit consensus that accommodated the regime's dissidents, e.g. Hungary and Poland, which resulted in a negotiated, or pacted, transition allowing the incumbent rulers an opportunity to leave their footprint on the new constitutional choices. Finally, where Leninist rule was maintained via patrimonial and clientelistic ties and networks between the elites and the masses, a characteristic feature of less developed societies such as Bulgaria and Romania on the periphery of communist Europe, there was little effective and independent opposition to speak of. In these cases, democratic reforms were promoted and pushed by particular factions within the communist leadership resulting either in a more peaceful palace coup, as in Bulgaria, or a violent overthrowing of the incumbents followed by mass turmoil, as in Romania. Either way, the contained transition from patrimonial-style Leninism resulted in limited institutional innovation and departure from the general communist practice of strong executives and non-proportional elections.

Scholars have debated whether or not, and if so to what extent, the political, social and economic conditions that characterized the pre-democratic period would also define the social basis and the programmatic nature of party competition once the transition to democracy has been completed (Evans and Whitefield 1993; Kitschelt 1995; Toka 1996, 1997; Whitefield 2002; Rohrschneider and Whitefield 2009). On the one hand some argued that in the wake of the depoliticizing legacy of communist rule, the new post-communist reality presented a *tabula rasa,* a clean slate where political parties would be formed by fickle and volatile political entrepreneurs without clear and firm attachment to identifiable bases of political support, which in the long run would make the formation of a program-based party competition extremely difficult if not well-nigh impossible (Elster et al 1998; Whitefield 2002; Evans 2006). In contrast, others have shown that there is no single post-communist trajectory; instead, based on the mode of democratic transition, the new institutional architecture, the type of communism, and the structural consequences of longer-term pre-communist conditions, specifically the timing of industrialization, the likelihood for the formation of a programmatic party system was far stronger in some than in other polities (Kitschelt 1995).

According to the latter view, constitutional design played a very important role in this regard: where parliamentary forms of government were combined with closed list proportional representation electoral systems with no or only limited preference votes allowed, the institutional conditions for the creation of cohesive depersonalized parties were ripe. Conversely, presidential constitutions and electoral systems that encourage the cultivation of personal as opposed to partisan reputation, such as those with multiple preference votes or a single transferable vote (Carey and Shugart 1995), promoted the development of a more personalized style of party politics at the expense of programmatic competition.

Over time, the ideological and programmatic orientation of political parties in the new democracies of ECE has turned out to be quite strongly based and anchored in existing social cleavages. Drawing on Lipset and Rokkan's (1967) canonical work about the emergence and freezing of West European party systems rooted in historically defined and specific social cleavages, scholars of electoral behavior and party competition in ECE have demonstrated that the ideological basis of partisanship varies systematically with the underlying social and economic divisions:

> . . . although economic differentiation was common to all countries (if not always to the same degree) . . . the religious and ethnic composition of countries in the region varies markedly. As a consequence . . . the connection of social division to ideological division also varies; religiosity appears to matter much more to social liberalism in Catholic than in Orthodox states; and issues of ethnic rights are more firmly rooted where minorities exist and where the sense of social difference between ethnic groups is more strongly felt. (Whitefield 2002: 187–8)

1.4 THE ORGANIZATION OF THE BOOK

The organization of the book is as follows. *Chapter Two: Post-Communist Institutional Design: Electoral Systems, Parliaments and Presidents*, provides a detailed comparative assessment of the independent variables, i.e. the electoral, parliamentary and executive institutions that constrain coalition politics in ECE. The central point of this chapter is to establish the three groups of states with regard to the power concentration of their institutional design: those with low concentration (Czech Republic, Lithuania, Poland, and Romania); those with high concentration (Bulgaria, Estonia, Hungary, and Slovenia); and those that are in-between (Latvia and Slovakia).

Chapter Three: Political Institutions and Electoral Coalitions, is the first substantive chapter that looks at the effect of political institutions on coalition politics. In this chapter, I will argue that the most favorable institutional environment for the formation and success of electoral coalitions is provided by the electoral systems with relatively small districts, more restrictive electoral formulae; and positive parliamentary government formation rules. An important conclusion of this chapter is that electoral coalitions play a much less recognizable role in states where the level of institutional power concentration is low than in those states where political institutions produce a high degree of power concentration. Hungary stands out as the only state where electoral coalitions have consistently defined the two main competing government alternatives. The process and the history of electoral coalitions in Hungary will be discussed in detail in the *Chapter Four: The Electoral Origins of Hungarian Governments, 1990–2002,* where I highlight that even facing the same institutional constraints and incentives political parties may adopt very different strategies to form electoral coalitions. Hungary also provides an excellent case to show how the electoral system can push parties to start the effective government formation process during the electoral stage of competition rather until after the polls are over and the final and complete allocation of parliamentary seats becomes common knowledge to all parties.

Chapter Five analyzes *The Institutional Sources of Minority Governments* in the ten democracies. I will argue that four institutional variables, large assembly size, a strong presidency, bicameralism, and negative parliamentary rules of government formation, weaken the incentives for political parties to form majority coalitions because they limit the authority of the first legislative chamber over the executive. The combination of these variables explains the relatively high frequency of minority governments in the Czech Republic, Poland, and Romania, three states where the political institutions are designed to disperse political power.

Chapter Six looks at *The Institutional Sources of Cabinet Duration* in the ten post-communist democracies. In this chapter, I identify the following political institutions as responsible for cross-national variation in the rates of government stability: the power of the presidency, bicameralism, and the government investiture and termination rules. In addition, I show that the level of party system fragmentation in the legislature, the majority status of the governing coalition, and whether a given government is formed immediately after the election, or sometime later in the legislative term, shape cabinet duration. The chapter concludes that states that have the lowest institutional concentration of political power (Czech Republic, Poland, and Romania) have some of the least stable governments in the region.

The last substantive chapter is devoted to the study of presidential selections. In *Dividing the Executive? Party Coalitions and Indirect Presidential Elections* I argue that the rules of indirect presidential selection in four states (Czech Republic, Estonia, Hungary, and Latvia) shape the ability of the incumbent governing coalition to elect its presidential candidate. In terms of their institutional power concentration, two of the four states belong to the high category (Estonia, and Hungary), and one each to the intermediate (Latvia) and the low one (Czech

Republic). The central finding in this chapter, namely that election rules shape the ability of the incumbent coalition to keep the presidency under its control, reinforces the central argument of the book by showing that divided government is indeed less frequent in the two states where the institutions provide for a high level of power concentration.

At the end of the book, I provide four Appendices as detailed reference material about the key independent and dependent variables that are discussed in the text: Appendix A surveys the development of electoral systems of the ten states; Appendix B summarizes cross-national variations on positive and negative parliamentary government formations rules; Appendix C provides a detailed account about the formation of electoral coalitions; and Appendix D reviews the formation and governing coalitions.

NOTES

1. This figure includes all prime ministers, both acting and serving a regular mandate.
2. Although not covered in my analysis, it is important to note that in 2012 the Czech Republic also switched to direct elections to the presidency.
3. It is important to add that Norway, while not a EU member, is also a constitutional monarchy. It is further worth mentioning that the last descendent of Bulgaria's former ruling dynasty, Simeon Saxo-Coburg-Gotha, entered Bulgarian politics and became a democratically selected head of government following the parliamentary elections of 2000.

2

Post-Communist Institutional Design

Electoral Systems, Parliaments, and Presidents

2.1 INTRODUCTION

An important characteristic of post-communist party systems is the striking institutional diversity that defines the rules and conditions under which political parties compete with each other, form and terminate governments. While all ten new democracies in ECE have adopted fundamentally parliamentary systems, the degree to which political power is concentrated in their parliaments, more precisely in a majority that controls the legislature, varies considerably. Based on a detailed comparative review of their institutional arrangements, I will identify the following three groups of post-communist democracies with regard to how favorable they are for the parliamentary concentration of power: (i) states with the most favorable conditions for power concentration (Bulgaria, Estonia, Hungary, and Slovenia); (ii) states with mixed conditions (Latvia and Slovakia); and states with the least favorable conditions (Czech Republic, Lithuania, Poland, and Romania).

The lifecycle of parliamentary government is conditioned and regulated by three sets of institutions: electoral, parliamentary, and executive (Laver and Schofield 1990: 62–6; Bergman 2010). The cycle starts in the electoral arena of party competition, where two important events get decided: (a) which political parties will be represented in parliament and can, therefore, participate in the formal government formation talks, and (b) which political parties contest the election as an electoral coalition, with either a tacit understanding or an explicit commitment to staying together during the ensuing government formation talks that follow the election. This embryonic stage in the government's lifecycle is primarily regulated by the electoral system; the rules and regulations that govern all aspects of a national election in a country.

Once the election is over, however, the cycle enters the parliamentary stage, where the institutions of the legislature exert their influence on coalition behavior and strategy. The first set of institutional constraints in the parliamentary arena is the formal structure of parliament itself, i.e. its size and the number of its chambers. Government formation, durability and termination are processes that are ultimately based in the logic of parliamentary arithmetic; they are about numbers. In order to form a government, political parties need to build a coalition that satisfies a certain threshold of winning (Riker 1962) or viability (Strom, Budge and Laver 1994). Likewise, to challenge the incumbent government and install a new one in its stead also requires careful and precise calculation of the number of parliamentary seats that will be supporting either side. The sheer size of parliament, that is the actual number of seats, defines the limits and boundaries of these calculations.

The presence of multiple legislative chambers also changes the dynamics of coalition politics because political parties know that either the investiture of the government (e.g. Romania) or the passage of bills in implementing the government's policy agenda, or both, will require the consent of additional veto players (Tsebelis 2000, 2002). Second chambers are particularly important in countries where a constitutional arrangement called *dual responsibility* is in place, meaning that both chambers are active in the investiture and termination of the government (Diermeier, Eraslan and Merlo 2007: 229). Although traditional studies on coalition governments have not looked at the effect of bicameralism, the few extant studies that do so agree that bicameralism leads to larger coalitions (Lijphart 1984a; Diermeier, Eraslan and Merlo 2007), however they disagree as to whether it reduces government duration (Tsebelis 2000, 2002; Druckman and Thies 2002; Diermeier, Erasln and Merlo 2007).

The third institutional constraint, i.e. executive institutions, on the government's lifecycle is provided by the rules and practices of government formation and termination. These rules are fundamental to representative parliamentary government, which rests on the twin notions of executive responsibility and accountability to the legislature. In order to be installed and to remain in office the executive must win and retain the confidence of a parliamentary majority; the rules of government formation and termination specify the exact ways in which this legislative confidence is expressed. In addition to parliamentary votes of investiture, the head of state may also play an important role in cabinet formation and termination. With regard to the former, the president may have the constitutional prerogative to determine the sequences in which multiple attempts to form a government are taken. Moreover, the head of state may also play a role in bringing about the termination of the incumbent government by affecting the early dissolution of parliament and calling for new elections. As we shall see, in some states the legislature may remove the incumbent government by an ordinary no-confidence vote, while elsewhere a constructive vote of no-confidence is required which expresses parliament's positive support for the next incoming executive.

Finally, another executive institution that shapes coalition dynamics and governance is the overall legislative and executive authority delegated to the head of state. As mentioned in the Introduction, none of the ten ECE democracies has a purely presidential system. Depending on the constitutional arrangement of presidential powers, the head of state may have considerable influence over the government, which, in turn, will have consequences for the government's ability to carry out its legislative agenda and ultimately hold its coalition of parliamentary support together. Such presidential powers include, among others, the president's veto over legislation; powers to appoint and dismiss members of cabinet; and the power to hold referenda (Shugart and Carey 1992).

These four sets of institutions (electoral rules; the structure of the legislature; rules of government formation and termination; and the powers of the presidency) constrain and influence political parties' coalitional choices because they determine how political power is organized in the political system. In addition to electoral support, i.e. votes, and policy, political power is one of the central goals and objectives that political parties pursue through their competitive interaction with one another. Therefore, the way in which that power is organized, divided, or concentrated, will affect what strategies and choices parties will make in the electoral, parliamentary, and executive realms of competition. Following a detailed review of the cross-national variation among the ten states on these institutional rules, I will provide a summary assessment of how combinations of these rules organize political power in each of these new democracies.

2.2 ELECTORAL INSTITUTIONS

Although the development of electoral systems in the ten post-communist democracies has not followed a uniform pattern, the fundamental institutional choices that were adopted at the time of the transition have remained fairly stable: most of these states adopted some variant of PR in the early 1990s and this type of system, apart from occasional modifications, has stayed in place. Two of the ten new democracies (Hungary and Lithuania) started out with a mixed-member electoral system and they also demonstrated remarkable resilience (Lundberg 2009). In fact, as I have argued elsewhere, the adoption of consensus, as opposed to majoritarian, democracy across the region has prevented large-scale electoral reform and acted as a built-in stabilizer of the key institutional choices negotiated at the time of the transition to democracy (Nikolenyi 2011). In several cases (e.g. Poland, Romania, and Slovakia) these initial PR systems underwent subsequent amendments that generally reduced their proportionality. However, in none of these new democracies was PR ever reversed in favor of a majoritarian electoral system (Juberias 2004), although Bulgaria switched from pure PR to a mixed system in 2009 and the Romanian reforms of 2008 also introduced single-member districts, which limited the proportionality of the system (Williams 2003; Coman 2008; Maxfield 2009). In other instances (Slovenia in 1996 and the Czech Republic in 2000), clear attempts were made to replace PR with a majoritarian alternative; however, they have all failed and a modified PR with multi-member districts has remained in effect. In one case, Hungary, repeated attempts at reforming a complex mixed electoral system also failed until the election of a conservative government in 2010 with a large two-thirds' majority finally allowed the reform to take place. While the Hungarian electoral system has remained a mixed-member system, the overall effects of the reform have reduced its earlier built-in proportionalities.

In short, the ten post-communist democracies constitute three clusters in terms of the stability of their electoral systems over the past twenty years. The first group comprises the three Baltic states which have had the most stable electoral systems. The second group includes the Czech Republic, Poland, Slovakia, and Slovenia. All four states started out with and have retained some variant of PR at the time of the transition; however, fairly major changes have taken place since in their rules. Nonetheless, all four of these states have retained a fundamentally list-based PR system. The third group consists of Bulgaria, Hungary and Romania, where the most far-reaching institutional changes were made: Bulgaria adopted a mixed system in 2009; Hungary reduced the number of seats in parliament by a half and limited the proportionality of her mixed system in other ways; and Romania introduced an ingenious system in 2008 which allowed voters to vote for candidates in single-member districts while still allocating most parliamentary seats on the basis of parties' combined vote shares.

Electoral systems are complex pieces of legislation including a variety of rules about electoral districts, the contenders, voters, the voting process and the allocation of seats once the voting has been completed, to name just a few. Following conventional wisdom in the electoral system literature (see, for examples, Lijphart 1994; Gallagher and Mitchell 2005; Farrel 2011), I assess post-communist electoral systems with reference to the following five institutional variables:

(i) the formula to convert votes into seats;
(ii) the average district magnitude;
(iii) multi-tier districting;
(iv) the openness of the candidate list to voter input;
(v) the nominal thresholds that political parties, and coalitions of parties, have to meet in order to secure seats in the legislature.

The main differences that have existed among the ten states as of 2010 are summarized in Table 2.1. For every state, I calculate average district magnitude by dividing the number of parliamentary seats, elected from the multi-member districts, by the number of such districts. In other words, the calculations do not include single-member districts and upper tier compensatory seats that are not allocated directly from the multi-member districts. The ten states form three distinct clusters in terms of their average district magnitude. The first one includes three states with large multi-member districts: Lithuania and Slovakia, both of which have a nation-wide district, and Latvia, with an average magnitude of 20 seats. The second cluster contains three states, the average district magnitude of which has hovered between 10 and 20 for most elections. These are the Czech Republic (25 seats before 2002 and 14.3 thereafter), Slovenia (11 seats per district

TABLE 2.1 *A comparison of electoral system features as of 2010*

State	District magnitude	Separate lists at PR tiers	Preference votes	Formula at first tier	Threshold for coalitions	Constitutional protection of electoral system
Bulgaria	7.7	No	No	D'Hondt	No	No
Czech R.	14.3	No	Yes	D'Hondt	Yes	Yes (PR)
Estonia	8.4	Yes	Yes	Hare	NA	Yes (PR)
Hungary	7.6	Yes	No	Droop	Yes	No
Latvia	20	No	Yes	Saint-Lague	No	Yes (PR)
Lithuania	70	No	Yes	Hare	Yes	No
Poland	11.2	No	Yes	Saint-Lague	Yes	Yes (PR)
Romania	8.2	No	No	D'Hondt	Yes	No
Slovakia	150	No	Yes	Hagenbach-Bischoff	Yes	No
Slovenia	11	No	Yes	Droop	No	Yes (PR)

Source: See Appendix A.

since 1992), and Poland (10.6 in 1991, 7.5 in 1993 and 1997, and 11.2 in 2001). Finally, the third cluster consists of the four states where the average number of deputies returned from a district has been of a single digit: Bulgaria (7.7), Estonia (8.4), Hungary (7.6), and Romania (between and 8 and 9.5).

There are very few cases where parties are allowed to submit separate lists of candidates at the different tiers. These include the mixed systems, which by definition have both a nominal and a list tier of candidates; the PR component of Hungary's electoral law; as well as the electoral systems of Estonia and Poland before 2001. At the first PR tier, half of the states have used the largest remainder method of seat allocation. As of 2010, the Hare quota is used in Estonia and Lithuania; the Droop quota is in place in Hungary and Slovenia, while Slovakia employs the Hagenbach-Bischoff method. Three of the four states are currently using the d'Hondt highest average method at the first tier: Bulgaria, the Czech Republic since 2002, and Romania since 1992; while Poland, since 2001, and Latvia employ the Saint-Lague method of highest averages.

In the large majority of cases voters have the opportunity to indicate their preference over candidates that are submitted by the parties. However, there is variation in both the number of preference votes per voter as well as the degree to which they can alter the eventual ranking of candidates once the votes are counted. In three states (Estonia, Poland, and Slovenia) preference voting is compulsory, while in four other states (Czech Republic, Latvia, Lithuania, and Slovakia) it is optional. Yet, in Latvia, as well as in Lithuania since 2008, voters' preference votes determine the ultimate ranking of candidates on the list, while in the Czech Republic and Slovakia, preference votes matter only if their overall number reaches a certain threshold. All but two of these seven states, the exceptions being Estonia and Slovenia, allow voters to indicate their preferences for multiple candidates. Overall, there are only three states where party lists are not open for voter input: Hungary, Bulgaria and Romania. However, in each of these countries, the nominal tier of competition provides an important avenue for voters to cast a candidate-oriented vote.

Most electoral systems in ECE impose a graduated threshold structure on electoral coalitions. The only state that explicitly bans electoral coalitions is Estonia, as of 1999, while three states, Bulgaria, Latvia, and Slovenia, make no distinction at all between parties and coalitions in terms of the nominal threshold. Of the remaining six states the Czech Republic imposes the highest and Lithuania imposes the lowest threshold on electoral coalitions.

Finally, half of the ten states have adopted constitutional protection of the fundamental principle of their electoral systems and in each case this protection applies to PR. Interestingly, mixed electoral systems are never mentioned in the constitution. In a couple of instances (Poland and Slovenia) such constitutional entrenchment of the electoral system has been part and parcel of the processes of electoral reform while in other cases it was adopted very early on after the transition to democracy.

2.3 PARLIAMENTARY INSTITUTIONS

2.3.1 Number of seats

Table 2.2 provides information about the size and the length of the mandate of each post-communist parliament in ECE. The entries in the third column in the Table show that there is considerable variation across the ten states in terms of the number of seats of their parliamentary chambers. These differences closely reflect the variation among the states in terms of the size of their population. The coefficient of the correlation between the number of seats in the first chamber and the size of the population in 2010 is extremely high (0.87).[1] The smallest states in terms of both variables are Estonia, Latvia, Lithuania, and Slovenia; while the largest ones are Poland and Romania, with the Czech Republic and Bulgaria situated in the middle. Hungary is something of an outlier given that its national parliament is considerably larger than expected given the size of the country's population.

In some cases, the number of parliamentary seats was modeled after the respective country's last pre-communist democratic constitutional framework dating to the inter-war period (Ishiyama 1997). For instance, in the Baltics, both Estonia and Latvia essentially revived their pre-war parliaments after the fall of communism; however, Lithuania took a different course and departed from her interwar model of constitutional arrangements. Reflecting the political and legal

TABLE 2.2 *The size and mandate of post-communist parliaments*

State	Chambers	Size of chamber (as of 2010)	Length of mandate
Bulgaria	*Narodno Sobranie*	240*	4 years
Czech Republic	*Poslanecka Snemovna*	200	4 years
Czech Republic	*Senat*	81	6 years
Estonia	*Riigikogu*	101	4 years
Hungary	*Országgyűlés*	386	4 years
Latvia	*Saeima*	100	4 years[+]
Lithuania	*Seimas*	141	4 years
Poland	*Sejm*	460	4 years
Poland	*Senat*	100	4 years
Romania	*Camera Deputatilor*	334**	4 years
Romania	*Senatul*	137**	4 years
Slovakia	*Narodna Rada*	150	4 years
Slovenia	*Drzavni Zbor*	90	4 years
Slovenia	*Drzavni Svet*	40	5 years

Notes: * The transitional parliament of Bulgaria, which also acted as the Constituent Assembly, was a far larger body of 400 seats. ** The size of the Romanian legislature has fluctuated slightly over time. The number of seats in the Chamber of Deputies changed as follows: 387 (1990), 341 (1992), 343 (1996), 345 (2000), and 336 (2004). The numbers of seats in the Senate were: 119 (1990), 143 (1992 and 1996), 140 (2000), and 137 (2004). [+] The Latvian parliament had a three year term until a constitutional amendment changed it to four years in December 1997 (Rose and Munro 2003: 196).

continuity that characterized the peaceful democratic transition in Hungary in 1989–90, the Roundtable Talks resulted in a small reduction in the number of seats from (350 to 386) in the unicameral parliament (Birch, Millard, Popescu and Williams 2002: 60). Since 1990, the number of seats has remained intact until the constitutional changes of 2010. Using its sweeping electoral mandate, the governing coalition of FIDESZ and the Hungarian Christian Democratic Party, passed a new electoral law, and a new constitution, which reduced the number of seats in the national parliament to 199. Post-communist Bulgaria did not follow either the communist-era or the inter-war models. The post-communist National Assembly was reduced to 60 percent of its communist-era size: from 1971 to 1990 the Assembly had consisted of 400 seats with deputies elected for five-year terms, thereafter the new constitution that came into effect in 1991 reduced the number of seats to 240 and introduced a four-year mandate for deputies. The new constitution that came into effect in 1991 was drafted by the Grand National Assembly, elected in 1990 via democratic multi-party competition, which was also the last one to select a president as the office became a directly elected one under the terms of new constitution. Prior to 1971, the number of seats in the Bulgarian National Assembly had never been the same in any two consecutive elections save the war-time elections of 1938 and 1940. The reason for this was the stipulation that every member of parliament had to represent the same number of voters; therefore as the population grew in size so did the number of seats increase in the Assembly (Ishiyama 1997).

In Poland and Romania, the most important change in parliamentary structure was the introduction of bicameralism whereas changes in the number of seats were marginal at best. Romania's Chamber of Deputies had approximately the same number of deputies after the transition to democracy as it had before: 349 (in 1970), and 369 until the election of the provisional parliament in 1990, which had 387 deputies. Although Romania's post-communist parliament has remained bicameral, a consultative referendum on parliamentary reform, which was held together with the presidential elections of 2009, approved to transform it into a unicameral body of no more than 300 seats (Stan and Zaharia 2010: 1145). In Poland, the 1921 constitution had established a bicameral parliament with a 444-seat lower house (*Sejm)* and a 111-seat Senate both elected by PR using the d'Hondt method (Polonsky 1972: 45–52). Deputies in the *Sejm* were elected for a five-year term. The size of the chambers remained unaltered in the next elections that were held in 1928 and 1930. However, the authoritarian constitution of 1935 reduced the size of both houses to 208 and 96, respectively, which remained in effect for the next two elections (1935 and 1938) that took place prior to the Second World War. After the War, the 1952 constitution of communist Poland created a unicameral parliament with a fixed number of 460 seats (Staar 1962: 33), which remained in place until the transition to democracy.

2.3.2 *Bicameralism*

Second chambers are much less varied in terms of their size. The directly elected Senates of Czech Republic, Poland and Romania are of nearly the same size consisting of 81, 100, and 119 seats, respectively. The upper chamber of the Slovenian parliament, is much smaller with only 40 indirectly elected members. Bicameralism was already in place during the communist federations of Yugoslavia and Czechoslovakia, and two of their successor states (Czech Republic and Slovenia) continued with this arrangement. It is worth noting though that Slovakia, another successor to a communist federation, did not opt for a bicameral parliament. Moreover, although the resurrection of bicameralism in Poland and Romania was the product of the democratic transition itself, i.e. prior to 1989 neither of these two states had a bicameral legislature, both states had had a bicameral parliament in the inter-war period (Olson 1999: 302).

The two major constitutional changes that took place in Poland since the demise of communism, the 1992 Small Constitution and the 1997 complete Constitution, affected the Polish *Senat* in important ways; however, its fundamental characteristics and relative powers remained intact. Both constitutions allowed the *Senat* to initiate legislation, however, only through the *Sejm*. The *Senat* was given 30 days to act on a bill passed by the *Sejm*; if the *Senat* took no action then the bill was considered as accepted.[2] If the *Senat* made any amendments to or decided to reject a bill, the *Sejm* could override it with an absolute majority vote although the 1997 Constitution changed this requirement to an absolute majority of half of the statutory members of the first chamber. In addition to its suspensive veto on ordinary pieces of legislation, the *Senat* has absolute veto on the president's request to hold a national referendum and it could also block the president from dissolving parliament. The *Senat* has no authority over the appointment and dismissal of the cabinet and it does not have suspensive veto over the government's budget bills. Given that the *Sejm* is more than four times the size of the *Senate*, the former remains much more powerful.[3]

The *Senat* is not a continous body, which means that the dissolution of the Sejm leads to an automatic dissolution of *Senat* and concurrent legislative elections to both chambers. Since the two chambers are elected by different electoral systems their partisan composition tends to differ. However, these differences simply mean that the largest party in the first chamber has an even larger margin of victory in the *Senat*, which makes the Polish parliament a case of congruent bicameralism (Lijphart 1999). While no single political party ever won a majority of the seats in the *Sejm*, four of the seven *Senat* elections produced such an outcome (1989, 1997, 2001, 2010) and in one other election (2005), the largest party was only a hair's breadth away from an absolute majority, winning forty-nine of the 100 seats. In every instance, the party that won the most seats in the *Sejm* also won the most or the majority of the seats in the *Senat*.[4] The absorption of both chambers by the same party coaliton reduces the abilty of the *Senat* to act as a veto player independent of the *Sejm*, reducing the potential of deadlock and disagreement between the two chambers and increasing the potential for policy change.[5]

Following the dissolution of the federal Czechoslovak state in 1992 the Czech Republic preserved a bicameral parliamentary structure while the Slovak parliament became unicameral. Although the new Czech constitution of 1992 provided for a directly elected second chamber, the first Senate elections would not take place until 1996 for lack of an agreement among political parties on the electoral system to be adopted. During this period, the political forces that opposed the creation of a bicameral parliament, such as the far-right SPR-RSC and the CSSD, tried to remove bicameralism from the new constitution (Filip 2001: 70–5). Although their efforts failed, it became clear that bicameralism was a contested issue. The new Czech Senate was designed to be a continous legislative body, in contrast to those of both Poland and Romania; the dissolution of the lower chamber has no effect on its term. In further contrast to the other two bicameral states, the Senate of the Czech Republic is incongruent with the first chamber. Different partisan control over the two chambers is promoted by the adoption of fundamentally different electoral systems and different electoral timetables: Czech Senators are elected for six-year terms with one-third of them elected every two years. As a result, governing parties in the first chamber have often faced opposition majorities in the second chamber.[6]

The Senate is a considerably smaller legislative body than the Chamber of Deputies; the latter has 200 members while the former only eighty-one. Although Senators can submit a draft bill, every piece of legisation must be initiated through the first chamber (Article 41) except for periods when the Chamber of Deputies is dissolved. However, even under such circumstances the legislative power of the Senate is highly limited as it is not allowed to pass measures related to the constitution, the electoral system, international agreements, the state budget and the state annual account (Article 33). Legislative measures passed by the Senate must be passed by the Chamber of Deputies at its first session after it has been re-constituted following a general elecion. Failure to do so results in the invalidation of those measures. The Senate is equal to the Chamber of Deputies in two areas: constitutional amendment and the election of the president of the Republic. Constitutional change requires a simultaneous three-fifths' majority in both chambers of parliament (Article 39) whereas in matters of ordinary pieces of legislation the Senate has only a suspensive veto which can be overriden by a majority vote in the Chamber (Article 46 and 47).

The rebirth of bicameralism in post-communist Romania originates in the decree issued by the Provisional Council of National Unity, on March 14, 1990. The decree called for simultaneous presidential and legislative elections in May 1990 and established two legislative chambers: the Assembly of Deputies and the Senate. According to the decree, the newly elected legislature was mandated to write a new constitution within the ensuing eighteen months to be followed by fresh general elections within a year thereafter (Crowther and Roper 1996: 136). Although the Senate was a much smaller body than the Assembly, having only 119 seats versus 396 in the latter, the constitution of 1991 made the two chambers co-equal in most respects. Most importantly, as we shall discuss later, the government was made responsible to both chambers. Until the 2003 amendment of the constitution, legislation could be initiated in either of the two chambers; thereafter the new constitution defined areas of competence where legislative initiative was assigned specifically to one or the other chamber.

The fourth ECE democracy with a bicameral parliament is Slovenia. However, in contrast to other three cases, the second chamber of the Slovenian national parliament, the National Council, is not a directly elected body. As a result, the role of the Council in policy and law-making as well as its overall political clout are minimal. Prior to the transition to democracy, the Slovenian Socialist Republic, a constituent republic of the federal Yugoslav state, had three legislative chambers each of them with eighty seats: the Socio-Political Chamber, the Chamber of Municipalities, and the Chamber of Labor. After the transition, the constitution of 1991 created a bicameral parliament with a weak second chamber that acts as a "typical corporate organ" (Zajc 1999: 383): the forty-member Council provides represenation to social, economic, professional and local interests (Article 96) although the majority of councillors (22) are elected by municipalities. The weakness of the Council vis-a-vis the Assembly is underscored by the provisions that it cannot decide on the electoral system used to elect its members (Article 98) and that its legislative role is limited to asking the Assembly to decide one more time on a law it has already passed within seven days of its passage (Article 91). While all legislation must originate in the Assembly, the Council may propose the passage of law to the Assembly. Furthermore, the National Council can also ask for a referendum which the Assembly cannot deny. Members of the National Council are elected for a five-year term during which the Council cannot be dissolved.

2.4 EXECUTIVE INSTITUTIONS

2.4.1 Government Formation and Termination Rules[7]

The central task in forming a new government is the selection of the prime minister who in turn leads the formation of the actual cabinet, the council of ministers. In each of the ten ECE democracies, the first move in this process belongs to the president: the head of state can either only recommend (Estonia, Hungary, and Slovenia) or actually designate/appoint the new prime minister (Bulgaria, Czech Republic, Estonia, Lithuania, Poland, Romania, Slovakia) subject to a subsequent vote of investiture. In three states (Estonia, Poland and Slovenia), the power of parliament is strengthened by a strong residual power to make a counter-nomination in case the president's nominee fails to win an investiture vote on the parliamentary floor. In the case of Romania, the *de facto* role of the president in the investiture process is strengthened by the fact that the constitution calls for *dual executive responsibility*, i.e. the government has to be approved and supported by both chambers of parliament simultaneously, which increases the coordination costs for the legislature. The constitution of Latvia is unique in that it leaves the selection and appointment of the prime minister at the exclusive discretion of the president. These variations notwithstanding, positive parliamentarism clearly prevails among the ten states. In only four states (Czech Republic, Latvia, Lithuania, and Slovakia) does the parliament have only a reactive role to confirm, or reject, the prime ministerial appointment made by the head of state.

Although political parties clearly play a crucial role in the actual process of government formation, including the selection of both the prime minister and the rest of the government, their position and role are formally acknowledged and specified in the constitutions of only three of the ten cases (Bulgaria, Romania, and Slovenia). In each of these cases, parties are mentioned only with respect to the selection of the prime minister. The Bulgarian constitution makes a particular point about stressing the role of parties by giving the party that won the most seats in the election the first mandate to form a government. In most ECE states, there is a fairly well established convention according to which the plurality party gets the first chance to try to form a government after a parliamentary election. The main exceptions to this pattern are the following post-election governments: Olszewski (Poland, 1991), Tariceanu (Romania, 2004), Paksas (Lithuania, 2000), Kristopans (Latvia, 1998), Dzurinda-1 and Dzurinda-2 (Slovakia 1998 and 2002, respectively), and Laar (Estonia, 1999). The specific reasons why the largest party failed to form a government after these elections vary considerably from case to case. However, in broad strokes we can sort these seven cases in two groups: the first one is made up by the Olszewski, Tariceanu, and Paksas governments. In each of these cases, the president played a critical role to prevent the formation of a government led by the largest parliamentary party (Fitzmaurice 2002; Downs and Miller 2005). The second group consists of the remaining four cases (Kristopans, Dzurinda-1 and -2, and Laar) where the central reason for the inability of the largest party to form a government had to do with its relative marginalization (the Center Party in Estonia, the Movement for Democracy in Slovakia, and the People's Party in Latvia) in the bargaining space and their genuine inability to attract coalition partners.

With regard to government termination rules, three groups of states can be identified. The first one consists of Hungary, Poland, and Slovenia, where parliament can censure the government only by passing a constructive vote of no-confidence against it but it cannot censure individual ministers, except in Poland.[8] The joint presence of these provisions renders the position of the head of government very powerful in the political systems of these two states both vis-à-vis the legislature as well as his/her own cabinet. In Poland, while the power of parliament to dismiss the entire cabinet is limited by the constructive no-confidence mechanism, the *Sejm* can still dismiss individual ministers by passing a vote of censure against him/her. By comparison with Hungary and Slovenia, this latter provision renders the institutional foundations of the Polish head of government somewhat weaker. The second group consists of Bulgaria, Romania and the Czech Republic, where the legislature can dismiss the government relatively more easily since the no-confidence vote does not have to be constructive. However, parliament cannot interfere with the composition of the cabinet by censuring its individual members. Finally, the constitution provides for a very powerful legislature vis-à-vis ministers in the third group of states, which includes the three Baltic democracies (Estonia, Latvia, and Lithuania) and Slovakia. Here, the legislature can dismiss both the government as a whole and its individual ministers by passing a simple vote of no-confidence.

2.4.2 The Presidency

The final institutional constraint on coalition politics is the overall power of the head of state beyond his/her role in the government formation and termination processes. Building on the pioneering work of Shugart and Carey, a number of techniques have been proposed to score and compare presidential powers. Two of these works, by Frye (1997) and Siaroff (2003), respectively, have attracted the most scholarly attention in the comparative literature The former builds on tabulations of post-communist presidential powers by Lucky (1994), McGregor (1994), and Hellmann (1996) and provides a much longer list of presidential powers, twenty-seven, compared to Shugart and Carey. The key distinction of presidential powers for Frye is not between legislative and non-legislative ones but between those that are specific and those that are residual. Specific powers are granted explicitly by the constitutions although they may not be owned exclusively by the president (Frye 1997: 525). Residual powers, on the other hand, are those which may allow the head of state to "make decisions in circumstances not specified in the constitution, such as a crisis, or to make binding decisions independent of the parliament" (Frye 1997: 526). The method of electing the president is included implicitly in Frye's list of powers; he decides to reduce by half the total score of powers in the case of indirectly elected presidents. In spite of their major differences, Frye's scaling of presidential powers, applied to twenty-four post-communist states, is very highly correlated with that of Shugart and Carey (0.814).

Siaroff (2003) adopts a very different approach to listing and measuring presidential powers. His list is the shortest yet, consisting of nine powers, which explicitly includes the method of electing the head of state. Siaroff's method is based on a dichotomous grading: on each of the nine dimensions a state receives a score of 1 if the president possesses the particular institutional power and a grade of 0 if the president does not. In contrast to the earlier tabulations, however, Siaroff (2003) does not consider the constitutional text as his sole basis of coding presidential powers. Rather he bases his assessment on both the legal text and on "actual political practice" (Siaroff 2003: 303). The nine presidential powers he considers are: the popular election of the head of state; concurrent election of the head of state and the legislature; discretionary appointment powers; chairing of cabinet meetings; veto powers; long-term emergency and decree powers; power to shape foreign policy; a central role in the government formation process; and the power to dissolve the legislature (Siaroff 2003: 303–5).

Table 2.3 compares the powers of post-communist presidencies in the ten ECE democracies as reported by the various studies mentioned above. The Table clearly shows that three states are consistently identified by the different scoring techniques as having relatively stronger presidents: Poland, Romania, and Lithuania. Of the remaining three presidents that are directly elected only Bulgaria receives somewhat higher scores in some of these studies but the Slovak and Slovene presidencies are no more powerful than most of the indirectly elected presidents.

As mentioned earlier, the ten states differ with regard to the mode of choosing the head of state: four of them elected the president indirectly for most of the

TABLE 2.3 *The powers of post-communist presidents*

State	Frye (1997) [0–27]	Metcalf (2000)*	Siaroff (2003) [0–9]
Bulgaria	10	2	3
Czech Republic	4.75	5	2.1**
Estonia	4.5	6	2
Hungary	7.25	10	1
Latvia	4.75	3	1
Lithuania	12	8	4
Poland	13	13.9***	6.3***
Romania	14	9	5
Slovakia	5	5	1.2 ****
Slovenia	5.5	3	1

Notes: * The numbers refer to the president's combined legislative and non-legislative powers respectively. ** The two numbers refer to the Czech Republic before and after 2000. *** The numbers refer to Poland before and after the constitutional changes of 1997. **** The numbers refer to Slovakia before and after 1999 when the presidency became a directly elected office.

1990–2010 period, while six states provided for a direct popular election of the head of state. Two states have changed their presidential elections method over the past twenty years: both Slovakia and the Czech Republic moved from indirect to direct elections in 1999 and 2012, respectively. Direct elections follow the two-round run-off rule: barring a first round majority, the top two candidates in the first round of the election advance to a run-off. Today, this rule is in effect in six states: Bulgaria, Lithuania, Poland, Romania, Slovakia, and Slovenia. In contrast, the rules of indirect presidential elections show considerably more diversity and complexity.

The specific rules of the Hungarian presidential selection game are described in Article 29 of the Constitution (Ludwikowski 1996: 421). Every citizen of at least 35 years of age is eligible to be nominated as a candidate for the presidency but the actual nomination must come from a minimum of fifty members of parliament. Members of parliament can lend their support only for the nomination of only one candidate at a time. The Constitution imposes a strict three-day limit on concluding the entire presidential selection but in practice it has never taken longer than two days to find the next head of state. In order to be elected a candidate requires the support of two-thirds of all members of parliament who vote in a secret ballot. Should no candidate receive such support a second round is held with new nominations having to be submitted. Once again, a two-thirds' majority is required to produce a winner on the second round. Should there be still no winner, a third round of polling is held between the top two finishers of the second round. At this stage a simple majority of the votes is sufficient to produce a winner.

Similarly to Hungary, the constitution of the Czech Republic (Article 58) provides for a maximum of three rounds of balloting in the presidential vote. However, the specific rules are very different since the Czech parliament is bicameral and both houses of the national legislature actively participate in the selection of the head of state. Moreover, the requirement for the nomination of a presidential candidate is much less stringent than it is in the case of Hungary; it takes only a minimum of ten members of either house of the Czech legislature to put forth a nominee. In the first round, the two chambers vote in separate sittings and the winner must secure an absolute majority of all statutory members in each chamber, i.e. to win on the first round a candidate must receive at least 101 votes in the Chamber and at least forty-one votes in the Senate. Should the first round fail to produce a winner, a second round is held within fourteen days between the candidates who received the most votes in each chamber. In case the same candidate receives the most votes in each house, but less than the required majority, then there can only be one candidate to vote for or against in the second round. As we shall see in Chapter Seven, this is what occurred in 1998 on the re-election of President V. Havel.

On the second round the majority requirement is a little more relaxed in that the winning candidate only needs a majority of the deputies and Senators present and voting. However, a bicameral majority is still required and the winner must have a majority in each chamber respectively. If the second round does not produce a winner either, a third and final round is held with the participation of the same candidates who had entered the second round. In order to win at this stage, the successful candidate needs to secure a majority of all deputies and Senators, sitting in a joint session, present and voting. If there is still no winner, the process starts all over again.

Since the Latvian constitution is the shortest of all constitutions among the ECE democracies, it is not surprising that there is but a single line devoted to the mode of electing the head of state. Article 36 provides that the president must be elected by secret ballot with an absolute majority of fifty-one members of parliament; the provision for a secret ballot allows for the possibility of undisciplined and uncoordinated voting by members of the *Saeima*. Apart from extending the term of the presidency (Article 35) from three to four years in the 1999 election, the rules have remained stable. Although the constitution is laconic about the rules on electing the president, the *Saeima*'s Rules of Procedure are quite a bit more straightforward. Except for the first election in 1993, when there was no restriction on the qualification of candidates to move to subsequent rounds of balloting, all other polls were regulated by Article 26 of the *Saeima* Rules of Procedure, adopted on May 6, 1996, which stipulates the elimination of the candidate with the fewest votes from each subsequent run-off.[9] If the final run-off between two candidates still does not produce the constitutionally required majority of fifty-one votes then a whole new election is held and unsuccessful candidates in the first election are eligible to re-enter (http://www.saeima.lv/en/legislation/rules-of-procedure).

The process to elect the Estonian head of state is defined in Article 79 of the constitution. The right to nominate a candidate for president rests with members of the legislature; since a minimum of twenty-one deputies have to submit a nomination there can never be more than five candidates running for the office at one time. In all three rounds of voting in Riigikogu, it takes a two-thirds' majority of the total membership to elect a winning candidate. If the first round fails to produce a winner then a second round is held with a newly nominated set of candidates. Should the second round also not produce a candidate with the required two-thirds' majority support, a third round is held between the top two candidates from the previous round. Although the competition is now reduced to two candidates, a two-thirds' majority is still required for victory. This is in stark contrast to the Hungarian rules, where the third round of parliamentary voting works with a simple majority rule. In case the *Riigikogu* cannot elect the president, an electoral college, consisting of all members of the *Riigikogu* as well as representatives from each of the local government councils, is convened to choose among the contenders from the third round of the *Riigikogu* vote as well as any other candidate who may be put forward by any group of twenty-one members of the college. In order to win at this stage, the winning candidate needs to secure an absolute majority of all voting members of the college in the first round. Should there still not be a winner, one more round is held between the top two candidates of the first round of the college vote using the same rules.

2.5 INSTITUTIONAL COMBINATIONS AND THE ORGANIZATION OF POLITICAL POWER

The electoral, parliamentary, and executive institutions that I have surveyed above have specific effects on the dispersion and concentration of political power in the respective polities. In some cases, these institutions are combined in such a way so as to reinforce the effect of one another while in other instances their effects are contradictory. Overall, however, three clearly identifiable groups of states can be identified with respect to their institutional organization of political power: (i) states where the institutions provide for a high level of power concentration in the legislature (Bulgaria, Estonia, Hungary, and Slovenia); (ii) states where the institutions provide for weaker concentration of power in the legislature (Latvia and Slovakia); and (iii) states where the institutions strongly divide political power either within the legislature (Czech Republic) or between parliament and the executive (Lithuania) or both (Poland and Romania). In this section I will explain the relationship between the four sets of institutions and the effect they have on the concentration of political power followed by an overall assessment of the institutional concentration of political power in the ten states.

It is well known from the literature on comparative electoral systems that more permissive rules, such lower thresholds, higher district magnitude, and the use of the largest remainder as opposed to the highest average method of allocating PR seats, led to the proliferation of smaller political parties and increased the level of party system fragmentation (Duverger 1954; Rae 1967; Lijphart 1984).

Conversely, higher thresholds, lower magnitudes and the use of the highest average formula tend to benefit larger political parties and, as a result, they lead to lower levels of party system fragmentation. *Ceteris paribus*, political power is more dispersed when the electoral system encourages the fragmentation of the party system among which power, both legislative and executive, will have to be divided. Under more permissive electoral systems the likelihood that fragmented multi-party coalition governments will be formed is greater than under electoral systems that discourage the success and survival of smaller parties. As discussed earlier, the ten states form three natural clusters with regard to their average district magnitude, which is the electoral system component that tends to have the strongest effect on party system fragmentation, and, therefore, the concentration of political power.

Assembly size has an inverse effect on the concentration of political power: the smaller the legislature the more difficult it is for smaller parties to get their proportional access to legislative seats, and, ultimately, to executive posts. Although the empirical relationship between assembly size and the party system fragmentation is much weaker than that between district magnitude and the number of parties, the general view is that as the number of seats in the assembly increases smaller parties have a greater chance to proliferate, legislative majorities will be harder to obtain (Lijphart 1994: 12–13), and that the seat share of the largest party will decrease (Taagepera and Ensch 2006) and party system fragmentation increases with the product of the number of assembly seats and district magnitude (Taagepera and Shugart 1993).

Political power is more dispersed in bicameral than in unicameral legislatures. In the former, the governing coalition that controls the executive in the first chamber needs to take into account the policy preferences and the partisan composition of the second chamber. Even when the same party or party coalition controls both chambers the potential for disagreement and need to coordinate and harmonize positions on issues increases. In short, the second chamber always acts as a check on the first chamber regardless of similarities or differences in their party compositions.

The rules of government formation and termination may or may not require a positive investiture or censure vote supported by a parliamentary majority. A positive investiture rule, as well as a constructive vote of no-confidence, requires that there be a clear and explicit legislative majority in support of the new government. In contrast, when the formation of the government is governed by the rule or tradition of negative parliamentarism or the dismissal of the government requires only a negative no-confidence vote, there is no need to build and maintain a majority coalition in support of the executive. In the latter instance, the government support can be diffused, while in the case of positive formation and termination rules, support for the government must be concentrated in and established through a clear majority. Therefore, positive formation and termination rules favor the concentration of political power while negative rules do not.

Finally, strong elected presidencies lead to more power dispersion than weak elected or unelected presidents who are not in a position to challenge or check the political will of the majority that control the legislature. While none of the ten states have a presidential, or even a purely semi-presidential executive, the powers of the Polish, Romanian, and the Lithuanian heads of state clearly stand out from the rest and as such they do balance the powers of parliament much more than the chief executives of the other states.

Table 2.4 summarizes this discussion and establishes a threefold classification of post-communist democracies with respect to their institutional power concentration. The top row of the table identifies the institutional conditions that are favorable for the concentration of political power: lower district magnitude PR elections, smaller assemblies, unicameral legislatures, positive government formation and termination rules, and a weak presidency. For each state I identify the presence (+) or the absence (−) of each of these conditions. The more conditions are present the greater the institutional power concentration in the given state and vice versa. For the district magnitude and assembly size I use two natural breaking points in the distribution of the otherwise continuous variables among the ten states in order to determine whether a favorable condition is present or not: I consider states with an average district magnitude below ten as low and an assembly size of less than 200 as small. These breaking points divided the ten states in nearly exact halves on both variables: four of the ten states have district

TABLE 2.4 *Institutional concentration of political power in post-communist democracies*

State	Small district magnitude	Small Assembly	Unicameralism	Positive formation/ termination rules	Weak presidency
1. Most favorable institutional conditions for power concentration					
Estonia	+	+	+	+/−	+
Hungary	+	−	+	+/+	+
Bulgaria	+	−	+	+/−	+
Slovenia	−	+	+	+/+	+
2. Mixed institutional conditions for power concentration					
Latvia	−	+	+	−/−	+
Slovakia	−	+	+	−/−	+
3. Least favorable conditions for power concentration					
Lithuania	−	+	+	−/−	−
Romania	+	−	−	+/−	−
Poland	−	−	−	+/+	−
Czech Republic	−	−	−	−/−	+

Note: As explained in the text, I consider Slovenia de facto unicameral because of the extremely weak powers commanded by an unelected second chamber.

magnitude below ten and exactly five states have a first legislative chamber of no more than 200 seats.

The table identifies three clearly distinguishable groups of states with respect to their overall institutional power concentration. The first group consists of Bulgaria, Estonia, Hungary, and Slovenia; each of these states has almost all the institutional conditions present that favor the concentration of political power. While the specific institutional make-up of each of these states is different, they all have unicameral legislatures (I include here the case of Slovenia where the second chamber is extremely weak and non-elected), positive government formation rules, and weak presidents. The most favorable conditions are present in Hungary and Estonia, with the other states of the group lagging only marginally behind.

The opposite group, where the institutional conditions for power concentration are the least favorable, consists of the Czech Republic, Lithuania, Poland, and Romania. This is a very mixed group in the sense that the four states disperse political power through different combinations of institutional rules. Poland and Romania do so mainly by combining large bicameral parliaments with strong presidents, while in Lithuania and the Czech Republic power is dispersed though negative government formation and termination rules and high district magnitudes. In addition, Poland also has relatively large districts although the dispersion of power is limited in this state by the application of positive government investiture and censure rules. Of the four states the Czech Republic has the least favorable conditions for power concentration, while power is a little less dispersed in Poland, Romania, and Lithuania.

Finally, the middle group includes Latvia and Slovakia which are perfectly identical in terms of the main features of their institutional design. Both states combine large electoral districts with relatively small unicameral assemblies that form and terminate government via negative rules. The powers of the presidency are weak in both states. The overall impact of these rules on power concentration is mixed: some conditions clearly favor it while others do not.

2.6 CONCLUSION

The central point of this chapter was to describe the cross-national variation among the ten post-communist democracies on the four main seats of institutions (electoral system, assembly structure and size, government formation and termination rules, and the presidency). Based on the descriptive material, I provided an overall assessment of the different combinations of these institutional rules with regard to the organization of political power. Clearly, there is no single dominant model of institutional design that characterizes the region; the ten states form three clearly distinct clusters. In the chapters that follow I will examine in detail how these institutional rules shape party choices in the electoral, parliamentary and executive realm of coalition politics.

NOTES

1. The population size of the ten states, in millions, as of 2010 was as follows: Bulgaria (7.6), Czech Republic (10.4), Estonia (1.3), Hungary (10), Latvia (2.3), Lithuania (3.3), Poland (38), Romania (21.5), Slovakia (5.4), and Slovenia (2). Source: World Bank (2010). *World Development Indicators* (http://data.worldbank.org/data-catalog/world-development-indicators ed.).
2. In the case of an urgent government bill, the *Senat* has only fourteen days to act but on constitutional bills it can take up to sixty days.
3. However, the processes that had led up to the constitutional changes of both 1992 and 1997 brought to the surface some of the potential and actual rifts between the two chambers. In fact, during the discussions leading up to the 1997 constitution the possible abolition of the *Senat* was taken up and a motion to this effect was only narrowly defeated (Olson 1999: 326). In 1992, as the Assembly was drafting and debating the Small Constitution that would at least in part abrogate the 1952 communist constitution, the *Sejm* was able to reject most of the long list of *Senate* amendments only after it had changed its internal rules of procedure precisely to ensure that the *Senate* modifications could be overridden (Gebethner and Jasiewicz 1993: 534).
4. The number of seats won by the largest party in the seven *Senat* elections are as follows: 60 in 2010; 49 in 2005; 75 in 2001; 51 in 1997; 37 in 1993; 21 in 1991, and 99 in 1989.
5. For the concepts of veto players, "absorption" and their effect on policy change, see Tsebelis (2002). Note though that the *Senat* cannot be regarded as a mere rubber stamp of the first chamber. Between 1989 and 2007, the *Senat* examined a total of 2,775 bills passed by the *Sejm* and made amendments to just about half of them (1,380). More importantly, the first chamber accepted almost all of these amendments (1,280). Furthermore, although the number of legislative proposals initiated in the *Senat* remains low (a total of 127 between 1989 and 2007), the *Sejm* has adopted about half of them (60) (Senate, 2007).
6. The percentage of Senate seats that governing parties and coalitions won after the respective Senate election is as follows: 64.2 percent in 1996; 28.3 percent in 1998; 27.2 percent in 2000; 32 percent in 2002; 62.9 percent in 2006; and 53 percent in 2008.
7. This sections draws on Fettelschoss and Nikolenyi (2008).
8. Article 66 of the 1992 Small Constitution of Poland provided for an optional constructive vote of no confidence.
9. The first run-off is an exception. If there is no candidate with a fifty-one-vote majority then the first run-off can be held with the same candidates running once more.

3

Political Institutions and Electoral Coalitions

3.1 INTRODUCTION

Through the formation of pre-electoral alliances and coalitions, political parties are able to directly influence and shape the environment in which the government formation game takes place once the parliamentary election is over (Nikolenyi 2004). The significance of pre-electoral coalitions is attested by a number of studies (Strom and Müller-Rommel 2000; Powell 2000; Golder 2006a,b) which report that a significant number of governing coalitions are in fact based on some kind of pre-electoral understanding among political parties in most European parliamentary democracies. Despite their obvious importance, the study of pre-electoral coalitions remains one of the most important uncharted areas of comparative party politics and electoral research (Powell 2000) and it has been given systematic scholarly attention only very recently (Kaminski 2001; Ferrara and Herron 2005; Golder 2005, 2006a,b; Blais and Indridason 2007).

Electoral coalitions, similarly to legislative and executive coalitions, vary in terms of their size and durability. Sometimes electoral coalitions become the central players in the election while other times they are relegated to a much more peripheral role. While my main interest lies in observing and understanding the cross-national patterns of electoral coalition formation, it is important to note that even within the same country there have been fluctuations and differences over time. Moreover, while some electoral coalitions become proto-coalitions in the government formation game others dissolve after the election and their constituent parties pursue their own agendas in the realm of parliamentary politics. Duverger expected that electoral coalitions and alliances would be temporary phenomena in the development of a party system and that they were merely a "prelude to . . . total fusion" (1963: 224) whereby parties merge and give up their separate identities to create a new organization. However, in a number of democracies, new and established alike, electoral coalitions have become a permanent part of the party system and the electoral landscape.

This chapter analyzes the impact of the institutional features identified in Chapter Two on the formation and size of electoral coalitions in the ten states. The next section provides a brief overview of the literature on electoral coalitions to identify the explanatory variables that have been proposed by other scholars.

Clearly, there is general agreement that electoral laws affect and shape the formation of electoral coalitions. However, the impact of the full range of electoral system variables on electoral coalitions has not yet been studied. At the end of the section, I propose a number of hypotheses linking specific parliamentary institutional and electoral system components to the likelihood of the formation and the success of electoral coalitions, followed by an operational definition of what constitutes and electoral coalition in the present context. The detailed presentation of the empirical record of the history of electoral coalitions in the ten states is left to Appendix C. In the fourth section I review the changes that have taken place in the institutional regulation of electoral coalitions and the reasons that led to these changes. The fifth section provides a comparative summary and analysis of the impact that particular configurations of electoral system features have on the formation of electoral coalitions.

The central finding of the chapter is that the most favorable institutional environment for the formation and success of electoral coalitions is provided by electoral systems that provide for relatively smaller district magnitude, the use of more restrictive electoral formulae, and a positive government investiture rule. Most of these institutional features are present in three states (Bulgaria, Hungary, and Romania), which together account both for the highest number and the largest electoral coalitions. Hungary stands out further from this group as the only state where the electoral coalitions dominate the party system and consistently define the two main competing government alternatives. A detailed examination of Hungarian electoral coalitions and their impact on government formation is left to the next chapter.

3.2 DETERMINANTS OF ELECTORAL COALITIONS: A THEORETICAL OVERVIEW

Although the topic of electoral coalitions, or alliances, received considerable treatment and attention in Duverger's (1959) seminal work on political parties, it was not until relatively recently that the literature began to study them more systematically. I start the review of the literature with a summary of Duverger's arguments about the formation and types of electoral alliances and then sketch the main directions in which the literature has developed subsequently.

Duverger identifies five conditions that promote the formation of electoral alliances. The first is the number of parties; here he expects that two-party systems would normally not lead to alliances whereas multi-party systems normally cannot manage without them. The second factor is national tradition according to which particular sets of parties, normally grouped together because of their shared ideological predilections, would join hands against others from time to time.

The third is the possibility of pressure from the government; however, Duverger observes this to be the practice of specific authoritarian regimes of the past (e.g. the Balkan states of the inter-war period of Wilhelmine Germany). Fourth, unique historical circumstances, such as major national economic and political crises, were also responsible for the formation of alliances. Finally, the fifth condition is the electoral system, which Duverger expects to have the strongest impact of all. Although his precise statement about the relationship between the electoral system and number of parties has received by far the most scholarly attention over time, Duverger is no less uncertain about the impact of electoral laws on the formation of electoral alliances. In fact he notes that this effect is

> sufficiently clear to be expressed in a precise formulae. In principle, the simple-majority second ballot system encourages the formation of close alliances; proportional representation, on the other hand, encourages complete independence. As for the simple-majority single-ballot system, its results are very different according to the number of parties functioning under it; in a two-party regime it encourages total independence; in a multi-party regime, on the other hand, it favors very strong alliances. (325–6)

In a neo-Duvergerian vein, Gary Cox (1997) specifically identifies two instances when the run-off system may encourage parties to form pre-electoral coalitions, both of them depicting particular party system formats: the first is the format of the *divided center* and the second is the format of *lopsided bipolarity* (Cox 1997). In each instance, Cox argues, the pole that is more divided and fragmented than its main competitor(s) will have an incentive to go through a coordination, or merger, process and a reduction in the number of parties offered to the voters. In turn, voters will find it easier to make their votes count and reduce the number of viable parties to its equilibrium level. As such, party system configurations of the divided center and the lopsided bipolarity type also constitute favorable conditions for the formation of electoral coalitions.

In his review of the history of West European electoral systems Carstairs (1980) notes that electoral coalitions, or *apparentment,* a party alliance that "the electoral law recognizes for the purposes of allocating seats to parties (23), was one of the three most commonly used methods by which changes in PR systems sought to affect the electoral chances of smaller parties.[1] Although he does not provide an analytical review of the different types of alliances that have been formed under the various electoral regimes of the continent, three points are worth extracting from his study. The first is that electoral coalitions were often associated with political opportunism and, as a result, became effectively banned in several states. Instead of extending positive assistance to smaller political parties, electoral coalitions could become a negative weapon to be used by some group of parties against others, typically by bourgeois parties against those of the left. The second is that while list-PR systems normally required the explicit recognition of *apparentments*, provided they were allowed, the single transferable vote system of

Ireland did not. Under this system political parties could form an electoral coalition simply by encouraging their supporters to give their lower preference votes to candidates of the other party or parties in the coalition. Accordingly, whether the coalition became effective or not remained ultimately in the hands of the voters.

Third, the regulation of electoral coalitions has varied considerably across Western Europe both in space and time. In some countries they were historically never allowed (e.g. Luxembourg, Denmark, Finland); in others they were allowed at some point in time but banned later on (Norway in 1949, Sweden in 1952, Austria in 1923); while in a third group of states electoral coalitions were not allowed at first but became introduced and permitted as a result of subsequent changes to the electoral law (Belgium in 1919, France in 1951, Holland in 1970, and Norway in 1985). The only state that consistently allowed electoral coalitions since the introduction of PR is Switzerland (Carstairs: 217). Although Carstairs does not formulate an explicit theory of these variations he notes that changes in the institutional and legal treatment of electoral coalitions was related to the use or abandonment of the d'Hondt rule: "[s]ince the D'Hondt system is imperfectly proportional and favors the larger parties, some electoral systems have, by way of compensation, permitted *apparentment* in order that smaller parties may share the same advantage by forming electoral alliances" (Carstairs: 217).

In a more recent work, Golder (2006a,b) offers two hypotheses that connect the type of the electoral system and the number of parties in the party system to the likelihood that pre-electoral coalitions will be formed. The first is the Disproportionality hypothesis, which posits that parties are more likely to form pre-electoral coalitions under disproportional electoral laws but only if the level of party system fragmentation is sufficiently high. Golder's second proposition about the formation of electoral coalitions is specified in her Signalling hypothesis, which suggests a positive relationship between the number of parties and the formation of pre-electoral coalitions. Here Golder expects that the need to identify a future coalition government is a positive function of the complexity of the party system, indicated by the degree of party system fragmentation, and the uncertainty about future government options.

3.2.1 What Constitutes an Electoral Coalition?

In spite of the growing interest in the study of electoral coalitions, there is still no clear definition and taxonomy of their different types and modes. In a very basic sense, electoral coalitions are a form of electoral coordination among political parties. However, not every form of coordination can be, or should be, considered an electoral coalition: political parties can engage in electoral coordination in a myriad of ways and we need to clarify which of these practices constitute an electoral coalition. *I propose that an electoral coalition is an organized and institutionalized form of electoral coordination among political parties that is made credible by the presentation of joint candidates, or lists of candidates, in the election.*

Golder's view of electoral coalitions is based on a dichotomy: there are "parties that compete independently at election time (no pre-electoral coalition) and parties that do not compete independently (pre-electoral coalition)" (2006: 16). While she suggests that there is a continuum of degrees of electoral coordination among political parties she refrains from providing a full taxonomy thereof. Golder (2006: 17) further states that the "specific form that electoral coordination takes in a particular country is likely to depend on the electoral rules, the regional distribution of the party system, and other factors relating to the relative strengths and ideological positions of different parties." Although she proceeds to describe five main types of electoral coordination among political parties, for the purposes of her analysis she ultimately considers all of them as one, i.e. instances of electoral coordination.

According to Golder (2006: 17–19), the highest levels of electoral coordination are nomination agreements and joint candidate lists. The former is tied to electoral systems that provide for single-member districts, while the latter form of coordination is possible only when there are multi-member districts. In the case of nominating agreements, the coordinating parties agree to run a single coalition candidate to represent them in the districts while in the case of joint lists the coordinating parties run a single list of candidates that come from the different parties. An intermediate form of coordination takes the form of dual ballot instructions and vote transfers. Again, the electoral system is crucial in making these types of coordination possible: dual ballot instructions assume that voters have multiple votes to cast while vote transfer instructions assume that the electoral law provides for open lists and the transferability of voters' preferential votes over candidates. Ultimately, however, all that parties do when they resort to this type of electoral coordination is to ask their supporters to cast their votes in a particular way. The third and weakest form of electoral coordination identified by Golder is the "public commitment to govern together" or not to govern together with certain parties (2006: 201).

While the notion of a continuum of electoral coordination among political parties is helpful, I disagree with Golder's claim that all forms of coordination constitute an electoral coalition. Instead, I build on the standard view in the coalition theoretic literature, which assumes that for a coalition to be present the contracting parties' agreement to cooperate has to be credible. At the stage of parliamentary politics credibility means that coalition partners must delegate ministers to the coalition government in order to be counted (Strom 1990). Similarly, an electoral coalition assumes that the coordinating parties do not run independently, i.e. they either run a single jointly supported candidate or they run a joint list of multiple candidates together. In the case of the latter three types of electoral coordination identified by Golder, i.e. dual ballot instructions, vote transfers, and the public commitment for or against governing together, this assumption is violated. In these cases parties do not coordinate in a credible fashion, they merely ask or instruct their supporters to vote in a particular way, which the voters may or may not follow. In other words, the latter practices are forms of electoral coordination but not electoral coalitions among political parties per se. Accordingly, an electoral coalition must be officially registered as such if the electoral regulations so require and/or it must be also explicitly identified as such to the voters either because the coalition has a specific name or because the constituent parties are clearly spelt out. Thus, so-called hidden coalitions, whereby a host party accommodates candidates of other parties on its own list and under its own name are not counted as electoral coalitions.

3.3 THE EXPECTED EFFECTS OF POLITICAL INSTITUTIONS ON THE FORMATION OF ELECTORAL COALITIONS

I expect that the institutions that govern inter-party competition in both the electoral and the parliamentary arenas will have an effect on the likelihood and success of electoral coalition formation. As we have seen above, the literature has dealt extensively with the effect that the electoral system has on these coalitions (Strom, Budge and Laver 1994; Golder 2006). I suggest, however, that forward looking parties also take into account the rules and structures that shape the post-election stage of inter-party relations. When those rules provide distinct benefits for larger players, political parties will be more likely to coordinate their actions and form electoral coalitions. The first three hypotheses link specific features of the parliamentary stage of party competition to electoral coalition formation, while the subsequent hypotheses identify expectations about the effects of particular electoral system variables.

Hypothesis 1: *Assembly size has a positive effect on the formation of electoral coalitions.* Political parties will be more likely to form electoral coalitions as the size of the electoral stake increases: the more seats are to be won in an election, the greater the resource constraints will be on individual political parties to find and nominate the candidates to fill them. By forming electoral coalitions, political parties can alleviate these constraints. The size of the stake in an election is defined by the size of the assembly, including both the first and second chambers, and the holding of concurrent presidential elections. Therefore, as the overall number of parliamentary seats increases political parties should have a stronger incentive to form electoral coalitions. Larger political parties may have less difficulty finding and nominating candidates for all seats; however, smaller parties may face particular constraints in their ability to run full slates on their own when there a lot of legislative seats to be filled. In new democracies where the institutionalization of the party system is weaker and, therefore, the ability of political parties to recruit and nominate candidates is more limited, competing for seats in a large parliament is likely to impose a particularly heavy burden on political parties.

Hypothesis 2: *Concurrent elections to both chambers of parliament (as in Poland and Romania) as well as concurrent elections to the parliament and the presidency (in Romania until 2008) should have a positive effect on the formation of electoral coalitions.* Similarly to assembly size, concurrent elections increase the size of the electoral stake that parties are competing for and benefit larger player over smaller ones. Therefore, they encourage parties to coordinate their efforts via the formation of electoral coalitions. Controlling for electoral concurrence, I will also examine if bicameralism or the relative strength of the presidency alone also promote electoral coalitions.

Hypothesis 3a: *Positive parliamentary rules of government formation provide stronger incentives for the formation of pre-electoral coalitions than negative formation rules do.* Government formation under positive parliamentarism can be a potentially chaotic process because of the inherent tendency for legislative bodies to generate cyclical majorities (McKelvey 1976). While the extent of such cycling is limited by the size of the generalized center of the space of competition, the yolk (Feld, Grofman and Miller 1988, 1989), cycles are well known to happen. In order to limit the occurrence of majority cycles which can lead to de-stabilizing and very chaotic outcomes in the government formation game, forward looking parties have an incentive to commit themselves to one another with regard to forming a coalition government.

Hypothesis 3b: *Government formation rules that privilege larger parties promote the formation of electoral coalitions.* Another feature of government formation rules that may have bearing on the formation of electoral coalitions is the provision, or informal practice, to give the party with the most seats the first opportunity to form a government. Cox (1997) has shown that such rules encourage cross-district linkages and coordination among candidates, which can lead to the formation of large political parties. Similarly, the same rules may encourage parties that are otherwise unwilling to give up their separate organization identities to coordinate their efforts and form an electoral coalition. By so doing parties send a clear signal to the voters about the likely government that will obtain if the largest member of this coalition will also emerge as the plurality winner in the election.

The following hypotheses disaggregate the Disproportionality thesis and identify how and why specific electoral system components may encourage or hinder the formation of electoral coalitions.

Hypothesis 4: *District magnitude has a negative effect on the formation of electoral coalitions.* It is well known from the literature on comparative electoral laws that district magnitude is positively related to the proportionality of the electoral system and, therefore, is inversely related to the proliferation of political parties, i.e. the fragmentation of the party system. Therefore, I expect that parties will be less motivated and pressed to form an electoral coalition when district magnitude is higher. Furthermore, when electoral coalitions are formed in systems of high district magnitude, I expect their size to be relatively smaller compared to those that are formed under more restrictive laws.

Hypothesis 5: *Closed list systems have a positive effect on the formation of electoral coalitions relative to open list systems.* Political parties that form an electoral coalition can pre-negotiate the allocation of seats among themselves with greater credibility when voters do not have the ability to change the ranking of candidates on the ballot. When voters have the ability to change the ranking of all or some of the candidates, party leaders' choices about the relative size of the coalition partners will be less credible, which in turn discourages the formation of electoral coalitions. Therefore, I expect that electoral systems that allow voters to cast preferential votes will limit the formation of electoral coalitions.

Hypothesis 6: *The proportionality of the electoral formula has a negative effect on the formation of electoral coalitions.* Similarly to the effect of district magnitude, the more proportional the electoral formula that is used to calculate the conversion of votes to seats, the weaker the incentive to form electoral coalitions. The least proportional rules are the majority and plurality formulae used in the nominal tier of the mixed electoral systems (Hungary and Lithuania), followed by the highest average (d'Hondt, Saint-Lague) and the quota-based largest remainder (Droop, Hare and Hagenbach-Bischoff) rules. Given that political parties will form electoral coalitions to overcome or at least reduce the barriers of disproportionality in the electoral system, I expect electoral coalitions to be more prevalent in systems with more disproportional formulae.

Hypothesis 7: *The formation of electoral coalitions is negatively affected by the imposition of special threshold requirements.* The nominal threshold is the electoral system variable that should have the most immediate effect on electoral coalitions. I expect that the higher the threshold for electoral coalitions, the weaker the incentives to form them. In those cases where the electoral law does not provide for a differentiated threshold, or such differentiation does not impose a significantly higher bar on coalitions, political parties should have a stronger incentive to form electoral coalitions, holding everything else equal.

3.4 THE INSTITUTIONAL REGULATION OF ELECTORAL COALITIONS IN POST-COMMUNIST DEMOCRACIES

Although the scale of electoral reform in the post-communist democracies of East Central Europe (ECE) has been limited by a variety of factors including international pressure, the normative commitment to proportional representation and the institutional logic of consensus democracy (Nikolenyi 2011), every state in the region has enacted some change in the initial electoral system that had been adopted at the time of the transition to democracy. As a matter of rule, electoral coalitions have been included in these reform packages and, since electoral reforms in the region have always aimed at reducing the fragmentation in the party system, the specific changes targeting electoral coalitions have been also more restrictive than the *status quo ante.* Overall, changes in the treatment of electoral coalitions have both reflected and have been part of the broader regional pattern to keep party proliferation in check and encourage the consolidation of individual political parties instead of ad hoc alliances and coalitions.

Increases in the institutional restrictions on electoral coalitions have resulted either (i) when existing electoral coalitions have failed to reduce the level of party system fragmentation which results in inefficiencies such as unstable coalition governments (e.g. Estonia before 1999, Latvia before 1998, Poland before 1993); or (ii) when the incumbent governing parties, or some set of parties that have the parliamentary strength to change the electoral system, perceive that the formation of a new electoral coalition signals the possibility of an adverse change in the balance of partisan power and the loss of their competitive advantage (e.g. Slovakia 1998, Czech Republic 2000, Romania 2008). Conversely, there was no incentive to change the existing restrictions on electoral coalitions (iii) when political parties behave according to the logic of a permissive PR system and contest the elections mostly on their own, rather than by forming electoral alliances, (e.g. Slovenia); or (iv) if there is already in place a balanced party system with regular alternation in power by the main partisan blocs and contenders (e.g. Bulgaria, Hungary, Lithuania, and Poland after 1993, Slovakia after 2002).

Table 3.1 summarizes the changes that have taken place in the regulation of electoral coalitions among the ten new democracies. The table reveals a very interesting pattern: while the regulation of electoral coalitions was virtually immune to change in the first group of states with a high level of institutional power concentration, all other states experienced some form of amendment to make the formation of electoral coalitions more difficult. Nonetheless, the most severe restriction on electoral coalitions, an outright ban, was implemented in Estonia, where political institutions otherwise promote the concentration of political power. This overall pattern makes good sense in terms of institutional logic. Electoral coalitions constitute the first stage in the lifecycle of the coalition formation process and as such they simplify the eventual formation of a

TABLE 3.1 *Electoral systems and changes in the regulations on electoral coalitions*

State	District magnitude	Change in the regulation of electoral coalitions
1. Most favorable institutional conditions for power concentration		
Estonia	8.4	Ban (1998, 1999)
Hungary	7.6	None
Bulgaria	7.7	None
Slovenia	11	None
2. Mixed institutional conditions for power concentration		
Latvia	20	Formal registration required (1998)
Slovakia	150	Threshold increased moderately (1998) and subsequently reversed (2002)
3. Least favorable conditions for power concentration		
Lithuania	70	None
Romania	8.2	Threshold increased moderately (2000)
Poland	11.2	Threshold increased moderately (1993)
Czech Republic	14.3	Threshold increased severely (2000)

parliamentary majority. If the prevailing logic of a state's institutional design aims at the dispersion of political power then it is reasonable that electoral coalitions would be discouraged. Conversely, if the prevailing logic of institutional design is to concentrate political power in a legislative majority then it makes sense not to introduce further restrictions in the rules that govern the formation of electoral coalitions. Indeed, three of the four states in the third group imposed additional restrictions on their electoral coalitions (Czech Republic, Poland, and Romania), while only one of the four states in the first group (Estonia) did so.

The most severe restrictions on electoral coalitions were introduced in the three countries (Estonia, Latvia and Poland) where the level of party system fragmentation reached extremely high levels leading to highly unstable governments. Until 1999, electoral coalitions clearly dominated and defined the Estonian party system. In 1992 the vote and seat shares of electoral coalitions were 76 percent and 89.1 percent, respectively. Three years later, however, both their vote and seat share dropped to 63.7 percent and 65.3 percent. The effective number of electoral and parliamentary parties in Estonia reached 8.9 and 5.9 in 1992 followed by 5.9 and 4.1 in 1995. Thus, although electoral coalitions dominated the electoral landscape, they were unable to produce strong and cohesive parliamentary parties, which also resulted in unstable governments. Although the largest electoral coalition in the 1995 election, the Coalition Party and Rural Union, was able win 40.6 percent of the seats, it quickly disintegrated as its constituent units formed their own parliamentary party groups. Government instability was also high; the *Riigikogu* elected in 1992 saw the alternation of two cabinets followed by four in the 1995–9 period. All the main arguments in favor of abolishing electoral coalitions in 1999 cited the inability of opportunistic alliances to become cohesive parliamentary entities as the main reason for the institutional reform.

The Polish and Latvian cases were similar in all regards. In Latvia, there were three electoral coalitions that succeeded to have their candidates elected to the parliaments after the 1993 and 1995 elections: the alliance of the National Harmony Party and Economic Rebirth, winning 12 percent of the votes and 13 percent of seats in 1993; the United List that combined the Farmers' Union, the Christian Democratic Union, and a splinter of the Democratic Party, which won 6 percent of the votes and 8 percent of the seats in 1995; and the coalition of the Latvian National Conservative and the Green Parties, which won together 6.3 percent of the vote and also 8 percent of the seats in 1995. In spite of allowing electoral coalitions to form and compete in the elections, both party system fragmentation and government instability remained at very high levels. The largest parties received only 36 percent and 18 percent of the parliamentary seats in 1993 and 1995 respectively and both elections were followed by the formation unstable governments: the *Saeima* elected in 1993 witnessed the alternation of two governments followed by four in the next *Saeima* elected in 1995.

In Poland, the period between 1991 and 1993 was similarly characterized by extreme levels of party system fragmentation and government instability: the largest party received a mere 13.5 percent of the seats in the *Sejm* after the elections of 1991 which was followed by the formation of three unstable governments. Among the 29 formations that entered the fractured *Sejm* in that election, there were five electoral coalitions with a combined vote and seat shares of 37.2 percent and 41.3 percent.

In one case (Slovenia), a high level of party system fragmentation did not lead to heightened restrictions on electoral coalitions because electoral coalitions have simply not played a major role in parliamentary elections and could not, therefore, be blamed for govenrment instability. Although political parties clustered into two distinct blocs in each of the country's post-communist elections, they submitted indiviudal candidate lists for the most part. Indeed, of all the contenders that have won seats in the country's five post-communist elections, I found only two electoral coalitions: the ZLDS and the coalition of the Slovenian People's Party (SLS) and the Youth Party of Slovenia (SMS). The central and dominant position of the Liberal Democratic Party, which led every government, together with smaller coalition partners, between 1992 and 2004 with but a brief interruption in 2000, lent a significant degree of stability to the executive. All in all, there was no reason in Slovenia to restrict the activities of electoral coalitions.

In three states restrictions on electoral coalitions were introduced because the incumbent party or coalition sought to prevent the formation of an opposition bloc of parties that could threaten its hold on office. As discussed by Cox (1997) such realignments are likely to take place either when the party system is characterized by a *divided center*, which gives an incentive for the centrist parties to coordinate and ally, or by *lopsided bipolarity*, when the member parties of the more fragmented and divided poles have an incentive to coordinate. The case of the *divided center* was exemplified by the Czech Republic between 1998 and 2002. The general election of 1998 resulted in a parliament with two large nearly equally sized parties, the CSSD of the left and the ODS of the right with the balance of power between them held by the smaller centrist KDU and the US; without the joint support of both of these smaller parties neither the CCSD nor the ODS was capable of forming a government (Nikolenyi 2003). In an effort to deprive the small parties of their blackmail potential, the two large parties sponsored a comprehensive package of electoral reforms in 2000 including changes to the district magnitude; the electoral formula and the threshold structures, with a specific provision to increase the threshold for electoral coalitions. In the end, it was only the restriction on coalitions that was upheld by the Constitutional Court (Crawford 2001).

Slovakia in 1998 and Romania in 2000 illustrated the cases of *lopsided bipolarity*. In both instances the governing coalition, the HZDS and its allies in Slovakia and the Democratic Convention with its allies in Romania, faced a fractionalized opposition that was regrouping to put up a united front against the incumbents in the coming elections. In both instances the government passed legislation that increased the threshold for electoral coalitions in an effort to hinder the chances of the opposition at the ballot box.

3.5 POLITICAL INSTITUTIONS AND ELECTORAL COALITIONS IN POST-COMMUNIST DEMOCRACIES

Table 3.2 provides descriptive statistics about electoral coalitions in ECE according to their size and frequency. I consider only the relevant electoral coalitions that have crossed the threshold of representation and won seats in the national legislature. The table shows that both the size and the frequency of electoral coalitions vary considerably across the ten states. During the two decades between 1990 and 2010, half of the states have held five and the other half have held six parliamentary elections, a total of fifty-three elections for the group. Since Estonia banned electoral election after her second national election, I only include the first two polls from that state. In these fifty-three elections I have identified seventy-six electoral coalitions, an average of 1.43 coalitions per election. While this number might not appear high, it is strikingly higher than what Golder (2006) reports for the twenty-three established democracies that she surveys. Even though Golder's definition of electoral coalitions is more inclusive of forms of inter-party coordination that I do not consider electoral coalitions, she can still find only 240 coalitions for 364 elections, an average of 0.66. At the same time, the average number of electoral coalitions per country is lower among the post-communist

TABLE 3.2 *Electoral coalitions in post-communist states, 1990–2010*

State	Number of elections	Number of electoral coalitions	% of seats for electoral coalitions	Size of electoral coalitions per assembly (in % of seats)
1. Most favorable institutional conditions for power concentration				
Estonia	2	12	12.9	30.9
Hungary	6	8	46.1	61.5
Bulgaria	6	17	22.3	58.1
Slovenia	5	2	10.6	4.22
Group average	***4.25***	***9.75***	***23.80 (18.52)***	***46.99 (38.18)***
2. Mixed institutional conditions for power concentration				
Latvia	6	7	11.9	13.8
Slovakia	6	4	23	18.4
Group average	***6***	***5.5***	***15.90 (9.92)***	***16.91 (18.52)***
3. Least favorable institutional conditions for power concentration				
Lithuania	5	8	12	19.3
Romania	6	7	32.6	38.1
Poland	6	10	21.6	36.1
Czech Republic	5	1	15.5	3.1
Group average	***5***	***6.5***	***21.64 (15.52)***	***25.30 (24.20)***
Total	**53**	**76**	**21.8**	**28.3**

democracies (7.6) than among Golder's samples of established democracies (10.43).

Three post-communist states (Bulgaria, Estonia and Poland) account for more than half of all observed coalitions (39 out of 76). While electoral coalitions have played an important role in all Bulgarian and Polish elections, they were no longer permitted in Estonia after 1999. Yet, there were so many electoral coalitions in Estonia's first two democratic elections that the country still has the second highest number among all ten states. In terms of their size, the largest electoral coalitions can be found in Hungary and Romania. In the former, electoral coalitions provided clearly defined government alternatives to the electorate and won a majority of the parliamentary seats in three most recent elections (2002, 2006, 2010). In Bulgaria, Poland, and Slovakia electoral coalitions, when they were formed, tended to win a little over 20 percent of the seats on average. However, while coalitions have been formed very frequently in Bulgaria, and a little less so in Poland, they have become non-existent in Slovakia following the 1998 elections. In fact, three of the four electoral coalitions in Slovakia were formed in the country's first elections after the Velvet Divorce. The average size of electoral coalitions in the remaining five states is much smaller, ranging from 10.6 in Slovenia to 15.5 in the Czech Republic.

The last column of the table takes into account both the size and temporal frequency of electoral coalitions by reporting the combined parliamentary seat share of all electoral coalitions divided by the number of elections held in the country. Once again, Hungary and Bulgaria stand out having the largest electoral coalitions. In both countries, political parties formed large electoral coalitions most of the time. They are followed by Romania, Poland, and Estonia where electoral coalitions have acquired between 30 percent and 40 percent of the parliamentary seats. It is striking that the relatively high percentage in Estonia is obtained from only two elections in which electoral coalitions were permitted. Finally, in the remaining five states electoral coalitions have been much smaller. In the Czech Republic and Slovenia electoral coalitions have been particularly marginal players.

Electoral coalitions in the post-communist democracies have not lasted long. The overwhelming majority of them contested only one legislative election and either dissolved or were reformed in some other composition in the next election. In two instances, the SLD of Poland and the SDS of Bulgaria, the electoral coalitions were transformed into genuine political parties. Out of the seventy-six electoral coalitions that contested the fifty-three elections only ten competed more than once. Four electoral coalitions contested and won seats three times (the ODS and the Coalition for Bulgaria; the SLD in Poland; and the MSZP–SZDSZ coalition in Hungary). The other six contested the polls successfully on only two occasions. These were the SDS in Bulgaria; CDR in Romania; the FIDESZ–KDNP and the FIDESZ–MDF coalitions in Hungary; the coalition of the Greens and the Latvian Farmers Union in Latvia; and the Moderates in Estonia.

Clearly, there is no strict systematic relationship between the overall institutional design of power concentration on the one hand and the size and frequency of electoral coalitions on the other. At the same time, it is worth noting that the average size of electoral coalitions per legislature is much higher in the first group of states (46.99 percent), where power concentration is the highest, compared to the third group (25.30 percent), where power concentration is the weakest. Curiously, the smallest electoral coalitions can be found in the intermediate group (16.91 percent). In each group, the standard deviations from the mean coalition size are very high: 38.18, 18.52, and 24.20 as we move from the first to the third group. Indeed, the groups are far from homogenous. In the first group of states we find cases with frequent and large (Hungary and Bulgaria) as well as rare and small coalitions (Slovenia). We find the same inconsistency in the third group of states in Table 3.2, which includes Romania and Poland, with relatively large electoral coalitions, as well as the Czech Republic, with negligible ones.

An important lesson from Table 3.2 as well as the analysis that follows is that specific elements of the countries' overall institutional design (features of the electoral system, assembly size and the government formation rule) are simply more important and relevant as far as the conditions that favor electoral coalitions are concerned while other elements of the overall design matter less if at all.

To estimate the effects of the institutional variables on electoral coalitions, I have run a series of bivariate OLS regressions, which are reported in Table 3.3.

I take the combined percentage of parliamentary seats secured by all electoral coalitions in a given election in a given state as the dependent variable. The total number of observations is fifty-three. I organize the institutional variables in three groups: parliamentary, executive, and electoral systemic ones. The group includes the following variables: *Assembly size*, which is defined and measured by the number of lower house seats in a given election; *Large assembly,* which is a dummy that gets a value of 1 for each election where the first chamber has at least 200 seats, otherwise it gets a value of 0; *Bicameralism*, which is a dummy variable with a value of 0 for each unicameral and a value of 1 for each election in a bicameral state; and *Concurrent elections,* which is also a dummy with a value of 0 for every instance when an election to the first chamber was held alone and a value of 1 for every instance when it was held concurrently with an election to either the second chamber or the presidency.

The executive institutions include the *Positive investiture* and *Weak president* variables, both of which are dummies. The former has a value of 1 for each election that is followed by a government formation process under positive parliamentary rules, otherwise the value is 0. Similarly, the latter has a value of 1 for each election that is held in a state with a weak president, otherwise the value is 0.

The third group includes the four electoral systemic variables that I identified earlier: district magnitude, formula, closed lists, and the imposition of special thresholds on electoral coalitions. District magnitude is measured in two ways. First I take the average actual district magnitude that was in effect at the time of the election. Second, I measure the *Low magnitude* variable as a dummy: a value of 1 for elections with a district magnitude below 10 and a value of 0 for each election where district magnitude was greater than 10. The variable *Closed list* is also a dummy. Elections conducted using closed party lists are coded as 1; open list elections are coded as 0. The two mixed systems (Hungary and Lithuania) are coded according to the nature of the party list that is used on the PR tier. Therefore, Hungary is coded as 1 and Lithuania is coded as 0. The *Electoral formula* is coded as 1 according to whether the d'Hondt rule is used in the PR tier, otherwise if a quota or the Saint-Lague divisor methods are used then the observation is coded as 0. Observations in the two states with mixed electoral systems (Hungary and Lithuania) are coded as 2 because single-member districts are by definition even more restrictive than any PR formula.

Table 3.3 shows that the most powerful effects are detected with respect to the following variables: *Large assembly, Low magnitude, Closed list, Electoral formula*, and *Positive investiture*. The coefficients for each of the variables are large, positive and their effects on the dependent variable are statistically significant. These regression results support the hypotheses that electoral coalitions are larger when the assembly is large, district magnitude is small, the party lists are closed, a more restrictive electoral formula is in effect, and the election is followed by a positive government formation process. The five variables explain 9 percent, 42.4

TABLE 3.3 *Bivariate OLS regression results (dependent variable = percentage of seats won by electoral coalitions per election; N = 53)*

Variable	Coefficient (St. error)	Intercept	r^2	H_0 rejected
1. Parliamentary variables				
Assembly size	0.082 (0.030)*	11.63	0.107	yes
Large assembly	20.638 (8.302)*	19.78	0.092	yes
Concurrent elections	7.609 (10.248)	29.45	−0.008	no
Bicameralism	−5.676 (9.318)	32.75	−0.012	no
2. Executive variables				
Weak president	−1.38053 (9.3506)	31.83	−0.0195	no
Positive investiture	28.752 (7.89)*	14.30	0.193	yes
3. Electoral system variables				
District magnitude	−0.245 (0.104)**	38.14	0.079	no
Low magnitude	41.708 (23.776)*	14.04	0.4238	yes
Closed list	32.352 (7.898)*	20.19	0.233	yes
Restrictive formula	13.113 (5.209)**	21.55	0.093	yes
Special threshold	6.718 (9.190)	26.61	−0.009	no

Note: * p < 0.01; ** p< 0.05.

percent, 23.3 percent, 9.3 percent, and 14.7 percent of the variation in the size of electoral coalitions respectively.

In Table 3.4 I report the effect of these five variables in a multivariate framework. This model explains over almost 40 percent of the variation in the dependent variable; however, all but one of the individual independent variables lose their statistical significance. The exception is low district magnitude, which as conventional wisdom in the comparative literature suggests should indeed be the main driver of electoral coalition formation. There are two important changes between Tables 3.3 and 3.4: the direction of the effect of the *Large assembly* and the *Closed list* variables are reversed and the magnitude of the coefficients of each variable, expect for *Low magnitude* drop considerably. In sum, we can conclude that low district magnitude, restrictive formula and a positive investiture rule consistently promote the formation of electoral coalitions, while the effects of assembly size and closed party lists are ambiguous.

These results help us understand the cross-national pattern that we discussed earlier. Regardless of their overall institutional design, the states that are characterized by a preponderance of electoral coalitions (Bulgaria, Hungary, and Romania) have relatively small electoral districts, a restrictive electoral system and a positive parliamentary government formation rule. As Table 3.2 showed, these states account for some of the most frequent and largest electoral coalitions. At the other extreme we find the Czech Republic, Slovakia, Latvia, and Lithuania, which are characterized by the preponderance of institutional factors that discourage the formation of electoral coalitions: large districts, permissive electoral formulae, and negative government formation rules.

TABLE 3.4 *A multivariate OLS regression model of institutional effects on electoral coalitions*

Variables	Coefficients (St. error)
Low magnitude	53.107 (14.879)*
Large assembly	−4.513 (9.108)
Closed list	−15.061 (14.895)
Restrictive formula	2.936 (5.437)
Positive investiture	1.833 (10.401)
Intercept	13.596 (6.359)
R^2	0.396
N	53

Note: the numbers in brackets indicate standard errors.* $p < 0.01$.

3.6 CONCLUSION

The central finding of Chapter Three is that political institutions have a clear effect on the formation of electoral coalition in the post-communist democracies. The extant literature on electoral coalitions, taking mostly the established Western democracies as its empirical pool, has focused almost exclusively on the role of the electoral system, specifically, district magnitude. As I have shown in this chapter, district magnitude also matters in the post-communist democracies. At the same time, other institutional variables, specifically the electoral formula and the mode of government investiture, are also found to have strong effects on the formation and the size of electoral coalitions.

Before turning to a detailed examination of the development of electoral coalitions in a single case, Hungary, an important observation is in order with regard to the relationship between the central finding of this chapter and the three-fold classification of the post-communist democracies in Table 2.4. Three of the four states where electoral coalitions have been an important part of the party system landscape (Bulgaria, Hungary, and Estonia at least until the ban was introduced) belong to the first group of states with an overall institutional mix in favor of power concentration. Conversely, two of the four states with the fewest and smallest electoral coalitions (Latvia and Slovakia) belong to the second and another two belong to the third group of states (Czech Republic and Lithuania) where political institutions are designed to increase the degree of power dispersion. The puzzling cases are obviously Slovenia, which belongs to the first group yet does not have significant electoral coalitions to speak of, as well as Poland and Romania where electoral coalitions have been important even though both states belong to the third group in Table 2.4. This chapter helps us understand that in some cases institutions are not designed consistently and will, therefore, have unexpected consequences. Whereas Slovenia's overall institutional mix promotes power concentration, it does not do so on the variable that is the most relevant for electoral coalitions, i.e. district magnitude. In the case of Poland and Romania, we see exactly the opposite: while the institutional mixes of these states are, overall, aimed at the dispersion of political power, they score favorably on specific institutional variables that are relevant for the formation of electoral coalitions.

The conventional view of the literature on electoral politics assumes that individual political parties are the proper units of analysis for scholars to focus on. Clearly, this chapter has shown that such a view may be misplaced and cannot be generalized: in several post-communist democracies electoral coalitions are just as, if not more relevant actors that structure the electoral competition and the party system. In turn, this raises important questions about the meaning of political parties and the party system, as well as about the future development of patterns of party government in the new democracies. As for the former, if electoral coalitions are the principal actors through which political competition is organized, to what extent is it valid to consider political parties as the proper units of analysis? When measuring degrees of party system fragmentation, volatility, nationalization and so forth, are we to take the individual parties, or the coalitions that they recurrently form, as the units of inquiry? Moreover, how do we conceptualize the boundary between party and electoral coalition especially when we find that in some cases electoral coalitions are but the embryonic stage of what later may become *de jure* distinct new political parties (see Appendix C for examples)?[2]

As for the development of patterns of party government, it is important to note that by encouraging political parties to form broadly-based large electoral coalitions, certain political institutions actually promote and push the party system towards the development of what Katz calls a bipolar model of party government. The cases in point are Hungary, Bulgaria, and Romania. In contrast, where political institutions encourage the development of distinct party identities as opposed to coalitions, they push the party system towards the development of Katz' coalitional or dominance models of party government, e.g. the Czech Republic or Slovenia. Whichever model of party government becomes the equilibrium model in the long run may have further consequences for the unfolding patterns of government formation and durability in the region: where electoral coalitions will continue to define the main competing government alternatives, the scope for the formation of a coalition government, other than the one by the winning electoral alliance, is extremely limited. Indeed, the next chapter about Hungary will highlight precisely this point: without paying proper attention to the formation of coalitions at the electoral stage, theories of coalition government formation cannot predict which parties would form a government in Hungary even though the relative simplicity of the party system keeps the range of possible options highly limited. Furthermore, since electoral coalitions reduce the numerical format of the party system, they also reduce the number of alternative coalition combinations that may replace the incumbent and by so doing they may plausibly promote government stability.

In this book, I do not examine these possible long-term effects of electoral coalitions on the party politics of the post-communist democracies as it would require the passage of several more decades to see what kinds of system will actually equilibrate. It is important, nonetheless, to sketch these possibilities because they help us appreciate and anticipate the longer-term indirect effects that political institutions may have, in the future, on the development of the party system, and party government, through the electoral coalitions that they engender.

NOTES

1. The other two devices being district magnitude and "exclusion clauses," i.e. the level of the threshold of representation (Carstairs 1980: 42).
2. I owe this point to Keith Dowding.

4

The Electoral Origins of Hungarian Governments, 1990–2002

4.1 INTRODUCTION

Institution-free theories of government formation assume that the coalition formation process starts after legislative elections are over and the distribution of parliamentary seats becomes common knowledge. It has been understood that following the declaration of the electoral results political parties engage in negotiations to form a government based on the policy positions they had announced before the elections and the number of seats they have won, unless a single party can do so on its own by virtue of having won a parliamentary majority. This conventional view has treated government formation as an essentially elite driven process with very little opportunity given to the voting citizenry to affect the composition of the government that will be formed after the election.

The institution-free perspective, however, provides an accurate modeling of the government formation process only in those democracies where political parties participate in the electoral competition strictly on their own. In other cases, political parties present voters with identifiable government alternatives by committing themselves to cooperating with a particular set of other parties (Huber and Powell 1994; Powell 2000; Shugart and Wattenberg 2001). Electoral alliances and coalitions are rarely broken after the election is over because of the high audience costs involved (Laver and Schofield 1990; Kohno 1997). Therefore, such commitments constitute binding proto-coalitions among the cooperating parties and exert an endogenous constraint on the government formation process (Strom, Budge and Laver 1994). In these democracies, predictions of government formation must take into account the electoral coalitions that parties have formed. Failure to do so may result in making unrealistic predictions about the outcome of the government formation game.

Electoral systems provide an important set of incentives according to which political parties form pre-electoral coalitions and electoral alliances (Strom, Budge and Laver 1994; Cox 1997; Kaminski 2001). For example, the transferability of the vote between candidates of different parties, run-off elections, or the possibility of joining and connecting parties' candidate lists are mechanisms through which the electoral rules encourage the formation of inter-party coalitions during or before the electoral process. This chapter illustrates the relationship between the electoral system and government formation through the case study of post-communist Hungary during 1990–2002. The Hungarian electoral system has encouraged political parties not merely to form electoral coalitions, in order to overcome its built-in disproportionalities, but also to build two major blocs, Left and Right, that have defined the competing government alternatives before the electorate. The actual composition of and the specific strategies adopted by the constituent parties of these blocs have varied over time. However, both the bipolar structure of the electoral competition and the electoral identifiability of government alternatives (Strom 1990) have remained recurring characteristics of the party system. This chapter examines how the Hungarian electoral system has effectively moved the game of government formation to the electoral stage of party competition. In so doing, the chapter also shows that by failing to take electoral commitments and coalitions into account conventional theories predict unrealistic outcomes about government formation in the country. Therefore, the chapter argues that the electoral system acts as a very important constraint on government formation in Hungary through its impact on strategic electoral coordination among parties.

The period between 1990 and 2002 is of particular significance because the development of the two electoral blocs occurred during that time, i.e. over the first four post-communist elections. In the first two elections, electoral coordination among parties was limited to strategic withdrawal of third and lower-placed candidates from the run-off. However, after the second election the League of Young Democrats (FIDESZ), the only parliamentary party that was not included in either of the first two coalition governments, started its gradual ascent to becoming the dominant party of the highly divided and fragmented center-right pole of the party system. FIDESZ's electoral strategy and success specifically hinged on the formation of pre-electoral coalitions with ideologically like-minded parties that could become prospective coalition partners in government after the election. At the same time, the parties of the center-left, a pole that was much less divided than the center-right, could afford to limit their electoral cooperation to the run-off. This pattern of asymmetrical electoral coalitions on the Left and the Right became firmly established by the 2002 election and was repeatedly played out in its essence in the next two polls of 2006 and 2010.

The chapter will start with a detailed description of the expected consequences of the Hungarian electoral system for party strategies. Next, I review the development of the Hungarian party system with particular attention to the changes in parties' electoral strategies. Finally, I shall analyze the formation of the coalition governments after the first four post-communist elections by explicitly showing that the outcomes were the result of the seat and policy maximizing choices that parties made under the constraints of the electoral system.

4.2 THE IMPACT OF THE ELECTORAL SYSTEM ON PARTY STRATEGY IN HUNGARY[1]

A detailed review of the Hungarian electoral system is provided in Appendix A. For present purposes let it be sufficient to summarize the three main features of the system, as it was in effect between 1990 and 2010, that have relevance for the formation of electoral coalitions during the period examined. First, the electoral system is a particular variant of the mixed-member systems: voters vote both for a regional (closed) list of party candidates as well as for candidates running in individual single-member districts. Second, the single-member races are decided by a run-off rule rather than in a single round. Third, there is also a national compensatory tier of seat allocation that qualifying national party lists participate in. However, voters never vote directly for any of these national lists. The only lists that voters see and vote for are those that parties present at the regional level; the threshold of representation in the national parliament was tied to winning 4 percent of this list vote in 1990 and 5 percent in the subsequent elections thereafter.

The electoral system allows Hungarian political parties to engage in six principal forms of cooperation depending on the type of the electoral district. First, in the single member districts, political parties may either run joint candidates or they may run separate candidates in the first round but engage in strategic withdrawal in each other's favor in the second. When running joint candidates, parties indicate their support of the given candidate by putting their label next to his or her name on the ballot to allow voters to understand that the candidate is endorsed by this party. The order in which the endorsing parties are listed is important for it indicates to the voter which of the cooperating parties the particular candidate is genuinely affiliated with. Moreover, the order of parties also suggests which parliamentary group the given candidate will join in case the cooperating parties decide not form a joint caucus after the election (called *frakcio* in the language of Hungarian legislative politics).

By running joint candidates parties can eliminate the problem of adverse vote splitting. Given the run-off component of the electoral system, an inefficient splitting of the vote in the first round could have a number of effects on the electoral race in the second round. First, vote splitting could cause the elimination of a contender from the second round who would stand the best chance to defeat the common opponent of these parties. For instance, too many Right candidates entering the first round could cause the elimination of a strong Right candidate who could otherwise stand a realistic chance to defeat the strongest candidate of the Left in the second round (Cox 1997: 123–38). Second, even if vote splitting does not lead to the elimination of an otherwise viable candidate, it could affect voters' perception of candidates' viability. Voters who take cues from the first round about the viability of the competing candidates in the second round may think poorly of the second-round chances of a candidate who had lost too many votes in the first round due to vote splitting. Third, switching from a strategy of competition to cooperation between the two electoral rounds may be too costly. Whereas the party elite may be able to do so at relative ease, voters may not follow along as easily. The absence of a consistent strategy of cooperation among like-minded parties throughout the electoral race may damage the perception that voters have of their potential and ability to work and govern in coalition with one another. By running joining candidates, parties can economize on such costs.

The run-off component of the electoral system also allows parties to engage in strategic withdrawals, the second kind of strategic cooperation, in one another's favor in the second round of the single member races. What is particularly important about this form of cooperation is that after the first round political parties have perfect information about both the partisan composition as well as the approximate distribution of legislative strength among parties in the post-election parliament. The partisan composition of the legislature is known because the result of the territorial list votes determines which set of parties has passed the mandatory threshold of representation. Therefore, electoral coalition building via strategic withdrawals will take place only among those parties that will be in parliament. Essentially, this means that party strategy in the second round can directly affect the distribution of seats in the post-election legislature. Since parties have perfect information about both the distribution of territorial list seats as well as the provisional results of the single member contests, they can gauge rather accurately each other's electoral support. This reduces the degree of uncertainty under which parties have to make their choices and, thus, makes their strategic calculations very well informed. In short, district-level vote management in the second round allows parties to have a very strong impact on the post-election distribution of seats in the legislature, and in consequence, on the government formation process as well.

The outcome of strategic withdrawals in the districts may either be a Duvergerian equilibrium, defined by the entry of two viable candidates in the second round, or a non-Duvergerian equilibrium, defined by the entry of more than two viable candidates (Cox 1997: 75–6). If the difference in viability between the second and third placed candidates is sufficiently large in favor of the second placed candidate then voters who would otherwise sincerely vote for the third placed candidates have an incentive to cast their ballot in support of whichever of the top two candidates they prefer. By casting a strategic vote, voters can prevent their least preferred candidates in the district from winning. The same rationale applies to candidates and their parties as well. Third and lower placed candidates, who may have advanced to the second round due to the 15 percent rule, but who are far behind the second placed candidates in terms of their vote share will have an incentive to withdraw from the second round if by so doing they can increase the probability that their more preferred opponent would win. Assuming that both parties and voters are motivated by policy, as well as office seeking, their strategic behavior should always be intended to benefit a competitor that is ideologically closer rather than one that is more distant.

In the first three elections, strategic withdrawals took place on a limited scale. Of the 176 single members districts, second rounds were held in 171 in the 1990, 174 in the 1994 and 175 in the 1998 elections. While the average number of candidates per district was 2.79 in 1990, it increased to 2.93 in 1994 and further to 3.02 in 1998. In sharp contrast, two-candidate races in the run-off became much more common after 1998. In the 2002 election the average number of candidates in the 131 districts where a second round had to be held was 2.05. Tables 4.1 through 4.4 present detailed information about this type of electoral coordination in the four Hungarian elections.

The remaining four types of electoral cooperation have to do with the party lists at the regional and national levels. At either level, political parties may either run joint lists of candidates or may choose to connect their own lists and form an inter-party cartel. Of particular importance are the regional lists since the threshold of parliamentary representation is determined as a percentage of parties' share of the regional party list vote nation-wide. Running a common party list is a rational strategy for parties when they expect to form a government together but some of them may have a low probability to meet the threshold (Cox 1997: 197–8). Such a strategy is mutually beneficial for both the smaller and the larger parties. On the one hand, the larger party can ensure that its ideal coalition partner will enter the parliament since the joining of lists essentially ties the fate of the smaller party to that of the larger one. On the other hand, the smaller party clearly benefits because its chances of entering the legislature might not have been quite as strong in the absence of such cooperation.

Technically speaking when a number of parties submit joint lists of candidates a new electoral entity is formed. However, parties may not necessarily want to give up their individual identity by merging into a new organization. Although the representational threshold is lower if the list were submitted as that of a single party rather than a joint one, this benefit may not exceed the costs that the

TABLE 4.1 *Strategic entry and withdrawal in the second round of the 1990 election, Hungary*

Party	Number of advancing candidates	Number of withdrawals	Number of entries in run-off
MSZP	61	2	59
SZDSZ	149	15	134
FIDESZ	19	9	10
MDF	162	8	154
KDNP	29	6	23
FKGP	78	8	70

Source: www.valasztas.hu

TABLE 4.2 *Strategic entry and withdrawal in the 1994 election, Hungary*

Party	Number of advancing candidates	Number of withdrawals	Number of entries in run-off
MSZP	174	0	174
SZDSZ	161	2	159
FIDESZ	10	5	5
MDF	99	1	98
KDNP	18	0	18
FKGP	46	0	46

Source: www.valasztas.hu

TABLE 4.3 *Strategic entry and withdrawal in the 1998 election, Hungary*

Party	Number of advancing candidates	Number of withdrawals	Number of entries in run-off
MSZP	175	6	169
SZDSZ	83	35	48
FIDESZ	94	12	82
FIDESZ–MDF	75	7	68
FKGP	116	71	45
MIEP	32	1	31

Source: www.valasztas.hu

TABLE 4.4 *Strategic entry and withdrawal in the 2002 election, Hungary*

Party	Number of advancing candidates	Number of withdrawals	Number of entries in run-off
MSZP	131	7	124
SZDSZ	78	70	8
FIDESZ–MDF	131	0	131

Source: www.valasztas.hu

cooperating parties might incur by losing the support of those voters who care very strongly about maintaining that separate party identity. For similar reasons, parties, especially when they expect to cross the threshold on their own, may choose to connect rather than join their regional and/or national lists. Similarly to the joint list, parties that connect their individual lists receive seats in proportion of the total vote that all of the connecting parties have received.

Finally, parties may also choose to combine these different forms of cooperation at different levels. For instance, two parties may run joint candidates in a number of single member districts without submitting a joint regional or national list, as the FIDESZ–MDF alliance had done in the 1998 election. Similarly, parties may submit joint regional lists in particular regions without running a joint national list and so forth.

4.3 PARTY SYSTEM AND GOVERNMENT FORMATION IN HUNGARY, 1990–2002

General elections have been held at regular four-year intervals in post-communist Hungary since 1990. Three of the first four elections, the exception being the 1994 poll, resulted in a parliament where no single political party controlled a majority of the seats. Figure 4.1 shows the left–right ideological location of the various political parties as well as their share of parliamentary seats after each election.[2] The bolded entries indicate parties that were part of the coalition government that was formed after the given election.

Alternation in office has been a recurring characteristic of Hungarian elections. The conservative coalition government, consisting of the Hungarian Democratic Forum (MDF), the Christian Democratic Peoples' Party (KDNP) and the Independent Smallholders' Party (FKGP), which had been formed after the first post-communist general elections of 1990, was replaced in office by the left-liberal coalition of the MSZP and the Alliance of Free Democrats (SZDSZ) four years later in 1994. Similarly, the 1998 election witnessed the defeat of the incumbents and the return to power of the center-right, this time including the Alliance of Young Democrats-Hungarian Civic Party (FIDESZ-MPP), the MDF and the FKGP. In 2002, the pendulum shifted once again and the left-liberal MSZP–SZDSZ coalition defeated the FIDESZ-led government and formed a new coalition cabinet. It is worth noting that the 2006 election would be the only exception to this pattern of regular alternation as the MSZP–SZDSZ coalition successfully prevailed at the polls after four years in power.

The first post-communist election of Hungary, held in 1990, was contested by three major political camps: (i) the conservative nationalist bloc led by the electoral alliance of the Hungarian Democratic Forum (MDF), the Christian Democratic People's Party (KDNP) and the Independent Smallholder's Party (KDNP); (ii) the center-left liberal Alliance of Free Democrats (SZDSZ) and the League of Young Democrats (FIDESZ); (iii) and the party of the reformed communists, the Hungarian Socialist Party (MSZP). Although the regime divide was very strong in the first post-transition election (Grzymala-Busse 2001), that is to say that the MSZP was not considered an acceptable coalition partner by any of the other relevant parties,

LEFT							RIGHT
	MSZP	SZDSZ	FIDESZ	MDF	KDNP	FKGP	MIEP
1990	8.8	23.8	5.4	**42.5**	**4.9**	**11.4**	N/A
1994	**54.1**	**17.9**	5.2	9.8	5.7	6.7	N/A
1998	34.7	6.2	**38.3**	**4.4**	**N/A**	**12.4**	3.6
2002	**46.1**	**4.9**	42.0	6.7	N/A	N/A	N/A

FIGURE 4.1 The left–right location of Hungarian political parties and their share of parliamentary seats, in percentages, 1990–2002

the expected electoral weakness of the reformed communist MSZP did not require coordination between the liberal and conservative blocs of parties. Therefore, the first post-transition election was a straightforward contest between the conservative alliance, led by the MDF, on one hand and the liberal parties, led by the SZDSZ, on the other.

The 1990 election ended with an impressive victory by the MDF, which won 42.5 percent of the parliamentary seats and proceeded to form a coalition government with the other two conservative parties, the FKGP and the KDNP, that crossed the threshold. The same three parties also agreed to elect Jozsef Antall, the leader of the MDF, to be the first Prime Minister of post-communist Hungary on May 23, 1990. Despite often tense relations between the MDF and the FKGP, as well as splits within the ranks of both, the coalition cabinet maintained its majority and survived in office for the entire duration of its parliamentary term. The stability of the coalition was also demonstrated by the ability of the three parties to ensure an orderly succession in the Prime Ministerial seat following Antall's death in 1993 (Ilonszki and Kurtán 1994: 320).

The two parties, the MDF and the SZDSZ, that had led the anti-communist opposition forces in the National Roundtable talks with the last Communist government in 1989, and dominated the electoral scene in 1990, steadily lost their ground to other parties after the polls. Although not entering into a formal agreement on power sharing, the two parties concluded a pact after the 1990 elections which guaranteed the stability of the basic institutions of parliamentary democracy during the difficult first years of Hungary's post-transition politics. The amicable relationship between the two parties, however, could not last long. In attempts to become the dominant party of the conservative Right and the liberal Left respectively, both the MDF and the SZDSZ adopted increasingly more radical and intolerant approaches towards each other. In February 1991, Janos Kis, president of the SZDSZ, announced at his party's annual congress that the conclusion of the pact with the MDF had been a mistake and the party should now be getting ready to terminate the current coalition government and replace the MDF in power (Bozóki 1992: 123–31). In an effort to mobilize against the government, the SZDSZ even reached out to the MSZP, which was at the time considered a virtual untouchable by all other parties for being the Communist successor party.

The strategy of radicalization cost both the MDF and SZDSZ considerable electoral support in the next elections held in 1994. Although the MDF still remained the largest party to the right of the SZDSZ, its electoral strength was reduced by more than half compared to what it had been four years before. This also meant that the party's parliamentary strength was reduced to less than a fourth of the number of seats it had commanded in 1990. As for the SZDSZ, the party won more seats than the MDF and became the second largest party in the new parliament. However, in the newly elected legislature, the SZDSZ ceded the leadership of the Left to the MSZP, which scored a resounding victory at the polls and secured a majority of parliamentary seats.

The second electoral and parliamentary cycle brought about the beginning of the fundamental transformation of the partisan landscape on the right-of-center. The central feature of this transformation was the repositioning of FIDESZ to shift from the liberal center to the right, and its emergence as the leading party of the latter. Whereas FIDESZ entered the second parliament with the fewest deputies, by the end of the term, it had become the single largest party in the entire opposition thanks to splits that had divided both the MDF and the KDNP. The former gave birth to a new parliamentary party, the Hungarian Democratic People's Party (MDNP), and the latter resulted in the complete disintegration and disappearance of the Christian Democrats from parliament. For its part, FIDESZ successfully attracted a number of Christian Democratic dissidents, which allowed the party to dominate the opposition by the end of the term.

FIDESZ contested the second parliamentary election as part of a four-member liberal alliance, which also included the SZDSZ, the Agrarian Alliance, and the Entrepreneurs' Party. The agreement did not commit the partners to continuing their cooperation in the legislature after the polls; however, it stipulated that they would coordinate and consult with one another before accepting a third party's offer of government formation. This clause was important as it reflected the uneasy relationship that had evolved between the SZDSZ and FIDESZ. The two parties had already clashed on their position towards the Communist successor party over the issue of establishing the Democratic Charta, a civic movement aimed the propagation of liberal values in Hungary. Furthermore, in contrast to the SZDSZ that was adamant to replace all members of the outgoing coalition government in office, FIDESZ did not rule out the possibility of post-election cooperation with the MDF and the KDNP. The two conservative parties reciprocated the attitude of both liberal parties: while they regarded the SZDSZ just as unacceptable a coalition partner as the MSZP, they remained open towards the possibility of closer relations with FIDESZ (Pető 1995: 176).

The MDF and the KDNP continued their cooperation in the 1994 elections also. In the second round of the polls, there was only one district where the two parties did not withdraw their candidates in one another's favor. In contrast, MDF and FKGP candidates clashed in five districts in the second round. In an attempt to balance against and weaken the MDF, the Smallholders reached out to the KDNP and offered closer cooperation with them if the latter were willing to distance itself from the Democratic Forum. As a result, the two parties ran candidates against each other in only one district in the run-off. These patterns of electoral coordination increasingly suggested that the KDNP occupied the pivotal middle ground between the MDF, to its left, and the FKGP, to its right.

The election resulted in a sweeping Socialist victory as the MSZP won an absolute majority of the seats by itself. Nonetheless, the MSZP congress authorized the party leadership on June 4 to start talks on forming a coalition government with the SZDSZ. In accordance with their pre-election agreement, the SZDSZ notified FIDESZ of its pending negotiations with the Socialists, which eventually resulted in the formation of a coalition government by the two parties. In its response, the FIDESZ leadership followed through with its earlier announcement in April, according to which it would sever its ties with the SZDSZ, despite their electoral alliance, should the party engage in any type of cooperation with the MSZP. Indeed, on June 6, Laszlo Kover officially terminated the SZDSZ–FIDESZ partnership. Shortly thereafter the Socialists concluded their negotiations with the Free Democrats and a new left-liberal coalition government was formed.

The formation of the new government left FIDESZ in a strategically challenging situation as suggested by the title of the party's agenda for its upcoming sixth congress: *From Opposition to Opposition*. Whereas the party had been in opposition to the previous conservative coalition government during the preceding four years, it found itself once again in opposition as a result of its relentless position not to share power with the communist successor party. Moreover, FIDESZ also ended up with the fewest seats among the opposition parties, which further suggested that the party was running the serious and very real risk of isolation and eventual disintegration.

In order to break out of this constraint, FIDESZ started making determined moves to establish itself as a credible member of the center-right bloc in the party system. The first visible indicator of this change in strategy was the electoral alliance that the party formed with the other two parties of the bloc, the MDF and the KDNP, in the municipal elections that were held in the Fall of 1994. The ability of the three parties to form this alliance was all the more impressive given the difficult hurdle that the governing coalition of the MSZP and the SZDSZ set up by changing the electoral system of the local polls. The electoral reform made inter-party coordination difficult by replacing the run-off system with a single round of plurality elections while maintaining a second tier of compensatory seats that were to be awarded to party lists. Nonetheless, the FIDESZ–MDF–KDNP alliance managed to overcome this obstacle in a number of municipalities. Very importantly, it nominated a joint candidate for the position of mayor of Budapest.

As the center-right parties were increasing and enhancing their coordination, their distance from the radical right end of the spectrum was also increasing. Indeed, the FKGP and MIEP formed their own electoral alliance in the municipal polls and fielded their own mayoral candidate in the Budapest race. Similarly, the FKGP did not join the other three opposition parties in supporting the candidacy of Ferenc Madl for president of the Republic in 1995. In the face of the overwhelming parliamentary majority of the coalition parties, the opposition alliance behind Madl's candidacy was merely symbolic. Nonetheless, the refusal of the FKGP to cooperate with the center-right once again provided further indication of the division within the Right.

The establishment of FIDESZ as a member of the center-right gained further credibility with the resolution of the party's seventh congress in 1995, which changed the party's official name to FIDESZ–MPP (MPP being the abbreviation for Hungarian Civic Party), its resignation from the Liberal International, and its adoption of a new tentative program at its 1996 congress, *For Civic Hungary* that clearly marked a movement away from advocating liberal individualism towards an emphasis on individual civic values within the context of the national interest of Hungary (Deutsch and Gyarmati 1999: 88–93). Finally, it is very important to mention that the party's seventh national congress resolved to authorize the party leadership to pursue talks with the MDF and KDNP about legislative and electoral cooperation. This resolution sought to give an institutional expression for coordination among the moderate parties of the center-right by creating the new Civic Alliance umbrella.

The three-party consultations that followed were centered on the FIDESZ proposal that sought to treat the three parties on the basis of parity. The FIDESZ leadership proposed that the three parties should field a single jointly supported candidate in every single-member electoral district in the next parliamentary polls as well as submit joint lists in the multimember districts. The principle of parity was apparent in the way the candidates were nominated and listed. According to the FIDESZ proposal each of the three partners in the Civic Alliance was to nominate one-third of the candidates in the first tier (i.e. single member districts) and one-third of the candidates on the joint lists. This proposal did not reflect the existing distribution of parliamentary mandates among the three parties: the MDF which had almost as many seats (thirty-eight) as FIDESZ–MPP (twenty) and

KDNP (twenty-two) together was to be seriously under-represented, while the junior partners of the Alliance would have been in a much more favorable situation than what their legislative strength would have suggested. Not surprisingly, neither MDF nor KDNP agree to this proposal immediately which would, for all intents and purposes, have made FIDESZ, the most recent and smallest member of the center-right camp, an equal footing with the other two more established and larger parties.

The idea of the Civic Alliance suffered its first important setback a mere one month later. In November 1995, the national convention of the KDNP adopted a resolution rejecting the idea of three-party cooperation. Instead of institutionalizing an inter-party alliance, the KDNP resolution advocated ad hoc cooperation among all like-minded parties with a Christian national orientation that were opposed to the left-liberal government, whether they were inside or outside the legislature. The wording of this resolution clearly suggested that the KDNP sought to remain equidistant from all opposition parties rather than follow the more specific type of cooperation that the FIDESZ proposal suggested. This rejection of the Civic Alliance by the KDNP revealed a deep rift between the organizational and the legislative wings of the party. Whereas the latter was dominated by party representatives who were sympathetic and supportive of the idea of collaboration with FIDESZ and MDF, the party organization remained under the control of the more radical group that was keen on maintaining ties with the radical right of the party system, namely the FKGP and even MIEP.

This division between supporters of Civic Alliance and those who advocated the idea of a broader cooperation that would include all parties to the right of the incumbent left-liberal coalition was also present within the MDF. The leadership contest between S. Lezsak and I. Szabo at the party's tenth annual congress was a straightforward fight between these alternative strategies that the leadership candidates and their supporters advocated: the former was in favor of the position that the KDNP congress had taken the previous year, while Szabo led those who wanted the party to develop closer ties with FIDESZ and remain at a distance from FKGP. The outcome of the leadership race, a victory by Lezsak, confirmed that the dominant position within the party was occupied by those forces that were interested in remaining open towards the FKGP and the establishment of a broader front of parties of the conservative right.

Two days after Lezsak's victory in the MDF leadership contest, Szabo and his followers quit the party, left the caucus and formed a new parliamentary group under the MDNP (Hungarian Democratic People's Party) label with fifteen representatives, the bare minimum required by the rules of parliament to form a new parliament group. However, the MDNP failed to establish an alliance with FIDESZ–MPP. In a surprising move, Lezsak announced in April 1996 that he was interested in cooperating with FIDESZ–MPP and to start building an alliance of moderate right parties, which the FIDESZ–MPP leadership accepted.

Similarly to the MDF, the cleavage between the moderate and radical members could not be contained within the KDNP for too long either. In the summer of 1997, the division eventually led to a split in the party's parliamentary group. However, in contrast to the MDF split, no new party was born of this both because the parliamentary representation of the KDNP was much weaker than that of the MDF and that the two factions drew the support of almost the same number of representatives (eleven moderates and nine radicals). In the end, the moderates joined the FIDESZ caucus while the radicals decided to sit as Independents.

By the end of the second parliamentary cycle, the establishment of center-right unity had a far stronger chance of realization than in the earlier part of the term of the legislature. The direct absorption of the moderate KDNP rebels after the MDF had gone through its traumatic split, left FIDESZ–MPP, the originator and strongest advocate of the idea of the Civic Alliance, in the position of being the largest opposition party in parliament. Furthermore, the two other center-right parties, KDNP and MDF, that had ambiguous positions towards the idea of the Alliance had split, making it easier for FIDESZ–MPP to push forward with the creation of the center-right front. Indeed, FIDESZ–MPP and the MDF entered the 1998 parliamentary race as strong electoral allies. The two parties ran common candidates in seventy-eight of the 176 single member districts; however, their regional and national lists remained separate. The majority of their joint candidates, fifty-six out of seventy-eight, were listed under a FIDESZ–MDF label, the rest under MDF–FIDESZ. The distinction was important both to indicate the primary partisan affiliation of the common candidates to the voters as well as to help in the allocation of seats between the two parties in the new parliament. Those who had FIDESZ listed first on their label were to join the FIDESZ caucus, while those which were primarily listed as MDF candidates were to join the parliamentary club of the Forum. The two parties also ran their own individual candidates in ninety-four and ninety-five districts respectively.

In Table 4.5 I present three OLS regression models that predict the electoral vote share of all FIDESZ and MDF candidates as a function of whether they were coalition candidates and the electoral support that the candidate's party list enjoyed in that election. The models show that coalitional status increased a candidate's vote share in the election. More importantly, we also find that the coefficient of the *Coalition* variable is far greater in Model Two, measuring the effect of coalition candidacies on the electoral vote share of the junior coalition candidate, than in Model Three, which measures the effect of coalition candidacies on the electoral vote share of the senior coalition candidate. The models also confirm that the party list vote has a strong impact on the votes of the same party's candidates; however, the magnitude of this effect is far greater, at least in this election, in the case of the junior coalition partner.

Hungarian voters went to the polls to elect representatives to their fourth post-communist parliament in April 2002. As in each of the three previous elections, the national polls once again resulted in the replacement of the incumbent

TABLE 4.5 *The effect of electoral coalitions on candidate performance in the first round of the 1998 Hungarian election (OLS regression)*

Variables	Model 1	Model 2	Model 3
	DV = Vote share of FIDESZ and MDF candidates in Round One	DV = MDF candidate vote in Round One	DV = FIDESZ candidate vote in Round One
Coalition	11.247 (0.822)*	21.26 (1.044)*	4.624 (0.821)*
Party list vote	0.542 (0.031)*	2.265 (0.747)**	0.905 (0.133)*
Intercept	5.968 (0.653)	−1.621 (2.357)	−1.687 (3.668)
Standard error	6.151	4.897	4.772
(Adjusted) R^2	0.689	0.780	0.373
N	266	120	146

Note: * $p<0.001$; ** $p<0.01$; *** $p<0.05$. The numbers in brackets indicate standard error.

coalition in power. The electoral coalition of the Hungarian Socialist Party (MSZP) and the Alliance of Free Democrats (SZDSZ) won a bare majority against the electoral alliance of the incumbent League of Young Democrats–Hungarian Civic Party (FIDESZ) and the Hungarian Democratic Forum (MDF). Despite following the pattern of alternation in power, the 2002 election was also unique because, for the first time since the inception of multiparty democracy in Hungary, it produced a four- instead of a six-party parliament.

The actual reduction in the number of parties took place on the political Right. Of the four parties of this ideological camp that were represented in the outgoing parliament only two, the FIDESZ and the MDF, managed to cross the electoral threshold to win parliamentary representation, while the far-right Party of Hungarian Justice and Life (MIEP), and the Independent Smallholders' Party (FKGP), a former member of the outgoing coalition government, failed to return to parliament. The de-fragmentation of the Right suggests that a balance between the two major political camps, the Left and the Right, was in the making in the Hungarian party system.

There was a sharp contrast in the pre-electoral strategies pursued by the parties of the governing coalition on the one hand and those of the opposition on the other. FIDESZ and the MDF not only repeated but also significantly improved on the pre-electoral alliance that they had formed before the 1998 elections. As mentioned earlier, FIDESZ and the MDF had run joint candidates in the first and the second round of the single member district races of the 1998 elections, however they joined neither their territorial nor their national lists. While their cooperation ultimately allowed the smaller MDF to win a sufficient number of single member districts to form a caucus in parliament, the particular method of cooperation that the two parties had chosen limited the number of list seats that they could win. By not running a common list the MDF fell below the 5 percent threshold and all its regional list votes were wasted. Assuming that the two parties would have received the same percentage of votes if they had run a joint slate as they did by running separately, their joint list could have won 32.28 percent of the total regional vote (i.e. 29.48 percent, which is what FIDESZ actually received, plus 2.8 percent, which is what the MDF actually won). By either dividing this vote between the two parties equally or in the same proportion as the joint candidates were, 65 percent to 35 percent, the MDF would have crossed the 5 percent threshold.[3] This would not only have allowed the two parties to receive regional lists after a higher combined vote share, 32.28 percent as opposed to the 29.48 percent which was won by FIDESZ alone, but would also have led to more national compensatory seats, from which the MDF was entirely excluded due to falling below the threshold.

Learning from this experience, FIDESZ and the MDF agreed as early as the summer of 2001 to contest the upcoming election by running joint candidates in each and every single member district, compared to only 44 percent of them in 1998, as well as joining both their regional and national lists. Clearly, FIDESZ had the upper hand in the alliance. On the 174-member joint national list only sixteen were nominated by the MDF, and only three of them were among the top forty. The highest ranked MDF candidate was Dr Ibolya David, Minister of Justice in the outgoing cabinet, who occupied the number two position on the list following Prime Minister Dr Viktor Orban. The next two MDF candidates occupied positions number fifteen and forty. Interestingly, the rest of the thirteen MDF candidates were listed at intervals of ten positions on the list. Thus, MDF candidates were numbers fifty, sixty, seventy etc. until 170. Similarly, on average, MDF candidates made up only 15.4 percent of the regional lists.

The formation of the FIDESZ–MDF pre-electoral alliance cannot be adequately understood without reference to parties' anticipation of the dynamics of cabinet formation after the election. By entering this pre-electoral alliance, FIDESZ and the MDF limited the range of potential outcomes in the post-election coalition formation game. More specifically, the formation of their alliance suggested that FIDESZ–MDF would either form a coalition majority government if they could win enough seats to do so, or they would form a coalition minority government by relying on the external support of any party located to the right of the MDF that crossed the threshold with enough seats to give FIDESZ–MDF a majority. Having contested the polls together, the two parties would not have to incur further costs to negotiate an agreement to govern together. In the second scenario, the two parties could form a coalition minority government by exploiting the spatially peripheral position of the party that enters to the right of the MDF, conceivably the far-right MIEP given that the third member of the outgoing coalition, the FKGP, had disintegrated shortly before the elections due to corruption scandals, leadership strife, and internal splits. Of course, the precondition for this would be that such a peripheral party wins enough seats to provide the allies with an overall majority. Finally, it is also worth mentioning that the formation of the pre-electoral alliance precluded the possibility of the formation of a FIDESZ minority government even if the distribution of seats had made it possible.[4]

In sharp contrast, the main opposition parties appeared to be less coordinated. Even though the MSZP and the SZDSZ had governed together before, from 1994 to 1998, and had cooperated in the 1998 election by strategically withdrawing candidates in favor of one another in the second round, the two parties did not form a nation-wide pre-electoral alliance in 2002. Indeed, there was no reason for them to do so. Pre-election public opinion polls found that of the smaller parties of the outgoing parliament only the SZDSZ had a reasonable chance to cross the threshold on its own. Expecting this to be the case, the SZDSZ could afford to run its own candidates and lists.

Furthermore, with regard to the post-election cabinet formation game, the alliance between FIDESZ and the MDF limited the options before the SZDSZ to forming a governing coalition with the MSZP anyway. The formation of the FIDESZ–MDF alliance meant that, even though they were spatially proximate, the SZDSZ could not form a coalition with FIDESZ without also joining hands with the MDF. Therefore the possible coalition options before the SZDSZ were either the MSZP, or FIDESZ and MDF together. Given this choice, the SZDSZ would opt for the MSZP because this choice would result in a more compact connected coalition. Knowing both that it was viable in terms of the likelihood of meeting the 5 percent threshold requirement and that it would have to form a coalition with the MSZP—provided, of course, that the final results permitted the two parties to have a majority together—it made sense for the SZDSZ to run on its own and create a strong bargaining position for itself vis-à-vis its expected coalition partner.

As election day drew closer, all four major public opinion polling firms (Tarki, Szonda-Ipsos, Median, and Gallup) suggested a convincing FIDESZ–MDF advantage. In their last pre-election polls, the four firms measured FIDESZ support to range between 43 percent to 48 percent among those voters who were decided about both their voting intentions and their party preferences. In contrast, the same survey showed MSZP support to range only between 37 percent and 39 percent. The first round of the 2002 general elections was characterized by two interesting features: an unprecedentedly high turnout rate and a very large number of single member districts where the election was both valid and conclusive. Defying expectations that the highly polarized and charged political atmosphere of the campaign might alienate voters from the electoral process, the polls saw an unprecedented number of Hungarians exercising their franchise on election day. The turnout rate, at 70.53 percent, was record breaking in comparison with Hungary's previous three post-transition parliamentary elections. Moreover, the first round of the election was also conclusive in forty-five districts, an unprecedentedly large number.

With the exception of the smaller Centrum Party, which contested the elections for the first time in 2002, all smaller parties experienced a net loss of votes between the two elections. Of the three small parties that were represented in the outgoing parliament (the SZDSZ, MIEP, and the FKGP), the FKGP lost the most votes followed by the SZDSZ and then the MIEP. What contributed to the failure of MIEP to cross the threshold of representation was the increase in the rate of electoral turnout between 1998 and 2002. Although the party retained more of its voters than the SZDSZ could, in absolute terms the SZDSZ still enjoyed the support of more voters. Therefore, no matter how barely, the SZDSZ managed to cross the threshold, despite the considerable shrinkage of its support base. It is also worth noting that, ceteris paribus, if the rate of electoral turnout had remained at its 1998 level, both SZDSZ and MIEP would have been likely to clear the threshold; however, the Centrum would still have fallen short of it by 8355 votes. In contrast, the two large formations were net beneficiaries of both the increase in electoral turnout and the vote losses experienced by the small parties. Both the MSZP and the FIDESZ–MDF alliance saw the number of their regional list votes increase by about 57 percent between the two elections.

A number of other indicators also confirmed the dominant position of the two large formations, the FIDESZ–MDF and the MSZP, after the first round. First, forty-four of the forty-five districts where the first round was conclusive were won by either the FIDESZ–MDF alliance (twenty districts) or the MSZP (twenty-four districts). The twenty-fifth seat was won by a candidate jointly fielded by the MSZP and the SZDSZ. Second, in all but one of the 176 districts the candidates of the same two formations finished second.[5] In fifty-six of the 131 districts where the results were inconclusive the candidates of the incumbent coalition finished first, while in the remaining seventy-five the MSZP candidates did so. Third, FIDESZ–MDF and the MSZP also dominated the party list votes by receiving 83.12 percent thereof between themselves. Whereas the difference between the first and second largest parties' share of the list votes was a mere 0.98 percent, the difference between the second and third largest parties was a staggering 35.5 percent. Fourth, in stark contrast to the previous three elections, only one additional party, the SZDSZ, managed to cross the threshold, and only barely so, besides the two large formations. Finally, the two large formations dominated the party list votes in all regions. Whereas FIDESZ–MDF received the largest number of list votes and seats in twelve counties, the MSZP did so in eight (including the capital city of Budapest). Moreover, there was no such county where these two formations did not receive at least the second largest share of the list votes cast.

Overall, the performance of the incumbent coalition in the first round was extremely successful. First, never in the history of post-communist Hungary have governing parties been able to increase their share of the popular vote between the two elections marking the beginning and the end of their term. FIDESZ and the MDF together almost doubled the number of list votes between the two elections: in 1998 the two parties together polled 1,467, 944 list votes, whereas in 2002 they collected 2,306,763. Second, the margin by which the MSZP was ahead of FIDESZ–MDF after the first round was far smaller in 2002 than the margin by which the then incumbent MSZP–SZDSZ alliance was leading after the first round of the 1998 elections. Given that FIDESZ, in alliance with its smaller supporters, managed to win the 1998 election despite a much less favorable first round performance than in 2002, the supporters of the incumbent coalition had reasons to look forward to the second round with optimism.

Finally, since FIDESZ–MDF emerged as the sole representative of the Right in the second round, it did not have to incur further coordination costs. Whereas the MSZP and the SZDSZ had to make adjustments and enter into strategic withdrawal in each other's favor, FIDESZ–MDF did not have to do so. The costs of such a mid-election alliance building could be quite considerable (Tsebelis 1990). Prior to and during the first round of a run-off election, parties in the same ideological bloc have to emphasize their differences in order to emerge as the winner within their bloc. However, once the first round is over, the same parties have to switch their strategies to cooperation in order to ensure the defeat of their common opponent, the representative of the other bloc. Changing strategies in the span of merely two weeks could be a difficult and costly exercise. FIDESZ avoided this problem by having built its alliance with the MDF well before the elections started, which allowed the two parties to save the costs of switching strategies midway through the elections.

Indeed, while the MSZP and the SZDSZ were preoccupied with working out the details of their cooperation in the second round, FIDESZ–MDF could focus on mobilizing voters directly. Although a total of 394 candidates qualified to enter the second round in 131 districts, only 269 did so. For its part, the MSZP expected to take advantage of the withdrawals offered by the SZDSZ, the Workers Party and most Centrum candidates. While the Workers Party withdrew each of its still standing candidates, the SZDSZ did so in 89 percent, and the Centrum in 78 percent of the cases. The perfectly disciplined behavior by the Workers Party was closely followed by the two small right-wing parties, the FKGP and MIEP, which had withdrawn all but one each of their candidates in favor of FIDESZ–MDF. To reciprocate the withdrawals that were made in its favor, the Socialist Party also had to make concessions by removing its candidates in seven districts, in each case in favor of the SZDSZ. The second round of the election resulted in a reversal of fortunes between the two leading parties; however, the gains made by FIDESZ–MDF were not large enough to allow the allies to win the election overall. In all but one of the nine districts where strategic withdrawal did not take place, the candidate that was leading after the first round ended up winning in the second round. In the overwhelming majority of the districts, the candidate who was winning the first round was able to preserve his/her lead in the run-off; only in twenty-five districts was the outcome of the run-off the reverse of the first round. The two largest parties were almost equally successful in terms of preserving their first round advantage. Whereas the Socialists preserved their lead in forty-eight districts, the FIDESZ–MDF alliance did so in fifty-two.

It is worth noting that the withdrawals made by the SZDSZ in favor of the Socialist candidates were successful only in a negative sense, i.e. they contributed to the Socialists not losing those districts where they had already enjoyed the first round lead. However, coordination with the SZDSZ was not sufficient for the MSZP to make further gains in the second round: there was only a single district where a withdrawal by the SZDSZ helped the Socialist candidate win despite being the runner-up in the first round. Moreover, in a paradoxical sense, strategic withdrawals by the SZDSZ allowed FIDESZ–MDF to retain its advantage in almost as many districts (twenty-eight) as it allowed the Socialist candidates (thirty-three) to do so. What was even more surprising was that SZDSZ withdrawals led to a reversal of positions in favor of FIDESZ–MDF candidates in more districts (eight) than it did in favor of the Socialist ones (one). Overall, the number of districts where the FIDESZ–MDF candidates ended up winning despite the removal of the SZDSZ candidate from the second round was greater (thirty-six) than the number of districts where Socialist candidates won (thirty-four). The limited success of the MSZP–SZDSZ cooperation is further indicated by the failure of the MSZP withdrawals to contribute to the fortunes of the SZDSZ: while the MSZP removed seven of its candidates in favor of the SZDSZ from the second round, only in two districts did this result in the expected SZDSZ victory.

Relatively speaking, the communist Workers Party made a more positive contribution to the second round performance of the Socialist party than the SZDSZ did. In six of the eight districts where the Workers Party removed its candidates from the second round the Socialist candidate preserved his/her leading position. In one of the two remaining districts where the Workers Party candidate stepped down, the SZDSZ candidate won despite having been the first round runner-up. The impact of the Centrum Party's withdrawals was more similar to that by SZDSZ, in that it contributed more positively to the fortunes of the FIDESZ–MDF alliance (nine districts) than to those of the Socialist Party (six districts).

The impact of withdrawals made by the two smaller right-wing parties was much more straightforward. Whereas the withdrawal of MIEP candidates contributed to a FIDESZ–MDF victory in thirteen out of sixteen cases, in each of the three districts where the FKGP removed its candidate the FIDESZ–MDF candidate won. Curiously, the withdrawal of Independent candidates also favored the FIDESZ–MDF alliance much more than the Socialists.

In sum, the fact that the FIDESZ–MDF alliance did not have to engage in costly negotiations between the two rounds paid off remarkably well. Of the 131 districts where a second round was held on April 21, the FIDESZ–MDF candidate won in seventy-five, while MSZP candidates were victorious in only fifty-four cases. This was a sharp reversal in party performance compared to the first round, when the Socialist won more seats in the single member districts than the FIDESZ–MDF alliance. Also, of the eight SZDSZ candidates who entered the second round, only two were successful. In the end, Hungarian voters did not deliver a clear verdict in the 2002 national elections. Although the FIDESZ–MDF alliance won the most seats, they could not claim to have won the election for they were unable to form a majority government. On the other hand, whereas the Socialist party won fewer seats than the FIDESZ–MDF alliance, it was in a position to form a bare-majority coalition government with the SZDSZ, which it eventually did. As a final note, it is important to mention the impact of the national compensatory seats on the final outcome of the election. In the absence of this tier of allocation, FIDESZ–MDF would clearly have won the election. However, by crossing the 5 percent threshold, the SZDSZ was able to translate all of its candidate and list votes that were wasted at the district- and regional-level of allocation and collect almost one-fifth of the compensatory seats.

4.4 AN INSTITUTIONALIST ACCOUNT OF GOVERNMENT FORMATION IN HUNGARY[6]

The formation of Hungary's first four post-communist coalition governments cannot be consistently explained in terms of institution-free coalition theoretic predictions. First, the formation of these governments generally defies the minimum winning coalition (MWC) prediction of the classic office-seeking tradition. This is particularly striking in the cases of the 1994 government, which was formed by coalitions of parties despite the fact that the largest party, the MSZP, could have governed by itself. Second, it is not clear either why in 1990, 1998 and 2002 respectively it was the actual set of parties that ended up forming the coalition government. For example, according to Figure 4.1, two other minimum connected winning coalitions (MCWCs) could have been formed in 1990 besides the one that was actually formed: MDF–FIDESZ–SZDSZ, or MDF–FIDESZ–KDNP. In terms of office-seeking, the former would have been a suboptimal outcome because of its extremely large size. However, the latter combination of parties would have been superior to the coalition that was eventually formed, because the combined size of the MDF–FIDESZ–KDNP coalition would have been less than that of the eventual MDF–KDNP–FKGP was. In 1998, the only other alternative MCWC coalition was FIDESZ–SZDSZ–MSZP, which on office-seeking grounds did not make more sense than the formation of the eventual coalition. However, this explanation is inconsistent with the formation of the 1990 coalition as suggested above. After the 2002 elections there were two alternative MCWCs and the one that was eventually formed was superior on office-seeking grounds to the other: the MSZP–SZDSZ coalition was smaller than the alternative MCWC consisting of FIDESZ–MDF–SZDSZ would have been. In the following sections, I spell out how electoral coalitions help us make sense of the formation of Hungarian coalition governments in an analytically consistent manner.

4.4.1 The First Conservative Government, 1990

In 1990, only six political parties crossed the 4 percent threshold in the first round of the election with the MDF and the SZDSZ leading the race. The results of the first round provided the four smaller parties an incentive to engage in strategic sequencing (Cox 1997: 194–5) to make sure that their favored large party would indeed receive the mandate to form the government. In particular, owing to their spatial location both the KDNP and the FKGP had an incentive to form an electoral coalition with the MDF because, of the two large parties, the MDF was closer to both of them (Hibbing and Patterson 1992). For similar reasons, the MSZP should also have had an incentive to support the efforts of the SZDSZ to become the largest party in the chamber. However, in the first post-communist election the divide between the Communist successor party, the MSZP, and the rest of the genuinely democratic parties was sufficiently strong to prevent any sort of cooperation with the MSZP.

The position of FIDESZ was a little more complex because the party was sandwiched between, and, therefore, spatially connected with both the SZDSZ and the MDF. Nonetheless, the expectation that the MDF would cooperate with the KDNP and the FKGP prompted FIDESZ to cooperate with the SZDSZ because forming a two-party coalition with the SZDSZ was "cheaper" for FIDESZ than forming a four-party coalition with the three conservative parties both in terms of ideological divergence and transactions costs. In other words, an SZDSZ–FIDESZ coalition would have been more compact than a MDF–FIDESZ–KDNP–FKGP coalition; therefore, it made sense that FIDESZ would support the cause of the former.

Interestingly, the MDF may have wanted to woo the support of FIDESZ since an eventual MDF–FIDESZ–KDNP coalition would have been a superior outcome from the perspective of the MDF than a coalition government with the two conservative parties. To see this, consider that in a three-party coalition with the FIDESZ and the KDNP, the MDF would be in the center and as such it would be able to control the policy agenda of the cabinet by exploiting the divisions between its partners. However, given that the first round showed the FKGP to be twice as strong as FIDESZ, in terms of seats secured, the MDF had an interest in seeking an alliance with the Smallholders' Party because FIDESZ may not have been able to provide the MDF with the sought-after parliamentary majority. In addition, a possible move by the MDF towards FIDESZ in the second round would have been vetoed by both the KDNP and the FKGP. The former would have opposed such a move because it would deprive it of the central position that it would enjoy in the three-party coalition government with MDF and the FKGP. The latter would have objected to it because a move towards FIDESZ would have moved the expected policy position of the coalition cabinet farther away from the policy position of the FKGP.

Due to these considerations, strategic withdrawals took place on both sides of the ideological spectrum, the Left and the Right. The largest number of withdrawals was made by the SZDSZ and FIDESZ in favor of one another. The coordination among the three parties of the Right was more difficult and costly because they were more successful in the first round and had more candidates qualifying to enter the second. Nonetheless, the three conservative parties managed to run an average of 1.4 candidates per district in the second round, which was only marginally greater than the average of 0.84 candidates run by the two left and center-left parties. These numbers also indicate that whereas the three conservative parties ran a little too many candidates, the SZDSZ–FIDESZ alliance ran a little too few. As expected, the "untouchable" MSZP did not withdraw its candidates; indeed, all but two of the party's qualifying candidates entered the second round.

In sum, responding to the incentives of electoral calculus, political parties formed electoral coalitions which, in turn, presented the electorate with two clearly identifiable government alternatives: the conservative MDF–KDNP–FKGP coalition on the one hand, and the liberal SZDSZ–FIDESZ coalition on the other. The MSZP was the sixth party that cleared the threshold and entered parliament; however, it was not part of either alternative. As such, the MSZP did not have a coalition potential at this time. Considering the impact of the electoral system on parties' calculations allows me to predict the formation of one of two coalitions, depending on which one will win a majority in the second round. This prediction is considerably more efficient than those based on MW and MCW coalitions.

4.4.2 The First Left-Liberal Coalition Government, 1994

The same six parties managed to clear the threshold, raised to 5 percent, in the first round of the 1994 election as in 1990. However, in contrast to 1990, the first round of the 1994 election was swept by the MSZP and the SZDSZ. The two parties together won almost a majority of the party list and the candidate vote. As a result, the MSZP and the SZDSZ had the largest number of candidates entering the second round: MSZP candidates qualified to advance to the run-off in 174 districts, while the SZDSZ candidates did so in 161. The party with the next highest number of surviving candidates was the MDF; however, its candidates qualified for re-entry in only ninety-nine districts.

Political parties had limited incentives to engage in electoral coalition building in this strategic context. Although the four smaller parties may have formed an electoral proto-coalition with the SZDSZ because this party was ideologically closer to each of them than the Socialist Party, the costs of this arrangement would have been very high both because of the relatively large number of parties involved (five) as well as the ideological diversity among them. Similarly, the SZDSZ would also find such an arrangement very costly and would, instead, opt to cooperate with the MSZP. An electoral coalition with the Socialists would make the SZDSZ better-off than a coalition with the conservatives essentially because the two parties were spatially connected, whereas the SZDSZ was not connected with any member of the outgoing conservative coalition government.

Likewise, the SZDSZ was the only political party having cleared the threshold that the MSZP was connected with; therefore, the Socialist Party was also interested in cooperating with the Free Democrats. However, despite their interest in forming a coalition, the nature of the results of the first round did not encourage the two parties to withdraw their candidates in favor of each other. The poor performance of the conservative parties, as well as FIDESZ, in the first round guaranteed that the run-offs in almost all districts were safe; that is, they were likely to be won by the candidates of the two largest parties. In other words, splitting the vote between the MSZP and the SZDSZ candidate in any given district did not risk losing the seat to the conservative parties, while at the same time it allowed the two parties to run a friendly race which would decide the distribution of power between them in the post-election cabinet that they would form. In short, whereas both parties were interested in strategic cooperation, their tactical choices made them appear as if they were competitors.

As a result of these calculations, far fewer strategic withdrawals were made in the second round than four years before. The partisan distribution of these withdrawals shows that with only two exceptions, all candidates of the two largest parties re-entered the second round. As expected, the three members of the previous coalition government did not withdraw their candidates, save for one exception by the MDF. The rest of the withdrawals were carried out by Independents; the Agrarian Alliance, a small party that did not clear the threshold; and FIDESZ.

The MSZP and SZDSZ candidates won in 94 percent of the districts where a run-off was held, with the former winning in 147 and the latter in sixteen of the 174 districts. This result has provided the Socialist Party with an absolute majority of seats in the new parliament. As such, the party was in in a position to form a single-party majority government, which is precisely what institution-free-models of coalition formation would predict. However, the analysis of parties' electoral calculations and choices suggests that the actual government alternative that parties presented to the electorate was the MSZP–SZDSZ coalition rather than the MSZP or the SZDSZ alone. Therefore, the predicted outcome is the formation of a coalition government by the two parties, which is indeed what took place.

4.4.3 The Second Conservative Coalition: 1998

In stark contrast to 1990 and 1994, electoral turnout in the 1998 election barely exceeded 50 percent, which resulted in invalid races in thirty-one single member and two regional multimember districts.[7] Despite the low turnout, only five political parties (the MSZP, FIDESZ, the SZDSZ, the FKGP, and MIEP) crossed the 5 percent threshold, as opposed to 6 in 1990 and 1994. The low turnout also limited further coordination among the parties in the second round because of the large number of districts where the first round was invalid. Since the allocation of seats among parties' national list seats is directly tied to the number of votes that parties receive in those districts where they are unsuccessful in terms of winning seats, smaller political parties had a strong incentive to re-enter their candidates in these districts. Of course, this logic applied simultaneously with the logic of strategic entry and withdrawal. In other words, notwithstanding the incentive to re-enter their candidates in the second round, where the first round was invalid, parties also had to consider the extent to which their doing so might result in adverse vote splitting.

The MSZP and FIDESZ were leading the race after the first round with the Socialists enjoying a slight advantage in terms of both the candidate and the list votes. Given their spatial location, the MIEP and the FKGP had an incentive to form an electoral coalition with the FIDESZ–MDF protocoalition in the second round in order to reduce the likelihood of a Socialist-led victory, while the SZDSZ had an incentive to cooperate with the MSZP. Incidentally, the SZDSZ was in precisely the same situation as FIDESZ had been in 1990: the party was sandwiched between the two large formations, and as such it could have chosen to cooperate with either of them. However, cooperation with the FIDESZ was not a credible option for the SZDSZ because entering an electoral protocoalition with that party would also have meant cooperation with parties located further to the right of FIDESZ. Therefore, forming an electoral coalition with the MSZP was "cheaper" for the SZDSZ because it required coordination with a single spatially connected party.

Of the two large parties the MSZP had very limited manoeuvrability due to its extreme spatial location. Its cooperation with the SZDSZ was in equilibrium because, as explained above, neither party had anywhere else to turn for allies. This, in turn, encouraged FIDESZ–MDF to seek a coalition with the FKGP instead of the SZDSZ, although both were spatially connected. Forming an electoral coalition with MIEP, however, was not equally necessary because given its extreme location the legislative support of MIEP could be taken for granted by FIDESZ–MDF anyway. Since MIEP was on the extreme right of the spectrum, it would have no choice but support a FIDESZ-led conservative coalition, no matter what.

In the run-off, the two large formations, the MSZP and the FIDESZ-MDF alliance, withdrew very few of their candidates, while the FKGP and the SZDSZ did so on a very significant scale. The latter two parties removed 62 percent and 42 percent of their candidates respectively from the second round. Not surprisingly, the MDF also withdrew a significant number of its own individually run candidates in support of a conservative victory. Of the two electoral coalitions that were formed between the two rounds, MSZP–SZDSZ on the Left and FIDESZ–MDF–FKGP in the Right, the latter proved victorious. As expected on the basis of their electoral cooperation, the three conservative partners proceeded to form a coalition majority government.

4.4.4 The Second Left-Liberal Coalition, 2002

Having realized the gains of efficient pre-electoral cooperation, FIDESZ and the MDF went further and submitted common national and regional lists in the 2002 election. The formation of the FIDESZ–MDF alliance made the formation of a similar alliance between the left-liberal parties, the MSZP and the SZDSZ, unnecessary. The joining of FIDESZ and the MDF meant that, even though they were spatially proximate, the SZDSZ could not form a coalition with FIDESZ without also joining hands with the MDF. Therefore the possible coalition options before the SZDSZ were either the MSZP, or FIDESZ and the MDF together. Given this choice, the SZDSZ would opt for the MSZP because it would result in a more compact connected coalition. Knowing that it would have to form a coalition with the MSZP, provided, of course, that the distribution of seats made it possible, it made sense for the SZDSZ to run on its own and create a strong bargaining position for itself vis-à-vis its expected coalition partner.

In stark contrast to all previous elections, only three political formations crossed the required threshold in the first round: the MSZP, the FIDESZ–MDF alliance, and the SZDSZ. With just one exception, the candidates of the MSZP and the FIDESZ–MDF finished first or second in all districts where a run-off had to be held. The distribution of vote shares in the first round also showed an unprecedented degree of bipolar concentration: the MSZP and the FIDESZ–MDF alliance together received around 80 percent of both the candidate and party list votes. Finally, owing to a very high turnout rate, 70.53 percent in the first round, the candidates of the two parties secured a conclusive victory in the first round in forty-five districts.

The first round of the election created a strategic context similar to that in 1998. The only small party that crossed the threshold, the SZDSZ, had no incentive to run candidates in the run-off. Since the party had already cleared the threshold, it was secure in terms of having parliamentary representation. However, given the tightness of the race between the two large formations, the SZDSZ could play a pivotal role in shaping the final outcome by withdrawing in favor of the MSZP. In short, the results of the first round encouraged the formation of two electoral coalitions among parties that already secured parliamentary representation: FIDESZ–MDF and MSZP–SZDSZ. In the run-off, the SZDSZ removed seventy of its seventy-eight qualifying candidates in exchange for the MSZP removing seven of its own. Explicit coordination between FIDESZ and the MDF was not necessary because the two parties had already been competing as a single entity.

Once again, political parties had a strong incentive to form two distinct electoral coalitions in the second round of the election, which also defined the two alternative governments that voters could choose between. Although the FIDESZ–MDF alliance won more of the single member districts in the run-offs than the MSZP–SZDSZ coalition, it was not sufficient to win an overall majority of the seats. Benefiting from the national compensatory tier, the SZDSZ acquired just enough seats to tilt the balance in favor of the left-liberal bloc. Therefore, the electoral coalition of the MSZP and the SZDSZ proceeded to form a coalition majority government after the elections.

4.5 CONCLUSION

This chapter has made two important contributions to the study of institutional design and post-communist party government. On the one hand, it has explored and demonstrated how political parties have developed strategies of electoral coalition formation in strict response to the hard constraints of the country's mixed-member electoral system. As we saw in Chapter Three, Hungary has all the conditions present that, in general, promote electoral coalitions in the region: it has an electoral system with relatively small districts, a highly restrictive electoral formula, and a positive government formation rule. As such, the Hungarian case study is helpful because it provides a micro-analytic insight into how parties respond to the institutional incentives and form electoral coalitions to better capitalize on their electoral following. Specifically, the case study highlights that the availability of a single seat through a run-off in the nominal tier of the electoral system plays a defining role in incentivizing parties to coordinate their candidate nomination strategies both before the election as well as between the two rounds. In other words, district magnitude clearly matters.

Second, this chapter has also shown that electoral coalitions can become extremely important actors in the government formation process. In fact, I have argued that the formation of governing coalitions in Hungary's post-communist democracy cannot be adequately understood without reference to the impact that the electoral system has on the choices and calculations that political parties make. By virtue of ignoring the electoral interplay among parties, institution-free models of government formation both fail to predict the outcomes accurately and predict coalition possibilities, which are unrealistic. Such shortcomings are overcome, however, when the impact that the electoral system has on parties' choices and strategic calculations is taken into account. It is important to note that the electoral system allows Hungarian voters to have a very clear menu of options in terms of government alternatives. Since the coalition formation process takes place before the electorate rather than behind closed doors after the election is over, the electoral system contributes to enhancing the legitimacy and the effectiveness of the nascent democratic process in Hungary. Whether this will remain a uniquely

Hungarian story or whether electoral coalitions will become similarly important in modelling and understanding the formation of governing coalitions in the region remains to be seen and analyzed in future work. For now, I will turn to an examination of how political institutions have shaped patterns of minority, and by default, majority government formation in the ten new democracies.

NOTES

1. This section draws on Nikolenyi (2004a,b).
2. For the left-right location of Hungarian political parties, see Korosenyi (1993) and Kitschelt, Mansfeldova, Markowski and Toka (1999).
3. The MDF would have received 11.3 percent of the regional list vote under the 65 percent to 35 percent division.
4. For instance, a FIDESZ-only minority government would have been conceivable, in the absence of a pre-electoral alliance under the following distribution of seats, in percentages: MSZP: 35 percent, SZDSZ: 10 percent, FIDESZ: 45 percent, MDF: 10 percent. In this scenario, FIDESZ could theoretically take advantage of a divided opposition.
5. The sole exception was District Number One in Komarom-Esztergom county, where an Independent candidate finished second after the MSZP candidate.
6. This section draws on Nikolenyi (2004b).
7. The two counties where the list voting was invalid were Hajdu-Bihar and Szabolcs-Szatmar-Bereg.

5

The Institutional Sources of Minority Governments

5.1 INTRODUCTION

Held under an extremely permissive and proportional electoral system in October 1991, the first post-communist parliamentary elections in Poland produced what became to this day the most fractured and fragmented legislature in all of East Central Europe. With the largest party controlling no more than 13.5 percent of the seats in the *Sejm*, it was not very surprising that political parties found it extremely difficult to put together a majority coalition that would be capable of looking after crucial legislative business involving social, economic and political reforms. Indeed, after two successive minority coalition governments proved unable to maintain majority support on the floor, the *Sejm* was dissolved, prematurely paving the way for fresh elections in 1993.

The same year Bulgaria also held the first post-transition elections to the *Narodno Sabranie*. Relative to Poland, the first Bulgarian parliament was considerably less fragmented in its composition than the Polish *Sejm*: only three political parties won legislative seats with the largest among them accounting for over 40 percent of the newly elected deputies. Similarly to the Polish case, however, the largest party, the Union of Democratic Forces (SDS), also opted to form a minority government, which, in retrospect, ended up being only slightly more durable than the minority coalitions in the Polish *Sejm*.

These examples suggest that political parties in the early post-transition legislatures of post-communist East Central Europe did not easily succeed, or were willing, to comply with the dicta of conventional coalition theoretic wisdom to form majority-size governments that either maximize their participants' office-related payoffs (Riker 1962), minimize the ideological distance among the coalition's partners, or both (Axelrod 1971). Instead, parties often opted to form undersized minority governments. Echoing earlier, and largely West European, explanations of minority governments (Taylor and Herman 1971), these examples suggest that undersized governments may well be the product of unpredictable unique, or crisis, situations in which the normal logic and dynamics of coalition bargaining are more difficult to apply.

Indeed, we might plausibly claim that the first post-transition elections of the respective new democracies presented parties with precisely the kind of unpredictability of circumstances to which these conventional "crisis" explanations attribute the formation of minority governments. From this perspective, it may not be very surprising to find that these first post-communist governments tended to be under-sized. Moreover, the well-known under-institutionalization of the party systems in new democracies might also seriously weaken the ability of political parties to carry out and implement the types of calculations that would lead to the formation of both majority-size coalition governments. Thus, in the case of the early post-transition East Central European legislatures, the formation of undersized governments may be merely reflective of the still nascent party systems where high electoral volatility and the high incidence of new party formation makes the precise calculation of the various coalition combinations particularly difficult.

If the formation of these early minority governments were truly the result and the artifact of historical time and context, then over the next several elections we should have witnessed post-communist parties conforming increasingly more to the logic and rationality of office- and policy-seeking and, as a consequence, forming majority governments as their national party systems stabilize and mature. If so, then the rate and frequency of minority governments in post-communist East Central Europe should also be very different from what we find in the established democracies of Western Europe, where "minority solutions have been chosen 42.8 percent of the time" and "[t]he frequency of minority governments has increased over time" (Strom 1990: 59). Indeed, we can see that whereas half of the ten new democracies witnessed the formation of a minority government after their first post-transition election (Bulgaria, Czech Republic, Latvia, Poland and Romania), the subsequent rate of minority cabinet formation after parliamentary elections declined to 18 percent (only eight of the forty-four subsequent elections up to 2010 resulted in minority governments). Yet, considering both post-election and mid-term governments, the frequency of minority cabinets is high: in approximately half of the instances that a new government is formed, either after a parliamentary election or during the same inter-election period, political parties have formed under-sized minority governments.

Whether the first post-transition government in a new democracy was under-sized or not seemed to have an effect on the frequency of minority governments in the future: all but one of the five states where the first post-communist election led to a majority government (Estonia, Hungary, Lithuania, Slovakia, and Slovenia) continued the same pattern after each subsequent parliamentary election. The only exception is Lithuania but even there we find only a single instance of a post-election minority cabinet in the year 2000. In contrast, six of the seven minority governments that were formed after later elections came about in those new democracies where the first post-transition election already produced such an outcome: two more elections led to minority cabinets in the Czech Republic and Romania respectively, and one more in Bulgaria, Latvia, and in Poland.

Important and relevant as context-specific explanations might be, the cross-sectional distribution of minority governments suggests that there are additional factors at work that may account for variation in the formation of under-sized governments across the new democracies. Why is it the case that some post-communist democracies never witness the formation of a minority government after a general election (e.g. Estonia or Hungary) while in other cases such an outcome is almost a norm rather than the exception (e.g. Czech Republic or Romania)? Indeed, minority governments in general are concentrated in four states: the Czech Republic, Poland, Romania, and Latvia; it was not until very recently that political parties started to arrive at minority cabinet solutions again in Bulgaria. An obvious candidate answer to this question would be the incentive structure provided by the prevailing institutional design of the new democracies that define both the rules of the government formation game and the constraints under which it would be played out. With respect to the institutional context of government formation, the ten new democracies have indeed shown sufficiently high variation which makes further analysis of their impact both worthwhile and justified. Specifically, the chapter will argue that *institutional features that hinder the concentration of power in, and as such weaken the relative authority of the first chamber of parliament over the executive, also reduce the incentives for political parties to form majority coalitions*. As discussed earlier, institutional features that promote the dispersion of political power include a large assembly size, bicameralism, negative parliamentary government formation rules, and a strong presidency.

This institutonalist argument about minority government formation stems from the central assumption that minority governments are formed for two reasons. On the one hand, there are potential members of a governing coalition whose entry could increase the size of the coalition to a majority but that decide to stay outside the government. On the other hand, it is also equally likely and possible that those members that are already inside the coalition choose not to increase the size of the coalition any further because they calculate that they would be able to govern from a minority position. Both of these calculations are shaped by the incentives provided by the prevailing institutional structures, specifically the limitations on the authority of the first parliamentary chamber. When the first chamber is the single source of authority of policy making and when there are few limitations on its overall political power, parties have a strong incentive to form majority coalitions that capture and control it. Conversely, when the authority and the powers of the chamber are more limited, the incentive to form a winning coalition becomes weaker as both the opposition and the governing parties may calculate that they can exercise control over policy and legislation through their access to those additional offices and sites of power that limit the authority of the first chamber. The institutions that may limit the overall power of the first chamber are its relatively large size, bicameralism, presidential power, and a negative formation rule.

The chapter starts with an overview of the main arguments in the literature about the causes for the formation of minority government with particular emphasis on the role of institutional arrangements. This will be followed by a comparative summary assessment of the history of government coalitions in the ten states. A detailed country-by-country review is provided in Appendix B. The third section evaluates the role of political institutions.

5.2 EXPLANATIONS OF MINORITY GOVERNMENTS

According to a long tradition of research on party systems and patterns of government formation, minority governments are associated with high degrees of fragmentation, polarization and instability in the party system, which reduce both parties' willingness to bargain with each other to form a majority coalition and the certainty of the information that they have about each other's strategies, preferences and goals (Dodd 1976). In this vein, Sartori argues that minority governments are particularly characteristic features of "moderate pluralism," a party system format defined by moderate degrees of fragmentation, with three to five relevant parties, and ideological polarization. In such systems, "minority single party governments do materialize, but they do so either as a result of miscalculated Indian wrestlings, or on the basis of a precise calculus (such as shedding unpopular, if necessary, policies), and otherwise as disguised coalitions and transitional caretaker governments" (Sartori 1976: 178).

A different line of explanation predicts that minority governments will be formed by a party that is located in the center of the issue space of the party system. Building on Black's (1958) well-known median voter theorem, which holds that the winset of the median player is empty in one dimension under majority rule, a number of authors have argued that a centrally located party can divide the majority opposition and form a minority government on its own (van Roozendaal 1992a,b; Crombez 1996; Laver and Shepsle 1996; Schofield 2007). By forming a government on its own rather than sharing office with its coalition partners, the center party can maintain control of the portfolio allocation process, which allows it to maximize its office benefits. At the same time, since the winset of the median player is empty, by forming a minority government the center party can also maximize the likelihood that government policy would reflect its own ideal point.

In this vein, Laver and Shepsle (1996) propose that a minority government will be formed by a *very strong party*, which is characterized by having "an ideal point such that there is no alternative government preferred by a majority to one that gives the very strong party all portfolios" (1996: 263). Van Roozendaal (1992a,b) predicts that the likelihood of both the formation and the stability of a minority government increase when the central party is also numerically dominant. Crombez (1996) arrives at essentially the same conclusion and predicts that the larger and more centrist the plurality party the greater the likelihood that it would form a minority government.

A more dynamic explanation of minority governments is offered by Grofman, Straffin and Noviello (1996) who model cabinet formation as a sequential process of proto-coalition formation. According to this model, a minority government will have a knife-edge quality to it in that it will be formed only when two proto-coalitions have reached equal size and no further expansion is possible. In a sense, this model provides a theoretical foundation for earlier observations by Taylor and Laver (1973) and Herman and Pope (1973) according to which most minority governments, in Western Europe, are formed by near-majority size parties because a "party, like a government, which controls over forty-five percent of the seats in a legislature is likely to receive the support necessary to provide it with a majority on crucial decisions. . . . This suggests that the effective decision point in these parliaments is a number smaller than a simpler majority" (Herman and Pope 1973: 203)

A third approach to understanding the formation of minority governments stresses the institutional incentives that encourage office- and policy-seeking political parties not to enter executive office and allow the formation of a minority cabinet instead of a majority coalition (Strom 1990; Laver and Budge 1992; Bergman 1993; Strom, Budge and Laver 1994). A number of different explanations have been proposed in this new-institutionalist vein. For example, Bergman (1993) links the formation of minority governments to negative parliamentary rules of cabinet formation, while Strom, Budge and Laver (1994) point out those restrictive legislative rules favor minority coalitions, while provisions for mandatory government size, as in the case of constructive no-confidence votes, rule out the formation of a minority government.

The most complete and influential account of minority government formation in the neo-institutional perspective is provided by Strom (1984, 1990) who identifies two institutions that provide incentives for political parties not to enter office: the influence of the parliamentary opposition on policy and the electoral decisiveness of government formation. The stronger the role of the opposition in the policy making process, the greater the likelihood that policy-seeking potential coalition partners may want to stay outside the formal structure of the executive in order to avoid incurring the electoral costs of incumbency. This disincentive to enter executive office is further exacerbated where electoral outcomes are decisive of coalitional bargaining power: instead of entering office now, which is costly in electoral terms, parties may strategically calculate that it is better to wait until their electoral chances will allow them to enter office on more advantageous terms in the future and let someone else incur the costs of incumbency in the meantime.

The literature on party coalitions in post-communist democracies has paid scant attention to the issue of minority governments. Instead, scholars have focused on how the regime divide, i.e. the bipolar competition between successors of the former communist parties and their opposition, has constrained parties' coalitional choices after the transition by imposing an electoral penalty on parties that cross this divide (Grzymala-Brusse 2001). An important finding in this stream of the literature is that coalitions that include communist successor parties tend to be oversized and that such parties tend to receive a less-than-proportional share of cabinet portfolios compared to other parties (Druckman and Roberts 2007). Other studies have pointed to the impact of institutional factors, such as the role of the president in appointing the formateur (Protsyk 2005), and the presence of dominant and central parties in the legislature (Nikolenyi 2004b) in affecting cabinet composition and duration.

One reason for the lack of significant scholarly interest in the study of post-communist minority governments may be that "[s]ince the new parties in the region have been initially described as having vague ideologies, few clear policy differences, and office as their main goal, there are . . . grounds to expect that the coalition in the region will follow the minimum winning coalition model" (Grzymala-Busse 2001: 86). If so, then minority governments are mere aberrations rather than patterned outcomes systematically and consistently generated by particular features of the new democratic political systems. Indeed, as we shall see in the following section, the majority of post-communist governments were of a majority size, and minority governments mainly proliferated in the first post-transition parliaments when policy constraints on coalition bargains were much weaker than later on as the party systems were becoming more institutionalized and ideologically patterned. Thus, although the lack of interest in post-communist minority governments is not entirely unjustified, it does create a lacuna in our current understanding of coalition dynamics in these new democracies.

5.3 MINORITY GOVERNMENTS IN POST-COMMUNIST DEMOCRACIES

Before providing a detailed description about minority governments in the new democracies a proper definition of the dependent variable is in order. In his seminal work on minority governments in parliamentary democracies, Strom defines a majority cabinet (or government) as "any cabinet that meets all appropriate constitutional requirements and that is composed of persons acting as representatives of political parties or parliamentary groups that collectively control no less than half of all seats in the national legislature, or that chamber of the legislature to which the cabinet is constitutionally responsible" (Strom 1990: 6). In turn, he defines minority cabinets (or governments) as those that "meet all of the foregoing requirements except the majority clause." Strictly speaking, this definition includes cabinet coalitions at the knife-edge, (Grofman, Straffin and Noveillo 1996), that is to say at exactly the 50 percent mark, among majority governments. Strom justifies this operational decision by explaining that "most parliaments have rules favoring the status quo in the event of tie votes. In parliamentary regimes this generally means the party or parties in office. Even in the absence of such a bias, the worst predictable outcome for the government would be a stalemate. But under no existing institutional rule would this suffice to bring down the incumbent government. And the crucial property of a minority government is precisely that the composition of parliament appears sufficient to bring down the government at any time". The formation of government coalitions rarely stops at the knife-edge, however, it does happen from time to time. In our dataset of post-communist cases, we find one instance of such a government, the Topolanek cabinet formed after the 2006 Czech parliamentary elections. Even in the established parliamentary democracies of Western Europe we can only find a handful of such instances in post-war Western Europe (in Italy, Ireland, Iceland, and Sweden).

A second operational question that needs to be discussed pertains to the exact nature of coalition partners' commitment to the government. Sometimes, parties may consider it prudent to commit only their external support to a minority government without formally accepting ministerial portfolios. The case of the Opposition Pact between the Czech Social Democratic Party and the ODS is perhaps the best known example of this in our sample (see Nikolenyi 2003); following the 1998 parliamentary election, the two parties entered into a formal contract which allowed the formation of a single-party CSSD minority government in exchange for ceding key legislative offices, such as the Speakership of the lower house and the chairmanship of important committees, to the largest opposition party, the ODS. Other instances where a party was formally committed to a governing coalition but to not to the government per se, which thus remained in a formal minority, include the Kristopans government of Latvia of 1998 (Davies and Ozolins 2001) and the Nastase government of Romania in 2000 (Popescu 2003). I agree with Strom that a party's commitment to a government is credible only if it is followed up by delegating at least one minister to the government; therefore, agreements of external support, including instances of coalitional membership that are not backed up by portfolio allocation, are not considered in our view as instances of partnership and membership in government. Therefore, I count each of the three instances above as cases of minority governments even though they were based on a negotiated majority coalition in the legislature.

The third issue relates to the presence of a majority party in the legislature, which effectively precludes the possibility that a minority government might form. In the language of cooperative game theory, majority parliaments constitute non-essential games, where the election has already produced a winner. Therefore, although we may witness the formation of oversized surplus majority coalitions

TABLE 5.1 *Minority governments in post-communist East Central Europe, 1990–2010*

State	Number of elections	Number of minority parliaments (%)	Number of post-election minority governments (% of minority parliaments)
1. Most favorable institutional conditions for power concentration			
Estonia	5	5 (100)	0
Hungary	6	4 (66.7)	0
Bulgaria	6	4 (66.7)	2
Slovenia	5	5 (100)	0
Group average	***5.5***	***4.5 (81.8)***	***0.5 (11.1)***
2. Mixed institutional conditions for power concentration			
Latvia	6	6 (100)	2
Slovakia	5	5 (100)	0
Group average	***5.5***	***5.5 (100)***	***1 (18.2)***
3. Least favorable conditions for power concentration			
Lithuania	5	4 (80)	1
Poland	6	6 (100)	2
Romania	5	5 (100)	3
Czech Republic	5	5 (100)	3
Group average	***5.25***	***5 (95.2)***	***2.25 (45)***
Total	**54**	**49 (90.7)**	**13 (24.1)**

Note: The numbers in brackets indicate average values in %.

even if a single party has won a legislative majority, such coalitions do not serve the immediate purpose of winning the government formation game per se. Of the fifty-four elections that were held in the ten post-communist democracies between 1990 and 2010 only five resulted in a majority winner: Hungary 1994 and 2010, Lithuania 1992, Bulgaria 1994 and 1997. In all but one instance, the exception being Hungary 1994, the majority party formed a government by itself.

Using these operational definitions, Table 5.1 shows the distribution of minority governments across the ten new democracies.

As mentioned above, the overwhelming majority (90.7 percent) of post-communist elections did not produce majority winners. This is hardly surprising given that none of these new democracies adopted plurality or majority electoral systems that are normally associated with the election of majority parliaments (Rae 1967; Lijphart 1994). As we saw in Chapter Two, with the exception of Hungary and Lithuania, which adopted mixed-member electoral systems, all other post-communist democracies use different forms of proportional representation. Since mixed-member systems incorporate a plurality/majority tier, it is hardly surprising that we actually find more than half of the majority election outcomes (three out of five) in these two states; also two of the remaining instances of majority election results are found in Bulgaria, which, interestingly, is also the state with the lowest magnitude PR system. It is well known from the literature on the political consequences of electoral laws that district magnitude has a positive effect on the degree of parliamentary fractionalization, which, however, has a negative effect on the likelihood of the formation of majority governments, *ceteris paribus* (Rae 1967; Lijphart 1994). Therefore, the election of so many majority parliaments in Bulgaria may not be so surprising.

Almost exactly one-fourth (thirteen out of forty-nine) of the elections that produced a minority parliament were followed by the formation of a minority government. While most majority governments are formed by multiparty coalitions, almost half of the minority governments (five out of thirteen) are formed by single parties, in each case by the party that won the most seats in parliament after the election. The five single-party minority governments are as follows: Bulgaria 1991, Czech Republic 1998, Poland 2005, and Romania 1992 and 2000.

In Western Europe, we find that minority governments are geographically concentrated in Scandinavia. Strom reports that sixty-one out of the 125 postwar minority cabinets were formed in the five Nordic democracies: Denmark, Finland, Iceland, Norway, and Sweden (1990: 58). In the new East Central European democracies, we do not find such a clear regional pattern. The three Baltic states (Estonia, Latvia, and Lithuania) account for three, while the five Central European states (Czech Republic, Hungary, Poland, Slovakia, and Slovenia) and the two Balkan democracies (Bulgaria and Romania) have had five post-election minority governments respectively. As individual countries, the Czech Republic and Romania stand out from the group by virtue of having no fewer of their elections followed by the formation of a minority cabinet than by a majority government.

Table 5.1 clearly suggests that the institutional concentration/dispersion of political power is related to the frequency of minority governments to form after the general elections: as we move from the first down to the third group of states the rate of post-election minority governments, i.e. the number of post-election minority governments divided by the number of all minority parliaments in the group, increases sharply from 11.1 percent in the first group (two out of eighteen), to 18.2 percent in the intermediate (two out of eleven), and reaches 45 percent in the third group (nine out of twenty). In other words, as the institutional dispersion of power increases so does the incidence of minority cabinets. Within the first and the last groups, however, there are anomalies to draw attention to. In the first group Bulgaria alone accounts for all post-election minority governments. Moreover, the number of these cabinets in Bulgaria is exactly the same as in those in Latvia, which belong to the next group. In the last group, Lithuania and Poland seem to deviate as they have similar numbers of post-election minority governments as states in the first two groups with high and intermediate degrees of power dispersion.

5.4 AN INSTITUTIONALIST ACCOUNT OF POST-COMMUNIST MINORITY GOVERNMENTS

I propose six specific hypotheses in order to evaluate the effects of institutional design on minority government formation.

Hypothesis 1a: *District magnitude is positively related to the likelihood of minority government formation.* As discussed above, party system fragmentation has been one of the reasons that conventional wisdom held responsible for minority governments. Since average district magnitude is well known to shape the number of parties in a negative way, i.e. the smaller the district magnitude the fewer the parties, it is reasonable to expect that district magnitude would have an indirect positive impact on the probability that a minority government is formed after an election. I will also assess the direct impact of the number of parties, measured by the Laakso-Taagepera index of the effective number of parliamentary parties, on minority governments.

Hypothesis 2: *Large assemblies promote the formation of minority governments.* As discussed earlier, assembly size inversely affects the concentration of political power. Since power gets more diffused as the number of seats increase, parties may be less likely to be motivated to invest in entering the executive. In addition, as the number of seats increases the sheer operational cost of coordinating more politicians around government formation increases. Simply put, it is easier to get fewer deputies together and form a majority coalition in smaller parliaments and ensure executive control over the legislature (Lijphart 1999).

Hypothesis 3: *Bicameralism promotes the formation of minority governments.* In contrast with other scholars (Lijphart 1984; Diermeier, Eraslan and Merlo 2007), I expect that bicameralism promotes the formation of minority governments either by virtue of limiting the policy authority of the first chamber, which reduces the benefit of government participation for prospective and potential coalition partners, or by encouraging the party that leads the government to keep power-sharing to the minimum if it has acquired a numerically strong position in the second chamber. (For the purposes of this analysis, I consider Slovenia *de facto* unicameral because the unelected nature of the National Council does not reduce the policy authority of the first chamber in any appreciable way.)

Hypothesis 4: *Constitutional provisions that provide a positive role for the legislature in the government formation process promote the formation of majority coalition governments while negative formation rules promote the formation of minority governments* (Bergman 1993). Under positive parliamentary formation rule, the party that is appointed to lead the government formation process needs to build a majority coalition before it can be invested in office. Under negative parliamentary rules, a government can be invested so long as there is no hostile majority coalition that can prevent it from passing a vote of confidence.

Hypothesis 5: *Strong presidencies promote the likelihood of minority government formation.* It is well known that minority governments abound in presidential systems of government (Cheibub 2007). Although none of the post-communist democracies have a presidential constitution, strong chief executives can promote the formation of minority cabinets for similar reasons as they do in presidential systems of government: since control over executive authority becomes increasingly more shared and contested between the legislature and the presidency as the latter becomes more powerful, political parties will have weaker incentives to focus their power-seeking efforts on establishing political control over the legislature.

Hypothesis 6: *The likelihood of minority government decreases after the first-post communist election.* As mentioned at the outset of the chapter, an important characteristic of post-communist minority governments is their temporal concentration in the first post-transition legislatures. It is not unimaginable that due to the novelty of representative and competitive democracy, parties may take longer to learn the art of building majority solutions in a recurring fashion. This view is supported by the descriptive fact that while half (five out of ten) of the first post-transition elections in the respective states (Bulgaria 1991, Czech Republic 1996, Latvia 1993, Poland 1991, and Romania 1992) produced a minority government, only eight out of the forty-four subsequent elections did so.

I evaluate these hypotheses first by running a number of bivariate logistical regressions; the results are reported in Table 5.2. Most of the variables are defined dichotomously as dummies. For the variable "First parliaments" I code 1 for every observation of a government that is formed after the country's first post-communist election and 0 for every other later election. The next three variables, i.e. *Large assembly*, *Bicameralism*, and *Positive investiture* are defined exactly the same way as they were in the previous chapter. The variable *Strong president* is the inverse of the *Weak president* variable from Chapter Three: for each election held in a state where the presidency is powerful I assign a value of 1 otherwise a value of 0. *Assembly size* is defined as the actual number of seats in the first parliamentary chamber at the time of the election. *Number of parties* is defined as by the effective number of parliamentary parties index proposed by Laakso and Taagepera (1979).

The bivariate equations show that the impact of most of the institutional variables on post-election minority government formation is in the expected direction. Thus, holding all else equal, minority governments are more likely to be formed after the first post-communist election; in states with a large a parliamentary assembly; in states with a bicameral legislature; and when the constitutional design established a relative more powerful presidency. At the same time, minority governments are less likely when government formation rules call for a positive parliamentary investiture. The only variables that have a statistically significant effect are *Large assembly*,

TABLE 5.2 *Bivariate logistical regressions of the likelihood of minority governments*

Independent variable	
First legislature	1.6094* (0.7781)
Small district	0.1005 (0.6674)
District magnitude	−0.0126 (0.0124)
Number of parties	0.0748 (0.2079)
Large assembly	1.6560* (0.7418)
Assembly size	0.0029 (0.0024)
Bicameralism	1.7228* (0.6969)
Positive investiture	−0.2978 (0.6530)
Strong president	0.9445 (0.6765)
N	49

Note: * $p<0.05$. The numbers in brackets indicate standard errors.

Bicameralism and *First legislature*; these three variables also have the highest odd ratios of minority government formation.

The important exception is district magnitude. When measured by the actual average district magnitude, this variable turns out to have an unexpected negative effect on minority government formation. When measured by a dummy, with districts of fewer than ten average seats coded as 1 and all else coded as 0, the effect of the variable remains in the unexpected direction and retains a modest magnitude. The *Number of parties* variable has the expected positive but very modest effect on the probability that a minority cabinet is formed after the election.

Table 5.3 reports the results of multivariate logistical regressions, which lead to a number of important observations. First, the *Bicameralism* variable behaves inconsistently: it has a negative effect on minority government formation in Models Two and Three but a positive one in the other three Models; however, the effect is very small is Model One. It is important to note that all three models where *Bicameralism* behaves in this unexpected fashion also includes the *Large assembly* variable. This is a very important point because there is a high overlap of states that have both of these institutions present, i.e. three of the five states with large first chambers (Czech Republic, Poland, and Romania) are also bicameral. Therefore, to ensure that they do not cancel each other out, I do not include them together in Model 4. Indeed, the effect of *Bicameralism* becomes significant and positive in that Model.

A second important observation is that four variables (*First legislature*, *Large assembly*, *Positive investiture*, *Strong president*) have a consistent predictable effect on the probability of minority government formation: large assemblies with at least 200 seats in the first chamber make it more likely that the post-election government will be of a minority size, as do relatively more powerful presidencies and the first post-transition elections. Positive government formation rules, on the other hand, have a consistent negative impact on minority

TABLE 5.3 *Multivariate logistical regression models of the likelihood of minority government formation after the election*

Independent variables	Model 1	Model 2	Model 3	Model 4	Model 5
First legislature	2.4778** (1.0825)	2.3476** (1.1214)	2.4492** (1.0768)	2.2569** (1.0083)	2.4410** (1.0761)
Small districts	1.1255 (1.3225)	—	—	—	—
Number of parties	—	0.2209 (0.3884)	—	—	—
Large assembly	2.6415 (2.0521)	3.5329 (2.0943)	3.1325 (2.0120)	—	2.7620** (1.1320)
Bicameralism	0.1790 (1.6576)	−0.4309 (1.5399)	−0.3598 (1.5614)	1.9127** (0.9008)	—
Positive investiture	−3.1613 (1.6464)	−2.4879 (1.4120)	−2.5516 (1.4391)	−1.1097 (0.8826)	−2.3673** (1.1591)
Strong president	1.7106 (1.2304)	1.5039 (1.2442)	1.6580 (1.2324)	0.6714 (0.9735)	1.4758 (0.9363)
N	49	49	49	49	49
Model chi square	17.1137*	16.7353**	16.3648*	13.1608**	16.3114*
Intercept	−2.5604	−3.6567	−2.5237	−1.9507	−2.4688
Correct predictions	40 (81.6%)	39 (79.6%)	39 (79.6%)	41 (83.7%)	39 (79.6%)

Note * p<0.01; ** p<0.05. The numbers in brackets indicate standard errors.

governments. In sum, institutions clearly have a very strong effect on the likelihood that the first government that parties form after a general election will be of a majority or a minority size. More specifically, since bicameralism, large assemblies, a stronger presidency, and negative government formation rules are institutions that are designed to disperse political power, it can be concluded that institutional design that reduces the concentration of political power in a parliamentary system will also promote the formation of minority governments. What happens to these cabinets thereafter, how durable they are likely to be is a matter that will be examined in the next chapter.

5.5 CONCLUSION

This chapter has made two important contributions to the study of how institutional design shapes party government in ECE. First, it has shown that political institutions notwithstanding, political parties were more likely to form minority governments early on after the transition to democracy. Overtime, in most states, majority coalition combinations, of both the minimum winning and the oversize majority type, have become the norm. In a small number of states, however, this has not been the case. The second important contribution of this chapter has been to show that the institutional design of power dispersion matters as far as the formation of post-election minority governments are concerned. Of the institutions reviewed, bicameralism has a particularly interesting effect. It is important to reiterate that although bicameralism comes in different varieties (Lijphart 1999), there are good reasons why political parties may not want to form majority coalitions, where they otherwise could, when the government formation game takes place in a bicameral setting: the second chamber, depending on its partisan constitution, may provide either those parties that are forming the government and/or those that are in opposition with resources that will reduce their incentive either to expand the coalition or join it in the first place. Either way, the overall legislative authority and political power of the first chamber is weaker in bicameral legislatures relative to unicameral ones, and, therefore, it is not surprising to see that political parties will be much more likely to form minority cabinets there.

What is very surprising, however, is that bicameralism seems to work very differently in Western Europe where such legislatures tend to lead to larger governing coalitions rather than smaller ones. An examination of why this is the case does not fall within the scope of this book. It is quite plausible, however, that bicameralism may have become an instrument of power sharing and consensus (Lijphart 1999) in the established democracies precisely because their party systems are established and stable. In the new democracies, however, parties are less stable, their electoral followings are more volatile, and they may be less predisposed to power sharing in general, which in turn may be reflected in the preponderance of minority governments under bicameralism. In any event, it remains an important finding that bicameralism in ECE does not seem to be the same instrument of power-sharing as it is in Western Europe but that it actually encourages a more narrowly based coalition of parties to capture and hold onto executive office.

6

The Institutional Sources of Cabinet Duration

6.1 INTRODUCTION

The ten post-communist democracies vary considerably in terms of the stability and duration of their governments. In some states, such as Hungary, the government that is formed and invested in office after the election tends to last for the entire or nearly the entire term of the legislature. Elsewhere, such as Latvia, post-election governments never last for a long time. In this chapter, I examine how the set of political institutions that disperse or concentrate political power in the electoral, legislative and executive arenas of party competition affect government duration. The central finding of this chapter is the several institutions that disperse political power also reduce cabinet duration: specifically, bicameralism, a more powerful presidency, and negative government formation rules. In addition, government stability inversely varies with the fragmentation of the legislative party system, and both majority and post-election governments are more stable than minority and later mid-term cabinets.

The organization of this chapter follows the same order as the previous ones. The first section reviews the key arguments in the comparative politics literature about the effects of political institutions on government stability. The second section reviews the data on cabinet stability by using a number of alternative measures of the dependent variable. The third section evaluates a number of hypotheses on government stability.

6.2 EXPLANATIONS OF GOVERNMENT STABILITY AND INSTABILITY

Arguments about the institutional causes of government stability have proceeded at three hierarchically ordered levels of analysis moving from the most immediate cabinet-level characteristics to more remote regime-specific attributes. At the first level we find arguments that attribute government stability to particular characteristics of the cabinet in power, specifically its size, composition, coalitional status, as well as the time of its formation in the context of lifespan of the legislature. In a classic statement that originated the myth about the inefficiencies of multipartism, Lowell argued that only the single-party majority governments that are formed in a two-party system can remain stable, while the coalition and minority governments that characterize multiparty systems are doomed to instability, because by their very nature, minority cabinets and coalition cabinets are transient (Lowell 1896). Several decades later Blondel (1968) echoed the same conclusion adding the nuance that single-party majority governments will be stable even if they are formed in two-and-a half or multi-party systems. At the same time, Blondel notes, that "[c]oalition, whether small or large, appears directly antagonistic to stable government..." (Blondel 1968: 199).

Dodd (1976, 1974) and Laver (1974) point out that the distinction between single-party and coalition cabinets provides a less powerful explanation of cabinet stability than the distinction among the types of coalition cabinets that are formed. Dodd specifically proposes that cabinet durability is the function of the minimal winning status of the governing coalition: whereas minimal winning coalition cabinets are stable, minority coalitions and surplus majority coalitions are not. Dodd attributes the inherent stability of minimum winning coalitions to the combination of two characteristics of the bargaining environment that produces governments of this of this type: strong willingness by political parties to bargain and the availability of certain and reliable information about parties' relative policy positions. Thus, oversized coalition cabinets are unstable because their formation reflects a party system in which parties' willingness to bargain is coupled with low information certainty. Finally, undersized cabinets are unstable because the party system in which they are formed is characterized by low information certainty and low willingness to bargain (Dodd 1974, 1976). A different explanation links the stability of minimum winning coaliton cabinets to the mutually credible exit threats that every member of such a coalition possesses: if the coalition is minimally winning then every member thereof can threaten to leave and cause the termination of the coaliton (Grofman and Roozendaal 1997: 431).

The empirical record seems to support these arguments. For example, using five different measures of government stability, Lijphart (1984) finds support for both sets of explanations in the context of West European governments: (i) single-party govenrments are more stable than coaliton governments and that (ii) minimum winning coalitions significantly outlast both minority and oversized cabinets (Lijphart 1984: 275, 276). The relatively shorter duration of minority governments is also confirmed by Strom (1985) although he notes that this does not mean that minority governments are transient and irrational cabinet solutions. The studies in Budge and Keman (1990) show that single-party governments are the most stable type of all in Western Europe. However, these studies also show that in some countries minimum winning coalitions may not be more stable than either minority or surplus majority governments. The significance of distinguishing between within-country and cross-country effects of cabinet stability is stressed most forcefully by Grofman (1989) who claims that the relationship between minimal winning status and cabinet durability is the "artifact of the high average duration of cabinets in countries where there are only two or three significant political parties (where minimal winning coalitions are the norm) and the low average duration of cabinets in countries with a very large number of parties (where minimal winning coalitions are rare)" (Grofman and Roozendaal 1997: 431). Grofman further proposes that it is not the type of cabinet that determines cabinet durability but rather the format of the party system, namely, its fragmentation and polarization, that determine both. Therefore, the relationship between cabinet type and cabinet durability, according to Grofman, is at best spurious.

In addition to the size and coalitional type of the government, three other cabinet-level institutional variables have been linked to cabinet stability. The first is the fragmentation of the cabinet, which originally Taylor and Herman (1971), and Sanders and Herman (1977) showed to have a negative effect on cabinet durability. Subsequent studies have provided strong empirical support for these initial findings. The second cabinet level explanation of stability has to do with the time and the number of attempts it takes to form a government. While the relevance of this variable is generally recognized, the nature of its relationship with cabinet stability is not clearly understood either theoretically or empirically. For instance, Strom (1985) reports that a long drawn out formation process leads to a stable government because the coalition partners can afford to work out the terms of their cooperation in more detail. On the other hand, Laver and Schofield (1990) claim that a long formation period is indicative of a tense and polarized bargaining environment that, in general is less conducive for cabinet stability. Finally, a third cabinet-specific variable related to the stabilty of the government is whether the cabinet is the first post-election govenrment or not. Grofman and Roozendaal (1997) note that post-election govenrments tend to be more stable than those that are formed later in the term and that caretaker governments are particularly short-lived.

Moving away from the level of the individual cabinets, the next institutional source of cabinet stability is the format of the parliamentary party system, i.e. the balance of powers among political parties in the legislature. It has been well established in the literature that there is a negative relationship between the fragmentation of the party system and cabinet stability (Lijphart 1984; King et al 1990; Grofman and Roozendaal 1997). However, as mentioned above, Grofman notes that the effects of the party system on cabinet stability may well be indirect and mediated through the format and the type of the cabinet formed. Moreover, Laver and Schofield (1990: 149) point out that while it is true that "countries with bigger party systems have less stable cabinets . . . variation in cabinet stability within individual countries reveals little or no relationship between party system size and cabinet stability."

Institutions at the third level are the least likely to change over time and will, therefore, have the potential to have the most lasting effect, while both the legislative party system and the characteristics of the cabinet in office may vary in the light of the result of every new parliamentary election. At this level we find institutions that regulate the length of the term of the legislatures; the rule of the government formation and termination processes; as well as the nature of legislative organization (Strom, Budge and Laver 1994). In countries where the incumbent government can dissolve the legislature and call fresh elections fairly easily, cabinets will be less durable than in those states where early elections are difficult to call. Furthermore, constitutional provisions for a constructive vote of no-confidence in the government may make it more difficult for the opposition to defeat the incumbent on the floor of the legislature, which should, ceteris paribus, the level of cabinet stability. With regard to the rules of cabinet formation, Bergman (1993) finds that positive parliamentary rules of government formation, which are defined by a formal investiture vote, lead to fewer instances of minority government which, in turn, tend to be less stable than majority cabinets. This would then suggest that the investiture requirement would correlate with higher levels of cabinet stability. In a somewhat different sense, Grofman and Roozendaal (1997) point out that government formation processes that are particularly determinate will lead to more unstable cabinets than rules that create more uncertainty about the outcome of the government formation process. Specifically, government formation rules can reduce cabinet stability by allowing a party or parties "to expect to have no other chance to put together a cabinet" (440) which will in turn cause them to consider cabinet breakdown relatively less costly.

It is important to note that there are two streams of non-institutional explanations of cabinet stability in the literature (Grofman and Roozendaal, 1997). The first one is characterized by relating cabinet termination to critical events that take place outside the legislature and that may trigger a cabinet crisis by changing the preferences that actors have and the incentives that they face (Robertson 1983; Browne et al 1988, 1986; Frendreis 1986; Laver and Shepsle 1998). Such events can be both political or economic, such as riots, rising levels of inflation, unemployment etc. However, there is no theoretical reason to expect a priori an event to become eventually critical in the sense of causing the premature termination of a government. Moreover, as Laver and Schofield (1990: 162) have noted, although events are important in affecting the durability of cabinets their effect is mediated through structures which make a particular cabinet potentially more or less resistant to a shock or crisis.

A second stream of non-institutional explanations (Grofman and Roozendaal 1994; Narud 1995) attribute cabinet durability to "the calculations made by rational actors in considering what the alternatives are to the continuation of the status quo and who has an incentive to prefer which of those alternatives" (Grofman and Roozendaal 1997: 442). Based on the assumptions that parties care about controlling seats in the legislature; that parties value power within the governing coalition; and that parties can value some coalition partners more than others, Lupia and Strom (1995) develop a model that specifies the kinds of calculations that affect cabinet stability. They predict that a critical event will lead to the dissolution of the cabinet if and only if there is a legislative majority that prefers an election to leaving the governing coalition in power and all offering parties prefer an election to the best acceptable offer they can make to others to join the coalitions.

6.3 GOVERNMENT DURATION IN POST-COMMUNIST DEMOCRACIES

Before presenting the data on cabinet stability in the post-communist democracies, a couple of operational notes on the dependent variable are in order. The first pertains to the definition of what a cabinet is, i.e. when it starts and when it ends. Lijphart (1984: 265) notes that such a definition requires conceptual clarification about the event or events that mark(s) the end of one government and the beginning of a new one. He identifies seven such events in the literature: a new general election; any change in the partisan composition of the governing coalition; change in the parties that support the cabinet from the outside but do not formally participate in it; change in the coalitional status of the cabinet; change of prime minister for political reasons; change in prime minister for any reason; and the resignation of the cabinet. After an empirical test of the different measurements using data from twenty West European democracies, Lijphart states his preference to define cabinet duration in terms of changes in the partisan composition of the governing coalition (1984: 278). In fact, he notes that nearly every work he has surveyed uses this event, in combination with others, in defining a cabinet. Budge and Keman (1990, 1993) have added change in the prime minister, a general election, and formal resignation to mark the beginning and the end of a cabinet. This definition has actually become the conventional norm in studies on cabinet government (Woldendorp et al 1998, 2000) including the two extant surveys of post-communist cabinets (Blondel and Müller-Rommel eds. 2001; Müller-Rommel 2004).

The second operational question concerns the measurement of time for which the cabinet is in power. The key question here is not whether one uses months or days as the basic units of accounting for time, although the latter has become the norm. Instead, a much more important decision to make is whether to count the actual length of time a cabinet lasted or the length of time a cabinet lasted as the fraction of the maximum length of time that it could have lasted (Lijphart 1984: 270). For instance, imagine a post-election government that is invested in office immediately following a general election that lasted for exactly 365 days. Following the collapse of this government, a new cabinet is invested that lasted for the same length of time. In terms of the actual number of days both cabinets have lasted the same length of time. However, assuming a four-year legislative term, the duration of the first government was only one-quarter of the maximum time it could have lasted while the duration of the second government was exactly one third. As such as the second cabinet was *relatively* more stable even though in actual terms both cabinets lasted for the same length of time.

In the following overview of cabinet stability in the post-communist democracies, I adopt the conventional defintion of cabinets as discussed above. That is to say that I shall consider any of the following changes as a change in the standing cabinet:

1) change in the partisan composition;
2) change in prime minister;
3) resignation of the government when followed by the re-formation of the same cabinet;
4) a general election.

As for the unit of time, cabinet duration is measured by the actual number of days. When a cabinet ends because of a general election, I take a date of the election as the end of the cabinet's tenure in office. The start date of each cabinet is the day when it was offcially invested in office either by appointment of the head of state or by a parliamnetary vote of investiture.

Table 6.1 shows the average duration of all cabinets in each of the ten states. The Table also distinguishes two types of governments; those that are formed immediately after a general election and those that are formed later in the term. The last row of the Table shows that the overall duration of post-communist cabinets is very short: the average duration of the 106 cabinets is only 551 days with post-election cabinets lasting almost exactly twice as long as cabinets that are formed later in the term (790 versus 382 days). However, there is variation among the ten states. Specifically, it is worth noting that in three states (Czech Republic, Lithuania, and Romania), mid-term cabinets last a little longer on average than cabinets that are formed immediately after the general election. In the case of the Czech Republic the difference is small, however in the other two states the difference is 100 days or more.

Table 6.1 provides strong preliminary evidence in favor of the view that the institutional foundations of power dispersion matter for the relative duration of governments. As we move down from the first to the third group of states, i.e. as we move from lower to greater degrees of institutional power dispersion, average cabinet duration clearly drops. The last column of Table 6.1 shows that the average number of days a cabinet lasts in the first group is 701 followed by 509.08 in the second and 473.96 in the third group. We find the same order in the second

TABLE 6.1 *Cabinet duration in post-communist democracies, 1990–2010*

State	Post-election cabinets	Mid-term cabinets	All cabinets
1. Most favorable institutional conditions for power concentration			
Estonia	714.00	380.67	514.00
Hungary	980.40	530.25	780.33
Bulgaria	1114.20	284.33	803.00
Slovenia	820.25	666.75	743.50
Group average	***937.66 (432.62)***	***451.41 (331.79)***	***701 (454.34)***
2. Mixed institutional conditions for power concentration			
Latvia	466.20	288.00	337.50
Slovakia	1321.25	147.50	930.00
Group average	***787.66 (532.13)***	***304.4 (195.75)***	***509.08 (423)***
3. Least favorable conditions for power concentration			
Lithuania	455.50	540.29	509.45
Poland	552.80	313.78	399.14
Romania	361.00	469.60	438.57
Czech Republic	604.25	631.75	618.00
Group average	***635.82 (406.49)***	***382.23 (296.27)***	***473.96 (357.74)***
N	44	62	106
Total	**790.36**	**382.10**	**551.56 (416.22)**

Note: The numbers in brackets indicate standard deviation values.

column, which indicates the average number of days that post-election governments lasted. However, with respect to mid-term governments, this pattern is no longer as clear: while the most stable mid-term cabinets are still found in the first group, the average duration of mid-term cabinets is longer in the third than in the second group. The contrast between the first and third groups is particularly obvious and striking. In terms of post-election cabinets, each and every state in the first group has a higher value of duration than any state in the third group. Almost the same holds true with regard to the overall level of cabinet duration with the exception of the deviant cases of Estonia and the Czech Republic.

Minority governments in general are more durable than minimum winning coalitions as they last for an average of 537 days as opposed to the latter's 423 days. However, the most stable governments are those that are formed by a single majority party (820 days) followed by oversized coalitions (652 days). Controlling for the post-election status of the cabinet changes these relations somewhat. Single-party majority cabinets are still the most durable, whether they are formed immediately after an election or later in the term, but minority governments are the least stable type of cabinet in both groups. Of the two types of majority coalition cabinets, minimum winning coalitions are relatively more durable than oversized coalitions only when they are formed immediately after a general election.

These patterns vary across the ten states considerably partly because the four cabinet types are not present in each and every state. In fact, minority governments are the only type of government that can be found in all ten states, followed by minimum winning coalitions which can be found at least once in all but one state (the exception being Romania), and oversized coalitions which were formed at least once in seven states (the exceptions are the Czech Republic, Estonia, and Poland). There are only two states (Bulgaria and Lithuania) where political parties have formed each of the four cabinet types at least once. In both of these states minimum winning coalitions are actually the most durable while minority cabinets are the least durable types of government. Thus, even though single-party majority governments appear to be the most stable type of government when we consider all 106 cabinets in all ten states pooled together, in the two states where they were actually formed they are not the most stable type. Furthermore, Bulgaria and Lithuania also differ with regard to the relative stability of their oversized coalitions and single-party majority cabinets.

Although minority governments are generally unstable, they are actually the most durable type of cabinet in two of the ten states (the Czech Republic and Romania) while everywhere else minority governments are the least durable cabinet type. There are similar variations with regard to the relative stability of minimum winning and oversized coalitions. Minimum winning coalitions are the most stable type of government in five states: Bulgaria, Estonia, Lithuania, Poland, and Slovenia, although the actual duration of these governments varies tremendously across the states. In the remaining three states (Hungary, Latvia, and Slovakia), oversized coalitions are the most stable.

6.4 AN INSTITUTIONALIST ACCOUNT OF GOVERNMENT DURATION

In this section I evaluate the effects that the four main institutions of power concentration/dispersion have on cabinet duration in the ten post-communist democracies. Specially, I will examine the following hypotheses:

Hypothesis 1a. *District magnitude will have a negative effect on government duration: the lower the magnitude the longer lasting the cabinets will be.* Democracies with more restrictive electoral systems will have fewer parties in their legislatures and, therefore, in their executive cabinets as well. With fewer parties, holding the level of their ideological dispersion constant, there will be fewer fault lines along which the government can be internally de-stabilized.

Hypothesis 1b. *Party system fragmentation will inversely affect cabinet duration.* The electoral system affects cabinet duration indirectly, i.e. via the political parties that make up the legislature and the executive. Electoral systems with lower district magnitude should have fewer parties, which in turn should result in more durable cabinets. Conversely, electoral systems with larger magnitudes should lead to party proliferation and less stable cabinets. This hypothesis taps into the more direct connection between cabinet duration and a consequence of the electoral system, i.e. the number of parties.

Hypothesis 2: *Assembly size will inversely affect cabinet duration.* For similar reasons as the electoral system, assembly size is expected to exert its impact on cabinet duration through the party system. Since larger assemblies are more likely to lead to greater degrees of party system fragmentation in the legislature than smaller assemblies do, I expect that larger assemblies will also reduce cabinet duration relative to smaller parliaments.

Hypothesis 3: *Bicameralism will inversely affect cabinet duration.* Bicameralism increases the number of veto points and veto players relative to unicameral legislatures, which, in turn, increase the coordination costs of keeping the government in office and in control of the policy and legislative agenda. It creates an additional institutional setting where the unity of the incumbent majority has to be tested and maintained. Relative to unicameral settings, this puts more stress and strain on the government and thus increases the likelihood of its premature termination.

Hypothesis 4a: *Positive government formation rules will lead to more durable cabinets.* Since positive investiture rules require the careful negotiation of a legislative majority that will support the government, it is more likely that the kinds of accommodations and concessions that might otherwise jeopardize the coalition mid-term would be addressed and taken care of before the government actually starts its term. In contrast, negative formation rules do not require such coordination and allow a government to enter office after simply having mustered an ad hoc support of partners on a single confidence vote.

Hypothesis 4b: *Constructive no-confidence provisions should lead to more durable cabinets.* This constitutional provision is normally entrenched with the precise intention of increasing cabinet duration by making it much more difficult to dismiss a government than what would be normally the case under ordinary no-confidence rules.

Hypothesis 4c: *Majority governments will be more durable than minority cabinets.* This hypothesis tests the relationship between cabinet status and duration directly. Majority cabinets are by definition winning coalitions, where every member receives positive power pay-offs as a reward for joining. In contrast, minority cabinets are not winning coalitions, although they may well be viable (Strom, Budge and Laver 1994), which in turn limits the degree and amount of power they can distribute to their members. All else equal, minority governments should lead power-seeking parties to search for alternative cabinet solutions more frequently relative to majority coalitions, resulting in higher levels of duration for the latter.

Hypothesis 5: *Strong presidencies reduce cabinet duration.* It is well known from the literature on the politics of presidential and semi-presidential systems that divided authority over the cabinet between the legislature and a directly elected president reduces cabinet duration (Shugart and Carey 1992). Maeda and Nishikawa (2006) report that governing parties in presidential systems face increasing hazard rates of the termination while those in parliamentary systems face declining hazard rates. According to them, this difference is attributed to the different types of goals that the two constitutional arrangements encourage political parties to seek: parties in presidential systems are primarily vote-seekers, which encourages oppositions parties to coordinate and stage a powerful challenge to the ruling party in the next election, while parties in parliamentary systems can balance the vote seeking imperative with the other two main goals of party behavior, i.e office- and policy-seeking. Although Maeda and Nishikawa do not speak to semi-presidential systems as such, the logic of their argument clearly implies that semi-presidential systems should also lead to less durable cabinets than parliamentary systems. In the context of post-communist states, Harfst (2000: 34) finds that parliamentary systems with an indirectly elected president have the longest lasting cabinets on average, followed by those with a directly elected president, premier-presidential and president-parliamentary systems.[1]

Presidential powers may also have an indirect effect on reducing cabinet stability through their negative impacts on the institutionalization (Mainwarring 1993), the strength (Shugart 1998), and the number of political parties (Mainwaring 1993; Clark and Wittrock 2005), all of which can, in turn, reduce the duration of cabinets. The impact of presidential powers on the number of parties is of particular significance: strong presidencies may encourage the fragmentation of the legislative party system by discouraging the formation of large parliamentary blocs, and the coalescence of actors behind large parties, given that both the policy-authority and the overall political power of the legislature are comparatively weak (Clark and Wittrock 2005: 175–6). Indeed, Maeda and Nishikawa also report that parliamentary systems tend to have less fragmented party systems than presidential ones (2006: 364).

Table 6.2 reports the results of a series bivariate OLS regression results. The dependent variable is the actual number of days a cabinet lasted in office. Most of the independent variables were defined in previous chapters except for the effective number of parties, which is measured by the Laakso-Taagepera (1979) index. The variable *Low Magnitude* is a dummy with a value of 1 for every election in which the average district magnitude is less than ten. Otherwise the value is 0. The results support most of the hypotheses, the exception being *Assembly size*. Cabinet duration is a negative function of the number of parties, which is an important outcome of the electoral system, when regressed on the *Effective number of parties*. Both bicameralism and a strong presidency, institutions that disperse

TABLE 6.2 *Bivariate OLS regression results of institutional effects on cabinet duration in post-communist democracies*

Variables	Coefficient	r^2
Low magnitude	142.792 (81.073)	0.019
Effective number of parties	−59.313 (24.065)**	0.0465
Large assembly	36.324 (81.908)	−0.008
Assembly size	−0.0954 (0.301)	−0.008
Bicameralism	−136.541 (85.304)	0.0145
Positive investiture	61.796 (83.136)	−0.004
Constructive no-confidence	65.042 (89.364)	−0.004
Strong president	−172.498 (83.115)**	0.031
Majority government	332.817 (75.831)*	0.149
Post-election government	416.926 (72.533)*	0.235
N	106	

Note: * $p<0.01$; ** $p<0.05$. The numbers in brackets indicate standard error.

political power, reduce cabinet duration relative to unicameralism and democracies with a weak presidency. Positive government formation and termination rules increase cabinet duration as does the cabinet's majority status. A dichotomous definition of assembly size (*Large assembly*) suggests that first chambers with fewer than 200 seats see more durable cabinets than those with fewer seats. However, measured by the actual number of seats in the first chamber results in a negative effect on the dependent variable. Finally, I also checked for the effect of post-election status on cabinet duration and found a strong statistically significant positive effect. In fact, of these bivariate relationships it is the last one that explains the highest percentage of variation in cabinet duration.

An important finding that emerges from Table 6.2 is that similarly to Western Europe the number of parties has a negative impact on cabinet duration in the post-communist democracies. In a survey of seventeen post-communist states that joined the Council of Europe, Harfst (2000) also finds that the fragmentation of the party system provides a more robust predictor of government duration than either the level of democracy or the type of executive–legislative relations enshrined in the constitution. Of the seventeen states he finds seven deviant cases where the number of parties does not correlate with cabinet duration in the expected direction. Three of these states, Bulgaria, Lithuania, and Romania, are also included in our sample; in each of these cases Harfst reports that cabinets are less stable than expected given the relatively low level of fragmentation in their party systems.[2] Similarly, Kluonis (2003: 107) also reports that the effective number of parties has a negative effect on cabinet duration ($r^2 = -0.44$) in the same ten states that I am examining; in fact, the correlation is very similar to what Taylor and Herman (1971) had reported for West European democracies almost three decades earlier. In two separate publications on post-communist cabinet stability, Nikolenyi (2004, 2005) shows that post-communist legislatures with a

TABLE 6.3 *Multivariate OLS regression results of institutional effects on cabinet duration in post-communist democracies*

Independent variables	Model 1	Model 2	Model 3	Model 4	Model 5
Low Magnitude	66.850 (76.018)	—	—	—	—
Effective number of parties	—	−43.875 (21.797)	−36.393 (23.281)	−46.27 (21.19)	−42.58 (20.06)
Large assembly	162.872 (116.722)	—	86.831 (128.965)	—	—
Assembly size	—	0.217 (0.4921)	—	—	—
Bicameralism	−105.333 (135.512)	−22.567 (112.861)	−68.266 (135.089)	—	—
Positive investiture	—	—	37.990 (81.102)	—	—
Constructive no-confidence	−14.003 (003)	10.858 (99.205)	—	—	—
Strong president	−74.862 (89.527)	−119.477 (93.827)	−93.549 (89.622)	−118.86 (72.85)	−85.45 (69.51)
Majority government	249.763 (72.886)*	231.954 (72.921)*	236.152 (72.036)*	—	246.95** (68.60)
Post-election government	336.169 (70.677)*	336.741 (70.262)*	334.329 (70.048)*	381.35** (71.71)	336.02** (68.97)
Intercept	231.658 (76.659)*	487.325 (156.015)*	444.936 (146.915)**	530.93** (117.92)	414.99** (116.06)
Adjusted R^2	0.326	0.332	0.3379	0.269	0.347
N	106	106	106	106	106

Note: * $p<0.01$; ** $p<0.05$. The numbers in brackets indicate standard error.

dominant player tend to have more stable cabinets, especially when the dominant player also occupies the center of the party space, than legislatures with no dominant player present. By definition, the latter are more fragmented that the former, which suggests that Nikolenyi's findings also support the conventional wisdom about the relationship between party system format, i.e. fragmentation, and government duration.

In Table 6.3 I estimate the effects of all hypothesized institutional variables on cabinet duration. Model 1 presents the most complete equation with seven dichotomously defined dummy variables. All but one variable points in the expected direction, however, only two of them have statistical significance: *Majority* and *Post-election* status. The puzzling exception is the *Constructive no-confidence* variable, which is curious, because, as I mentioned earlier, this is the only institution that is entrenched in the constitutions with the express purpose of promoting cabinet stability. Models Two through Five replace *Low magnitude* with the *Effective number of parties*; the variable retains its negative sign consistently although it is not significant in any of the models. There are four additional variables that have a consistent impact on cabinet duration in all models: *Bicameralism* and *Strong presidency* have a negative, while *Majority* and *Post-election* cabinet status have positive impacts.

6.5 CONCLUSION

Government duration is at the very heart of party government and coalition politics. To the extent that governments last and work, policies will be formulated and implemented which will not only contribute to the collective welfare of society but will also create the conditions for retrospective voting and allow political parties, both in government and in opposition, to develop their identity and electoral following along programmatic and policy lines. On the other hand, if governments do not last, if coalition infighting leads to frequent inter-election cabinet turnovers, then neither parties nor voters will be in a position to develop a programmatic orientation that can serve as the foundation for the development of a well structured and stable party system. Instead, voters will be fickle, elections will be volatile, and parties will have no incentive to remain unified and cohesive entities. In extreme circumstances, party/coalition government may undermine the viability of the new democracy if it adds too much stress to an already fragile and nascent framework of political competition. In short, government duration matters and its institutional underpinnings are particularly important to understand for those who seek to build and design well functioning newly democratizing polities.

This chapter has shown that institutional design has a strong impact on the duration of governments in the post-communist democracies. Specifically, the central findings of this chapter are as follows: (i) systems with a weak presidency have longer lasting cabinets than those with a strong presidency; (ii) bicameralism reduces cabinet duration relative to unicameralism; (iii) cabinets formed under positive investiture rules last longer than those that are formed under negative parliamentary rules; (iv) party system fragmentation has a negative effect on cabinet duration; (v) post-election cabinets last longer than those formed mid-term; and that (vi) majority governments are more durable than minority cabinets.

In sum, this chapter further confirms that the institutional design of power dispersion and power concentration matters for the unfolding pattern of coalition politics and party government in the post-communist democracies. As we saw earlier, political systems with institutions that concentrate political power tend to promote the formation of sizable electoral coalitions, followed by the formation of majority governments, which tend to last longer than minority cabinets, which are promoted by the institutional mix of power dispersion.

NOTES

1. It is worth noting that Harfst's sample includes non-democratic post-communist systems such as Moldova, in the premier-presidential category, Macedonia, in group of parliamentary systems with a directly elected head of state, and Albania, in the group of purely parliamentary systems. He finds a mean cabinet duration of 633 days in pure parliamentary systems, 590 days in those where the president is directly elected and 479 days in the group of premier-presidential systems. It is worth noting that the three president-parliamentary systems covered by his study (Croatia, Russia, and Ukraine) have the shortest mean cabinet duration at 408 days.
2. The other deviant cases are Albania, Croatia, Ukraine, and Georgia. In the latter, a high level of fragmentation coincides with relatively stable cabinets.

7

Dividing the Executive?

Party Coalitions and Indirect Presidential Elections

7.1 INTRODUCTION

Although there is no shortage of studies on post-communist presidencies and presidents (Lucky 1994; McGregor 1994; Baylis 1996; Hellmann 1996; Fry 1997; Beliaev 2006; Tavits 2009), a literature on the role that political parties play in the selection of the chief executive is noticeably absent. One reason for this lacuna is that most presidents in the East and Central European new democracies are elected directly by the voters, which means that presidential elections are normally examined as a matter of electoral studies. However, the head of state is selected indirectly by the legislature, or a special electoral college, in four states (Czech Republic, Estonia, Hungary, and Latvia). In these cases, political parties are the key players in deciding the outcome of the presidential selection game; in fact, the presidential contest becomes another round of renegotiating coalition agreements, under new rules, not only within the incumbent government but also with the opposition. Invariably, these rules are considerably different from those that govern the investiture of the cabinet and the prime minister and require that the winning candidate should secure a special majority. The objective of this chapter is to examine how the rules of indirect presidential selection in the four states shape the ability of the incumbent governing coalition to have its presidential candidate elected. In particular, based on the expectation that similarity in rules leads to similarities in outcomes, I will show that *the more congruent the presidential and prime ministerial selection processes are the greater the likelihood that the same coalition will capture both offices*. If and when the presidential selection requires a special majority that is very different from what the selection of the prime minister required, then the outcome of the two processes should reflect this difference.

A clear understanding of when and why incumbent governing coalitions succeed or fail to capture the presidency is not only a theoretically interesting issue but it also has clear political and practical relevance. Tavits (2009) has shown that divided government accounts in a large degree for presidential activism both in new and in established democracies with a non-hereditary head of state. However, her analysis does not extend to uncovering the reasons why co-habitation or a split executive might emerge in the first place. Furthermore, whereas Samuels and

Shugart (2010) have explicitly discussed the relationship between political parties and the head of state from the perspective of a principal-agent framework, they fail to address how principals arrive at selecting, or why they fail to do so, their specific agents. This chapter will fill both of these lacunae.

7.2 INDIRECT PRESIDENTIAL ELECTIONS IN HUNGARY

The Hungarian presidency represents an extreme case in terms of incumbent control over the office. Of the five presidential selections that took place to date (1990, 1995, 2000, 2005, and 2010) all but one of them were won by the candidate that was nominated and supported by the governing coalition. The 1990 selection was an uncontested process with a single presidential nominee, A. Goncz, whose candidacy was supported jointly by the government and the opposition. In three other instances (1995, 2000, and 2010) the government faced little difficulty to ensure the selection of its nominee to the highest public office of the post-communist state. The only exception to this occurred in 2005 when the candidate of the conservative opposition, L. Solyom, was able to defeat K. Szili, the candidate of the governing Socialist Party, thanks to the abstention of the party's junior coalition partner, SZDSZ.

The case of Hungary lends strong support for the hypothesis about the institutional effect of the presidential selection rules on the ability of the incumbent governing coalition to secure a favorable outcome. As mentioned in Chapter Two, the Hungarian constitution provides for a three-round selection process where the winning candidate is required to demonstrate a qualified majority support in the first two rounds. This supra-majoritarian requirement is much harder to meet than the simple majority that is required for the investiture of the head of government. As such, one might expect that a majority-based governing coalition, which was always in office at the time of the each of the five presidential elections, would have to negotiate and enter into a compromise with the opposition in order to elect its candidate, which was the case in 1990, unless its majority is large enough to meet the qualified majority requirement, which was the case on two occasions: in 1994 it was the left-liberal coalition of the Socialist and SZDSZ parties and in 2010 it was the conservative coalition of FIDESZ and the KNDP that succeeded in securing the election of their own nominees on the first round of balloting. However, as the events of the presidential election of 2000 showed a disciplined and strategic incumbent can win the game even if it fails to do so during the first two rounds. At the ultimate stage the constitution requires only a simple majority, which a unified majority coalition should have little difficulty in meeting. In other words, given its majority size the governing coalition can always block the game in the first two rounds and secure a victory in the last round as long as the coalition remains unified and disciplined, which with the passage of time may be harder to maintain.

Since the president is elected for a five-year term there are bound to be periods of divided government even though the incumbent coalition normally wins the presidential selection. Indeed, Hungarian governing coalitions had to co-habit with a president who was not their own candidate for nine out of the twenty years over the past five parliamentary terms. These years of co-habitation were (i) 1998–2000, when a center-right government elected in 1998 faced the Liberal president (Goncz) who had been invested in 1995; (ii) 2002–5, when the left-liberal coalition elected in 2002 had to work with President Madl who had been invested by the previous conservative government; and (iii) 2006–10, when the re-elected left-liberal coalition co-habited with President Solyom who had been elected by the conservative opposition in 2005. According to the design of the Hungarian constitution, a divided executive is effectively guaranteed as long as parliamentary elections produce majority coalitions which remain united for the purposes of the presidential election and as long as general elections result in regular alternation in government. If these three conditions are met then an incumbent party coalition will be able to prolong its executive presence by capturing the presidency whose term will last into the term of the next government. This is precisely what happened in 1998–2000 and 2002–5. In 2006–10, divided government was the unexpected result of an electoral outcome that returned the incumbent left-liberal coalition to office in 2006, which, however, had proved to be undisciplined and had failed to elect its presidential candidate in 2005. It is important to stress that divided government in Hungary, in contrast to Estonia and Latvia, has never been the result of shifting governing coalitions within the term of the same legislature.

Table 7.1 provides a comparative summary of the five presidential selections in post-communist Hungary between 1990 and 2010. The names in bold indicate the eventual winner and the columns show the number of rounds it took for the process to produce a winner. The presidential selection in 1990 was unique in

TABLE 7.1 *Presidential elections in Hungary, 1990–2010*

Selection year	Round 1	Round 2	Round 3
1990	**Goncz 295**		
1995	**Goncz 259**		
	Madl 76		
2000	Madl 251	Madl 238	**Madl 243**
2005	Szili 183	Szili 178	Szili 182
	Solyom 13	Solyom 185	**Solyom 185**
2010	**Schmitt 263**		
	Balogh 59		

Note: Entries in bold indicate the winning candidate. The numbers in brackets indicate standard error.
Source: http://www.parliament.hu

that it was governed by the terms of the two-party opposition agreement concluded after the first parliamentary elections between the MDF, the largest member of the new governing coalition, and the SZDSZ, the largest opposition party. According to the pact the two parties agreed to support the SZDSZ's candidate for president, A. Goncz, in exchange for the party's support for a constitutional amendment that would ensure that individual ministers could not be censured by parliament but only by the prime minister. Upon his nomination Goncz had to give up his party membership in the SZDSZ, however, he never really severed ties with his party and would continue to attend SZDSZ caucus meetings well into his term as head of state (Tavits 2009). Eventually, Goncz was nominated by 143 members of parliament, almost three times the minimum requirement, which clearly showed the strong support that his candidacy enjoyed. Indeed, he was the only candidate nominated for the office. On August 3, 1990, he received 295 of the 308 valid votes and was immediately declared the first president of the nascent Republic of Hungary.[1]

None of the next four presidential elections proved to be as consensual as the first one was. Although the size of the respective governing coalitions ensured a first round victory for Goncz in 1995 and for Schmitt in 2010, both of these candidacies were formally contested. Moreover, on the two occasions when the governing coalition did not have the two-thirds majority required for a first or second round victory, it took three successive rounds of balloting to produce a winner even though, at least, in 2000, the candidate of the governing coalition ran unopposed. Table 7.1 also shows that there has been a steady decline from 1990 to 2005 in the margin by which the eventual winner secured his victory pointing to the increasingly competitive nature of the selection process in the context of an increasingly more competitive party system.

7.3 INDIRECT PRESIDENTIAL ELECTIONS IN THE CZECH REPUBLIC

Table 7.2 shows the outcome of the three presidential votes that have taken place in the parliament of the sovereign Czech Republic. The first time that the elected parliament of the sovereign Czech Republic held a presidential vote was in January 1998. The incumbent was President V. Havel who had been elected to the office five years earlier by the national legislature of what was still at the time a federal Czechoslovak state. In stark contrast to his first election, Havel's candidacy was neither uncontested nor was it free from criticism leveled from all corners of the party system. The political context for the presidential vote was defined by the deep crisis that beset the Czech political system in late 1997 as a result of the corruption scandal that ultimately led to the resignation of Prime

TABLE 7.2 *Presidential elections in the Czech Republic, 1998–2008*

Election year and date	Candidates	Round 1		Round 2		Round 3
		Chamber	Senate	Chamber	Senate	Chamber and Senate
January 20, 1998	**V. Havel**	91	39	99	47	
	S. Fischer	26	5			
	M. Sladek	22	1			
January 15, 2003	V. Klaus	92	31	77	32	113
	P. Pithart	20	35	46	43	84
	J. Bures	39	7			
	M. Krizenecky	44	2			
January 24, 2003	V. Klaus	89	32	85	33	127
	J. Moserova	25	43	32	42	65
	M. Zeman	78	5			
February 28, 2003	**V. Klaus**	115	32	109	30	142
	J. Sokol	81	47	83	46	124
February 8, 9, 2008	V. Klaus	92	47	94	48	139
	J. Svejnar	106	32	104	31	113
February 15, 2008	**V. Klaus**	93	48	93	48	141
	J. Svejnar	104	32	94	32	111

Note: Entries in bold indicate the winning candidate.
Sources: Brokl and Mansfeldova 1999: 350; Linek and Mansfeldova 2004: 980.

Minister V. Klaus's conservative coalition minority government. President Havel did not remain neutral during the cabinet crisis; he made his dissatisfaction with the ethical and moral character of Prime Minister Klaus very clear in a number of public statements and once the government resigned, he took urgent measures in an attempt to install a new government to be headed by J. Lux, leader of the KDU, a junior partner in the outgoing coalition. In addition to the faction of the ODS that had remained loyal to Klaus, the president, was also unpopular with the communist left due to his uncompromising negative predisposition against the KSCM.

On December 10, Havel was the first presidential nominee to declare his candidacy once he had secured the formal support of the four parliamentary parties that he considered democratic: the ODS, the ODA, the KDU, and the CSSD (http://www.rferl.org/content/article/1141554.html). The president had stated earlier that he would accept to be a candidate only if he were to receive the support from all democratic forces in parliament, which he clearly did. The day before the vote the newly formed parliamentary group (Freedom Union) that consisted of the dissident faction opposed to Klaus' leadership in ODS also confirmed its support for Havel's re-election. Yet, his candidacy was not unopposed. On December 15, the KSCM submitted the name of S. Fischer, a scholar of astrophysics, as the party's candidate in the upcoming race (http://www.rferl.org/content/article/1141557.html) and on January 16, only four days before the first round of the vote, the extreme right Republican Party also nominated its own candidate, party president M. Sladek, for the post. Thus (http://www.rferl.org/content/article/1141575.html), on January 20 there were three candidates in the race representing the extreme Left (Fischer), the broadly defined Center spanning from the left-of-center to the right-of-center (Havel), and the extreme Right (Sladek). Based on the nominations, it was widely expected that Havel would easily secure a first-round victory; Radio Prague reported an estimated prediction of 122 votes for Havel in Chamber and forty-seven in Senate on the first ballot.

On the day of the vote, the results defied these expectations. Although Havel won by far the most votes in both chambers, he failed to meet the strict majority requirement in the two chambers and fell ten and two votes short of the absolute majority in the lower house and the Senate respectively. While not sufficient for an outright victory, these numbers allowed Havel to be the single candidate on the second round, in which he easily met the weaker majority requirement in the two legislative houses.

The second Czech presidential election was one of the most complicated and drawn out affairs of all presidential searches in the region which virtually paralyzed the entire Czech political system for almost two months (Linek and Mansfeldova 2004). As Table 7.2 shows it took nine separate votes in three rounds for the two houses of parliament to elect the next head of state. The only politician who participated in each vote was the ODS' candidate and party chairman V. Klaus, the eventual winner of the race. With each successive ballot the number of contestants dropped: at the first attempt each of the four parliamentary parties nominated a separate candidate; at the second attempt there were only three candidates; while on the third trial only the two largest parties, the ODS and the CSSD, nominated candidates. It was indicative of the extremely tightly balanced nature of the Czech parliamentary party system at the time that even on the last vote, which was the third round of the third attempt to elect a president, Klaus was able to surpass the required majority threshold by only two votes.

The next presidential election in the Czech Republic took place in February 2008 (Linek 2009). It is worth noting that this was also the last time that the Czech parliament selected the country's head of state because a constitutional amendment passed in 2012 introduced direct elections for the presidency by 2013, when the next president is scheduled to be elected. In contrast to 2003, it took only two rounds of balloting to find a winner in 2008, possibly because of the presence of only two competing candidates from the very beginning: V. Klaus of the governing ODS and J. Svejnar of the Green Party (SZ). In further contrast to the previous election, however, both of these candidates were nominated by political parties that otherwise governed together in a knife-edge minority coalition in the Chamber. Therefore, the pattern of divided government continued to prevail in the Czech party system as coalition partners once again proved their unwillingness and inability to come together and jointly secure the presidency. Although the winner of the elections was a candidate of one of the coalition partners (Klaus), the outcome and the process leading up to it contributed to deepening the divisions within the coalition rather than providing an opportunity to create consensus and unity.

There were two novel features that characterized the 2008 presidential vote. First, for the first time since the creation of the Republic the presidential candidates engaged in televised debate, which took place in the Senate and had CSSD senators as its audience (Willoughby and Richter 2008.01.29). The alleged purpose of the debate, which was only reluctantly agreed to by Klaus, was to help undecided senators to get more information about the contenders. The second novel feature of the contest was the long drawn out debate about the method of voting. As the divisions within the different parties' ranks were becoming increasingly more obvious, there were calls for an open vote in both chambers. The constitution is silent about whether the vote should be secret or open, although on all previous occasions Czech lawmakers opted for the former, which, as we had seen, allowed for considerable disunity and undisciplined voting. The Chamber and the Senate were split on this question with a large number of deputies wanting an open vote while the Senate majority, controlled by the ODS, was comfortable with keeping the status quo (Cameron 2008.02.07). Given the internal party divisions and the tight balance between government and opposition, the implications of keeping the vote secret or opening it up were far-reaching:

> . . . essentially a candidate can only win if at least some MPs betray their party and vote for the other guy. This can only happen in a secret ballot, because no MP is going to raise his hand and vote for the other guy when all of his colleagues—and the general public—are watching. In the lower house, the Civic Democrats, who support Vaclav Klaus, are hoping enough Social Democratic MPs, who are supposed to be voting for Jan Svejnar, will vote for Mr Klaus instead. The easiest way to prevent that from happening is to force an open ballot. This is what the Greens, who support Mr Svejnar, and the Social Democrats, who will be embarrassed if some of their number vote for Mr Klaus, are doing. They appear to be supported by those Christian Democrats who support Mr Svejnar (the party is split between Klaus and Svejnar supporters). However, it also works the other way around, Jan Svejnar can only be elected if some Civic Democrats vote for him, so it's not clear whether this strategy will pay off for his supporters. A big unknown is the Communists . . . (Cameron 2008.02.07)

Since there were gains to be made by both camps from making the vote open, the new rule was eventually adopted; however, not without a long drawn-out ten-hour acrimonious debate on the first day of the presidential vote (Willoughby and Johnston 2008.02.08).

As Table 7.2 shows, the first attempt to elect the president was inconclusive. In the first two rounds Svejnar carried the Chamber majority while Klaus secured the majority in the Senate. In the third round Klaus got considerably more votes; however, due to the abstention of the Communists he fell two votes short of winning. Four days after the vote the KSCM made a surprise announcement to put forward one of its deputies, J. Bobosikova, as candidate for the next round of voting. Although it was evident that her chances were very slim, the Communist

Party appeared to use her candidacy to put pressure on the CSSD to make concessions in exchange for communist votes in the next round of balloting. The CSSD was not closed to such a trade-off (Linek 2009: 941); however, it noted with concern that if Bobosikova stayed in the race she might split the left vote, which could leave Klaus as the only candidate to move to the subsequent rounds (Richter 2008.02.13). In the end, she withdrew from the race before the next round, which resulted in a repetition of the first attempt for the first two rounds: Svejnar won the Chamber and Klaus carried the Senate. On the third round, however, Klaus was able to win just enough votes to be elected president thanks to substantial support from KDU deputies and senators as well as the dissenting votes of three CSSD lawmakers (Linek 2009: 942).

7.4 INDIRECT PRESIDENTIAL ELECTIONS IN LATVIA

Table 7.3 summarizes the results of the five presidential elections that were held in Latvia between 1993 and 2010. Except for the election of 1999, it never took the *Saeima* more than two attempts to elect the head of state and, except for 2003, the winning candidate normally passed the majority threshold only with a narrow margin, which reflected the extremely fragmented nature of the Latvian legislative party system where even governing coalitions proved to be very difficult to cobble together. Latvian governing coalitions were able to elect a common coalition

TABLE 7.3 *Presidential elections in Latvia, 1993–2007*

Election year and date	Candidates	Votes
July 6 and 7, 1993	G. Meierovics	35
	A. Jerumanis	14
	G. Ulmanis	12
July 7, 1993	A. Jerumanis	26
	G. Ulmanis	53
June 18, 1996	**G. Ulmanis**	53
	I. Kreituse	25
	I. Liepa	14
	A. Rubiks	5
June 17, 1999*	**V. Vike-Freiberga**	53
	V. Birkavs	20
	I. Udre	9
June 20, 2003	**V. Vike-Freiberga**	88
May 31, 2007	**V. Zatlers**	58
	A. Endzins	39

Note: * The election of Vike-Freiberga was preceded by inconclusive rounds of balloting.Entries in bold indicate the winning candidate.
Sources: EECR Summer 1999; Huang 1999; Ikstens 2008.

candidate only on two occasions (in 1993 and 2007), whereas in the other instances either the lack of a parliamentary majority or within-coalition instability resulted in winning candidacies whose parliamentary support cut across the government–opposition divide. Thus, in 1996 the incumbent president, Ulmanis, was broadly supported both by several parties of the governing coalition and some parties of the opposition against the candidate of the senior coalition partner, I. Kreituse of the DPS; in 1999 members of the governing coalition again ran their own candidates against each other; but in 2003 parties reached across the government–opposition divide to re-elect incumbent V. Vike-Freiberga with the largest margin ever.

The first presidential election took place one month after the conclusion of the first post-transition polls to the *Saeima* in 1993. It is important to point out that the election of both the head of state and the head of government happened almost simultaneously. On July 6, the *Saeima* had to choose among three candidates, none of whom was able to collect the required majority of fifty-one deputies. The following day a new election was held between Ulmanis, the candidate of the Farmers' Union, and A. Jerumanis, a candidate of the Christian Democratic Union. While a significant number of legislators (thirty-nine) had abstained from the first vote, including members of Latvia Way, the party that won the most seats in the election, the participation rate increased substantially in the second vote Bugajszki (2001: 119). With the consolidation of the coalition deal between Latvia and the Farmers' Union, Ulmanis was elected as the joint candidate of the governing parties, which in turn elected V. Birkavs as prime minister the following day.[2]

Three years later Ulmanis was renominated as candidate for the presidency. Although A. Skele, prime minister of the highly fragmented eight-party surplus majority coalition that was formed after the 1995 parliamentary election, confirmed his support for Ulmanis who also received support from most of the coalition partners and some opposition parties, the largest member of the governing coalition, the DPS, decided to run its own candidate in the person of I. Kreituse, the chair of the *Saeima* (RFE/RL Archives).[3] Yet, given that the governing coalition still had a majority of seats without the DPS, the dissent of the party did not make a difference to the outcome. In addition to these two candidates, the imprisoned leader of the Latvian Communist Party, A. Rubiks, and I. Liepa of the largest opposition party, the TKL-ZP, also entered the contest. As the table shows, Ulmanis received a first ballot majority even though the coalition was formally divided between him and Kreituse.

By far the most protracted of all presidential votes in Latvia took place in 1999 when it took six ballots for the *Saeima* to eventually settle on a winning candidate, Vike-Freiberga (Huang 1999). This was also the first time that the *Saeima* elected a head of state for a four-year presidential term. The election itself followed an important change in the line up of the governing coalition, initially formed by Latvia's Way, the Fatherland and Freedom Alliance and the New Party after the October 1998 elections, due to the inclusion of a Social Democratic minister in the cabinet even though the Social Democratic Union itself refrained from formally joining the coalition. All four parties that were represented in the cabinet nominated a presidential candidate as did the opposition People's Party. The first two rounds, held on June 17, did not produce a winner. Therefore, A. Kalnins, the candidate of the Social Democrats, who scored the fewest votes, was eliminated from the next run-off. Three more rounds followed with the successive elimination of J. Priedkalns, the Fatherland candidate, from the third and A. Gorbunovs, the Latvia's Way candidate, from the fourth rounds. The fifth round was a straight contest between the opposition candidate, V. Paegle of the People's Party, and a coalition party candidate, R. Pauls of the New Party. However, due to the formal withdrawal of a number of parties from participating in the final rounds of the election, the ultimate run-off failed to produce a winner: Pauls won thirty-three votes against Paegle's twenty-four which was well below the required majority threshold of fifty-one. The next attempt to elect the president was held the same night among three contenders: former prime minister V. Birkavs of the Latvia's Way, I. Udre of the New Party who held the economics portfolio, and V. Vike-Freiberga, a formally non-partisan candidate who had enjoyed the broad support of all of the other parties that had run unsuccessful candidates in the previous rounds of voting. Given the nature of Vike-Freiberga's support, she was elected easily in the first round by securing fifty-three votes against Birkav's twenty and Udre's nine. Four years later Vike-Freiberga ran unopposed and won an unprecedented majority of eighty-four votes from the Saeima in the first and only round of balloting in June 20, 2003. Apart from the opposition Socialist Party and some independents, all coalition and opposition parties supported and voted for her (http://www.rferl.org/newsline/2003/06/200603.asp).

The 2007 presidential election was a straightforward contest between A. V. Zatlers, the candidate of the four-party governing coalition (People's Party, Fatherland and Freedom, The Latvia Way Alliance, and the Union of Greens and Farmers), and A. Endzins, who was nominated by the opposition National Harmony Party. The ability of the governing coalition to rally behind a single joint candidate already suggested that the election itself would be a mere formality since the four parties together controlled a comfortable majority in the *Saeima*. The coordinated nomination of Zatlers as the coalition candidate followed an initial division between the People's Party, the senior coalition partner, and the LPP/LC, both of which had entered their own candidates. In fact, it was not until about a week before the date of voting that the two parties had agreed to withdraw their candidates and line up behind Zatlers. The public reaction to this move was extremely negative as people assumed that the governing parties had wanted to hide the identity of their real candidate until the last minute knowing Zatler's deep unpopularity due to his alleged corrupt behavior in his professional medical practice (Ikstens 2008: 1045–6). Nonetheless, for the first time since 1993 the governing parties agreed to run a single candidate for the presidency. Another opposition party, the New Era, had initially also proposed to run a candidate of its own, S. Kalniete; the party eventually changed course and lined up in support of Endzins. Yet, the opposition parties did not have the sufficient number of seats to ensure a successful bid for the presidency. The competitive nature of this election stood in sharp contrast to the huge consensus with which the outgoing incumbent had been elected in 2003. Moreover, whereas Vike-Freiberga enjoyed both parliamentary and overall popular support as well, the winning candidate of the 2007 election was perceived in an extremely negative light by many Latvians as mentioned above.

7.5 INDIRECT PRESIDENTIAL ELECTIONS IN ESTONIA

As discussed in Chapter Two, failure on the part of the Estonian parliament to elect a President results in the convening of a broader electoral college including local government authorities. Given the high special majority requirement that presidential candidates have to face in the *Riigikogu*, it is not at all surprising that three of the four Estonian presidential elections proceeded and were decided at the electoral college stage (1996, 2001, 2006) as Table 7.4 shows.

TABLE 7.4 *Presidential elections in Estonia, 1996–2011*

Election year and date	Candidates	Votes in Round One	Votes in Round Two	Votes in Round Three
August 26–27, 1996	L. Meri	45	49	52
	A. Rüütel	34	34	32
September 20, 1996	**L. Meri**	139	196	
(Electoral College)	A. Rüütel	85	126	
	T. Kelam	76		
	E. Tougu	47		
	S. Oviir	25		
August 27–28, 2001	P. Kreitzberg	40	36	33
	A. Tarand	38		
	P. Tulviste		35	33
September 21, 2001	P. Kreitzberg	72		
(Electoral College)	**A. Rüütel**	114	186	
	T. Savi	90	155	
	P. Tulviste	89		
August 28, 2006	E. Ergma	65		
	T. H. Ilves		64	
	T. H. Ilves			64
September 23, 2006	**T. H. Ilves**	174		
(Electoral College)	A. Rüütel	162		
August 29, 2011	**T. H. Ilves**	75		
	I. Tarand	25		

Note: Entries in bold indicate the winning candidate.
Sources: EECR Fall (1996: 12); Lagerspetz and Vogt (2004); Tavits (2009); Estonian National Electoral Committee.

The first completely indirect election to the Estonian presidency took place in the summer of 1996 following the constitutional amendment of 1995, which replaced the previous hybrid election.[4] The presidential election of 1996 was held a little over a year following the last parliamentary election, which resulted in the formation of a short-lived majority coalition government between the Coalition Party and Rural Union alliance (KMU) and the Estonian Center Party (K) in April 1995. It is worth noting that although the KMU's most preferred coalition partner was the pro-market Estonian Reform Party, the post-election coalition negotiations failed to bring these two partners together into government. The eventual premature collapse of the KMU-K coalition was intimately related to these failed coalition discussions: prime minister T. Vahi, of the Coalition Party, dismissed the Center Party's leader E. Savisaar from his portfolio as interior minister, and took his party out of the coalition, when police found evidence that Savisaar had illegally taped his phone conversations with other politicians during the coalition talks (EECR 1995 Fall). Following the collapse of the coalition government, president Meri reappointed Vahi as prime minister who managed to bring the Reform Party into the coalition this time.

As the time of the presidential election was drawing closer, differences between the new coalition partners started to loom larger. The Reform Party early on indicated its support for the re-election of incumbent president Meri, while a growing number of legislators in the KMU preferred Rüütel, the runner-up of the 1992 election (EECR 1996 Winter). According to the public opinion polls, Meri remained the most popular presidential choice; however his chances to be re-elected became overshadowed by his increasingly tenuous relationship with the prime minister thanks to his frequent use of the presidential veto. Nonetheless, by early 1996 Vahi's Coalition Party eventually came to back Meri's candidacy together with the Reform Party, the Moderates and the Progressive Party; with the formal support of these four parties the incumbent could count on forty-nine votes, far short of the sixty-six required. As in 1992, Meri faced a single opponent in the *Riigikogu*, A. Rüütel, whose candidacy was supported only by the Pensioners' and Families' League and the Rural Union, a member of the governing coalition, which controlled only twenty-three seats.

Meri's immediate re-election was prevented by the fact that neither the Center Party, which blamed the president for failing to prevent Savisaar's dismissal, nor Pro Patria, which had nominated Meri in 1992, offered their support for him (EECR 1996 4:12). With the additional votes of these two parties, the incumbent would have easily secured the necessary two-thirds majority in the *Riigikogu*. Although Meri's advantage over Rüütel remained consistent throughout the successive ballots both in the legislature and in the electoral college (see Table 7.4) it still took five complete rounds of voting before he was finally selected as the winning candidate.

The next presidential election started in August 2001, more than two and a half years after the last elections to the *Riigikogu* in March 1999, and was eventually concluded almost a month later in September with the final vote cast, once again, in the electoral college. The three-party right-of-center majority government, comprising the Pro Patria, the Reform and the Moderates parties, that had been formed after the March elections showed a number of strains by the time of the presidential election. From its inception the coalition suffered from two structural difficulties. First, that the party that won the most seats in the election, the left-of-center Center Party, remained in opposition, and second, that the three parties that made up the government were almost evenly balanced in terms of the number of their parliamentary seats: the Pro Patria, which supplied the Prime Minister, and the Reform Party had eighteen seats each while the Moderates had seventeen. Thus, an evenly fragmented coalition with no clear center of gravity faced an opposition that very clearly had the Center Party as its point of gravity. Apart from these structural disadvantages, another important source of policy disagreement among the coalition partners had to do with differences of opinion about the method and pace of economic liberalization; while the Reform Party insisted on a more aggressive strategy, including the abolition of corporate taxes, the coalition partners took a more cautious approach.

Although the coalition parties failed to agree on a single nominee, they agreed to run a single candidate against the Center Party's candidate in the *Riigikogu* (Pettai 2002: 950). In the first round, the Moderates' candidate, A. Tarand, ran against Kreitzberg; however, neither of them managed to get anywhere near the required two-thirds majority to win. In the second attempt, the coalition submitted a new nomination; this time it was the Pro Patria candidate, P. Tulviste, who ran against Kreitzberg in two extremely narrow and inconclusive rounds of voting. The last *Riigikogu* vote actually resulted in a tie between the two candidates. It is worth noting that the high abstention rate in all three rounds certainly contributed to the failure of parliament to elect the next president of Estonia. Of the 100 deputies only seventy-eight voted in the first ballot, followed by seventy-one in the second, and sixty-six in the third.

The first round of the electoral college vote was inconclusive with Rüütel scoring a surprise plurality of 114 followed by Savi's ninety. Although the coalition partners agreed to coordinate and ask their deputies and councillors in the electoral college to vote for Savi on the last round, this was not sufficient and Rüütel won the presidency over Savi with a convincing margin of thirty-one votes. The divisions within the coalition that became clearly visible during the presidential election proved to be unsustainable and led to the collapse of the coalition government in December 2001. The new minority coalition that was invested in January comprised the Reform and the previously opposition Center Parties (Pettai 2002: 951).

Similarly to the previous presidential election, the 2006 vote for the Estonian head of state was also held quite a bit later after the previous parliamentary polls, held in March 2003, which left a lot of time for inter-party and intra-coalition differences to come in the open and prevent a coordinated coalition nomination. As a matter of fact, the parliamentary landscape was so fractured and divided in the *Riigikogu* after the 2003 elections that two coalition governments followed each other in quick succession within a short span of three years. Prime Minister J. Parts (Res Publica), who led the three-party majority coalition of the Res Publica, the Reform and the People's Union parties, was defeated in a vote of no-confidence after two years in office and was replaced by A. Ansip (Reform) at the helm of a Reform–Center–Peoples' Union coalition. The size of the government remained intact because two of the three coalition partners remained the same (Reform and Peoples' Union) and the Center Party had exactly the same number of seats in the *Riigikogu* as the Res Publica.

Five of the six parliamentary parties, the left-leaning People's Union being the exception, started early discussions about the possibility of nominating a single candidate whose election by the *Riigikogu* would be guaranteed as long as the five parties remained united. Indeed the five parties had a total of eighty-eight seats, well above the requisite sixty-eight (Pettai 2007). Although the People's Union indicated its continued support for Rüütel, the four parties of the right (Res Publica, Reform, the Social Democrats previously known as the Moderates, and the Pro Patria) were adamant to replace the incumbent. Their ability to do so, however, hinged on the cooperation of the Center Party, which did support Rüütel in 2001 and also indicated on this occasion that "it was not absolutely against Arnold Rüütel, although it would also nominate its own candidate" (Pettai 2007: 944). The possibility of a five-party consensus broke down on June 28 when the roundtable meeting of these parties' representatives voted to support E. Ergma and T. H. Ilves as the joint candidates in the successive rounds of the parliamentary vote. Since both of these candidates were initially nominated by center-right parties, the Center Party defected from the five-party coalition, indicated its support for Rüütel and instructed its deputies to join the People's Union deputies in abstaining from the *Riigikogu* vote altogether. In accepting the support of the same two parties who got him elected in 2001, Rüütel announced that he would not contest the parliamentary stage of the election but would enter only through the electoral college (Pettai 2007: 945).

Since the combined seat total of the two pro-Rüütel parties was well above one third of all the seats, their abstention guaranteed that the next president would also be elected by the electoral college. Indeed, although the deputies of the four parties that had nominated Ergma for the first and then Ilves for the second and third rounds cast their ballots in a disciplined fashion, both candidates fell a few votes, three and four respectively, short of the required two-thirds majority. In contrast to the 1996 and 2001 elections, only two candidates entered the first round of the electoral college vote. Therefore, with the full participation of all parties, the first round was also conclusive and decisive as it yielded the narrowest majority victory, a margin of twelve votes, for Ilves over Rüütel.

The fourth election to the Estonian presidency was the most straightforward of all previous contests: it took a single round of voting in the *Riigikogu* to re-elect the incumbent T. H. Ilves with a large majority of seventy-five votes against the candidate of the opposition Center Party, I. Tarand. The elections took place in August 2011, five months after the latest legislative election gave a renewed mandate to prime minister Ansip's two-party majority coalition comprising the Reform Party and the Pro-Patria–Res Publica Union that had been in government since the 2007 elections. The stability of the coalition, the temporal proximity of the presidential to the parliamentary polls and the reduced fragmentation in the *Riigikogu* all helped to streamline the 2011 presidential contest. Three of the four parliamentary parties, the two members of the governing coalition as well as the Social Democrats who had nominated Ilves in the first place in 2006, quickly agreed to support his re-election. Although the Center Party nominated its own candidate, the overall parliamentary size of the three pro-Ilves parties pre-determined the result of the first and only vote in the *Riigikogu* on August 29, 2011.

7.6 DIVIDING THE EXECUTIVE? A COMPARATIVE ANALYSIS

The four post-communist democracies that I have surveyed in this chapter held seventeen indirect presidential elections between the early 1990s and 2011. Of these elections four can be considered uncontested: the 1990 and 2000 elections in Hungary, the 1998 Czech, and the 2003 Latvian elections. Of the remaining thirteen elections eight were characterized by deep divisions within the governing coalition while in five cases the coalition was united behind a common candidate. In each and every one of the latter five cases the coalition candidate was successfully elected: Goncz (1995) and Schmitt (2010) in Hungary; Ilves (2011) in Estonia; Ulmanis (1993) and Zatlers (2007) in Latvia. In three out of the eight instances when the governing coalition was divided the opposition was able to elect the next president three times (Rüütel 2001; Klaus 2003; and Solyom 2005); in the remaining five cases the next president enjoyed at least some support from some of the members of the governing coalition.

An important variable that emerges from the narrative to have shaped the outcome of indirect presidential elections is whether the incumbent runs for the office or not. In every country there is a two-term limit on the presidential office, which means that every second contest could theoretically have the incumbent run again. However, incumbents were not always nominated or chose not to enter. In Hungary the only incumbent who ran for a second term, and successfully so, was Goncz in 1995, while in the Czech Republic and Latvia both incumbents who were eligible to run for a second term (Havel in 1998 and Klaus in 2008 in the former case; Ulmanis in 1996 and Vike-Freiberga in 2003 in the latter) did so and won. Estonia is the only case where an incumbent who ran actually lost (Rüütel in 2006); however even in that country the other two incumbents who ran for a second term (Meri in 1996 and Ilves in 2011) got elected. In sum, in seven out of

MOST CONCURRENT RULES		**MOST DIVERGENT RULES**
HUNGARY	LATVIA	CZECH REPUBLIC
		ESTONIA

FIGURE 7.1 Indirect presidential election rules in East Central Europe

eight cases the current president who ran for a second term was successful. The partisan support that these seven re-elected incumbents enjoyed varied considerably: two of the seven re-elected incumbents (Goncz and Ilves) were candidates of the governing coalition; two (Vike-Frieberga and Havel) were consensus candidates who received substantial support from both the governing coalition and most or all of the opposition parties; while the remaining three (Ulmanis, Klaus, and Meri) did not have a clear cut support from either the coalition or the opposition.

In the remainder of this section, I will show that the degree to which the presidential election rules deviate from the way in which the prime minister and the new government are elected in the legislature consistently explain whether and when the governing party or coalition succeeds to elect the new head of state, or at least prevent the opposition from doing so. More specifically, the four states can be conveniently ranked on a continuum from having the most to having the least concurrent presidential and prime ministerial election rules.

The most concurrent rules can be found in Hungary where, in the ultimate round of the presidential election, it only takes a simple majority of legislators to choose the head of state. Since the prime minister is invested in office with the support of an absolute majority of all deputies, a governing coalition that can win and maintain an absolute majority of the voters in the legislature should also be able to elect its head of state for which, technically speaking, fewer votes are required. As mentioned earlier, since the first two rounds in Hungary use a two-thirds majority rule, any member of the governing coalition, or any party to that effect, with at least one third plus one of the seats can block a victory in those rounds. Then, in the ultimate round, a united coalition should be able to secure the election of its candidate. Since it is relatively easy for a governing coalition to ensure the election of its candidate to the presidency, these election rules can actually promote and encourage coalition unity and discipline.

The narratives of the five Hungarian presidential elections support the expectation that governing coalitions should ordinarily remain united and able to elect their candidate to the presidency. The elections of Goncz in 1995, Madl in 2000 and Schmitt in 2010 are clear cases in point. In the first and last of these cases the governing coalitions were extremely large and had a two thirds majority to secure the first round election of these candidates. In 2000, the governing coalition was far from having such a majority. Nonetheless, by remaining united it was able to secure the election of Madl to the presidency. The fact that Madl ran unopposed bears further testimony to the incentive that the election rules provide for political parties: anticipating that the ruling coalition would prevail in the end made the nomination of an opposition candidate redundant. In the other two cases (1995 and 2010) when the opposition did nominate a candidate in spite of facing a united coalition of government parties their move was merely symbolic and served the sole purpose of denying the winning candidate the appearance of a consensus.

The only presidential election that seemingly does not conform to our institutional explanation, is of course, the one held in 2005 when the ruling coalition parties, the MSZP and the SZDSZ, failed to agree on a joint candidate, which allowed the opposition to ultimately seize the initiative and prevail in the contest. Why did this happen? More specifically, why did the presidential election rule fail to encourage the coalition partners to stick together and ensure the election of a joint candidate? One explanation to this puzzle highlights the importance of the democratic deficit of the Socialist Party and the continued importance of the regime divide as a cleavage in Hungary's post-communist politics (Csizmadia 2006). According to this explanation, since the presidency is an important symbol of the new democratic regime, the SZDSZ, known for its historic opposition to the communist system and its crucial role in bringing it to its end, understood the importance of vetoing the election of a candidate connected with the communist past, e.g. Szili.

I propose an alternative explanation that is much less connected with the contextual specificity of Hungary's post-communist politics. Instead, I suggest that the election of Solyom as the opposition candidate in 2005 points to the extremely tenuous state of affairs that characterizes a governing coalition where the dominant and central parties are not one and the same (Nikolenyi 2004b). It is well known that coalitions that are formed by dominant and central parties tend to be unstable because such parties have equally powerful and credible claims to power: the power of the dominant party stems from its numerical size, which allows it to form alternative winning coalitions that can exclude its current partners, while the power of the central party comes from its control of the median legislator (van Rozendaal 1992). As I showed elsewhere, the median legislator in the Hungarian parliament after the 2002 election was controlled by the SZDSZ (Nikolenyi 2004b), the junior coalition partner. In contrast to the aftermath of the 1994 election, when the MSZP and the SZDSZ formed their first coalition government, the relative power of the SZDSZ vis-à-vis the Socialist Party was much greater after 2002 thanks to its spatial location and to the fact that the MSZP did not have a majority on its own. The median location of the SZDSZ suggested, as per Black's well-known median voter theorem, that under a simple majority rule, its preferred candidate would beat any other candidate in a presidential vote. Knowing this, the party insisted on nominating an SZDSZ politician as the coalition candidate against Solyom. As for the MSZP, the largest and dominant party in parliament, and the only one that has never had a claim to the presidency, it also made sense to hold out and insist that its nominee should become the joint coalition candidate.

This clash between the dominant and central players that formed the coalition government over the choice of the presidential candidate was quite simply the continuation of their extremely tense and troubled relations from the inception of their government. As mentioned in the narrative, the MSZP–SZDSZ coalition was in fact the first one not to have lasted for a complete term in office due to the forced resignation of prime minister P. Medgyessy a little over two years into his mandate. The inability of the MSZP–SZDSZ coalition, which was the only coalition government in post-communist Hungary that was formed by a dominant player that did not control the median legislator at the same time (Nikolenyi 2004b), to settle on and elect a joint candidate to the presidency suggests that the structure of the coalition may limit the extent to which the election rule can induce cooperation among the coalition partners. In this sense the Hungarian case is particularly important because the presidential election rules here are the most concurrent and we would therefore expect it to always produce a presidential election outcome that the governing coalition favors.

At the other extreme of the continuum we can locate Estonia and the Czech Republic. In both cases the rules by which the head of state is elected and the prime minister and government are invested completely diverge. In Estonia, the *Riigikogu* can elect the president only if there is a two-thirds coalition of all deputies in support of a candidate. Given the fragmented nature of the Estonian electoral and party systems such a large coalition could not be obtained prior to 2007. However, in the two elections that have been held since then, the governing parties managed to win a two thirds majority in the *Riigikogu* and, consequently, also secured the election of their presidential candidate in 2011. Similarly to Hungary, the two thirds requirement also means that any party with one third plus one of the seats, which in the *Riigikogu* amounts to a mere fifteen deputies, can effectively block the parliamentary election of the president. In contrast to Hungary, however, this veto is much more powerful because all three rounds of the balloting retain the two thirds majority rule. In the electoral college, where all but one of the presidents were elected, the *Riigikogu* has a minority, which further weakens the ability of the governing coalition to secure the election of the head of state. These election rules provide a strong disincentive for members of an Estonian governing coalition to stay united in an effort to capture the presidency. Since members of the coalition know that their unity cannot ensure victory, unless they have a combined majority of two thirds of the deputies, the expected benefits of their cooperation decline. Indeed, successive Estonian coalitions disintegrated in the presidential elections with its members running candidates against each other until a large coalition with a two-thirds majority was eventually formed that elected a president in a single round of legislative voting in 2011.

Similarly to Estonia, the rules of choosing the Czech president diverge significantly from the way in which the prime minister and the government are invested into office. Being a bicameral legislature, both houses of the Czech parliament have a say in choosing the head of state, however, in contrast to Estonia, in the ultimate round of voting, when the two chambers meet in a joint session, members of the first chamber constitute a significant majority (of 200 out of 281 seats). Yet, the size of the Senate is large enough to make it unlikely for any governing coalition that controls the Chamber of Deputies to also control the joint session of the two chambers. In fact, a governing coalition would have to have an extremely unlikely 70.5 percent majority in the Chamber of Deputies (141/200) in order to ensure its control of the joint session and secure the election of its candidate to the presidency. Under these rules, the only thing that a united Czech governing coalition can guarantee is that its presidential candidate will advance to the successive rounds of voting by virtue of being the candidate with the most votes in the first chamber. However, the very fact that in the last round it takes a much larger coalition to ensure the victory of the candidate actually reduces the incentives for such a coordinated and disciplined behavior.

Indeed, except for the re-election of President Havel, who was the consensus candidate of all but two of the parliamentary parties, the winning presidential candidate was never the common choice of the parties of the governing coalition. In 2003, the governing coalition was split according to which chamber its parties had a numerically stronger position: the centrist coalition of smaller parties (KDU–US–ODA) had a strong incentive to run their candidates because their plurality position in the Senate allowed them to advance to the final round of the vote where they could expect a compromise to be struck in their favor. Similarly, the senior coalition partner, the CSSD had an incentive to run its own candidate because the party was in a plurality position in the Chamber where its candidate could advance as long as the party's deputies would vote in a disciplined fashion, which, as we saw, they did not do. Nonetheless, the bicameral institutional structure of the presidential election explains consistently why the members of the governing coalition kept splitting instead of running a joint candidate. The eventual coalescing of the coalition partners behind Sokol's candidacy came too late in the game; by the time the third round of the presidential ballot was held Klaus proved to have staying power as he emerged with the most votes from the previous two attempts. Furthermore, the continued isolation of the KSCM by the center-left coalition also gave Klaus the time that he needed to mobilize the Communist vote in his support. Whereas Klaus' ODS and the KSCM were far apart in the ideological left-right space they shared a common suspicion of deepening integration with the European Union, which made an alliance between the two parties possible.

The 2008 presidential election seemingly resulted in a coalition victory as Klaus emerged the winner once again. However, the ODS and its junior coalition partners, the KDU and the Green Party, were badly split on this issue. In fact, the election was a choice between two candidates nominated by two coalition partners: Svejnar of the Green Party and Klaus of the ODS. Once again, the split nomination was possible because of the bicameral structure of the election. The Green Party understood that its centrist position between the two parties to its left (the KSCM and the CSSD with combined blocking power of exactly 50 percent of the seats) and the two parties to its right (the KDU and the ODS with a combined 47 percent of the seats) made it a pivotal player for the formation of any ideologically connected majority coalition in the Chamber. In other words, the Green Party was a central player exactly as the SZDSZ was in the Hungarian parliament after the 2002 election. At the same time, the ODS had a number of reasons to insist on its choice of candidate. First, Klaus was the incumbent and incumbents, as we have seen, almost never lose a re-election. Second, like the MSZP in the Hungary after 2002, the ODS was also a dominant player in the Chamber, that is to say that it was in a position to form distinct majority coalitions behind its candidate that could allow it to divide both the opposition and its coalition partners to its advantage. Third, and most important for our purposes, the ODS had a one-seat majority in the Senate, which, as long as deputies would vote in united fashion for their parties' candidates, guaranteed Klaus's survival until the last round. In short, the requirement to have a majority in the two chambers separately in the first two rounds of the balloting led members of the governing coalition to calculate that their relative positional advantages in the respective chambers would lead them to the final round.

Given how the 2003 and 2008 presidential elections unfolded, it remains puzzling why Czech political parties from both the government and the opposition benches were able to support Havel as a consensus candidate in 1998. Indeed, one might have expected that the same institutional conditions that prevailed then would have led to the splintering of the governing coalition as it happened on the two future occasions. Why did it not happen? A plausible answer might be that by virtue of being the incumbent, Havel was the obvious choice to support. His national and international stature, and untainted credentials as life-long critic and opponent of communist rule were difficult for any candidate to match. Indeed, the very fact that the four parliamentary parties that were clearly committed to building a competitive liberal democratic regime and making a clear break with the communist past lent their support to his re-election supports this idea. The only two parties that ran candidates against him were the KSCM and SPR, neither of which belonged to this group of democratic parties; the KSCM was for all intents and purposes an unreformed orthodox communist party at the time, while the extremist overtones of the SPR made the democratic credentials of that party questionable.

An alternative explanation, one that is more consistent with the logic of party choices based on institutionally derived incentives, has to do with the state of the party system in the Czech parliament at the time of the presidential election. As mentioned in the narrative, the minority coalition government of the ODS, ODA, and KDU headed by Klaus resigned at the end of 1997 and was replaced with a six-month caretaker government that was to remain in place until early elections in

June of 1998. While the appointment of a caretaker government and the holding of early elections were supported by the three members of the previous coalition, the newly formed Freedom Union, as well as the CSSD, the largest opposition party, those elections were to be preceded by the election of the president, which was scheduled to take place during precisely this six-month caretaker period. Under these conditions, the only choice that made sense for the main government and opposition parties was to support Havel's re-election for a number of reasons. First, the disintegration of the coalition government and the splintering of the ODS meant that there would be no scope to build the kind of majority coalition that would be required for a partisan candidate to be elected in case the presidential election became a competitive race. Therefore, under the present conditions a competitive race would have been very likely to end up in a stalemate which would have created a constitutional crisis that no parties was ready to be responsible and pay the electoral price for. Second, and related to this, all major political parties were concerned to prepare for the early elections, which Havel was also committed to. Allowing him to stay on was, therefore, a vey low-cost way to ensure that the fresh elections would not be postponed and unduly otherwise delayed by any unexpected turbulence that a competitive presidential elections might cause. Third, the expectation of an imminent legislative election also created a veil of uncertainty that gave a certain advantage to the incumbent president. By agreeing to Havel's candidacy as a consensus choice, all four major parties could be assured to have a "friend" in the presidential palace in case they ended up losing in the June parliamentary elections. In short, the re-election of Havel to the Czech presidency as the consensus candidate of the four main parliamentary parties in 1998 shows that even under an otherwise extremely demanding institutional rule it is possible for political parties to cooperate and find a compromise that results in a conclusive outcome in one round of balloting. However, such consensus was made possible only because the overall political climate in the party system was characterized by a government crisis and political instability.

The fourth case, Latvia, falls in between the two extremes although much closer to Hungary than to either Estonia or the Czech Republic. As in Hungary, the national parliament is the sole body that has the mandate and power to choose the head of the state; in case of repeated failure the voting continues without recourse to having another college or body determine the outcome, which is the case in the latter two countries. Also, the margin of victory is very similar: while there is no hard constitutional requirement as to the investiture of the prime minister and the cabinet, the winning presidential candidate must have the support of an absolute majority of members in the *Saeima*. Since the rules make it very likely that a viable governing coalition would be able to secure the election of its candidate to the presidency, coalition partners in Latvia have an incentive to work together towards this goal. Indeed, the only time when the coalition completely fell apart on the presidential vote was in 1999; the remaining cases included broad consensus between government and opposition (2003); a straightforward victory by a united governing coalition (1993 and 2007); and dissension by a single coalition partner (1996).

The election of Ulmanis to the presidency in 1993 was a straightforward affair facilitated by the convergence of two favorable conditions: the two parties that agreed to form a government after the parliamentary election were only three seats short of the required fifty-one seat majority and the presidential election was held in the immediate aftermath of the legislative polls. The temporal proximity of the two elections and the fact that there were only two parties to coordinate meant that Latvia's Way and the Farmer's Union could effectively trade the presidency and the prime ministership between themselves. As such, the support of Latvia's Way to Ulmanis became an important element to cement the coalition deal that the party was making with the Farmers' Union. This was also the only election that was not held under the sequential run-off rule adopted in 1996. Three years later, a much broader and much more fragmented coalition got into power. Although the DPS defected, the remaining coalition partners still had enough seats to secure the re-election of Ulmanis to the presidency. In this, the nomination of a separate candidate by the DPS amounted to no more than a symbolic gesture.

The 1999 election constitutes the central puzzle in the history of Latvian presidential elections: in this instance the governing coalition completely fell apart and almost every party ran its own candidate; clearly, the rules of the game failed to hold the coalition together this time. In order to make sense of this puzzle, a number of important points are worth noting. First, the absence of an incumbent running for re-election made the contest extremely competitive and removed the possibility of a focal point on which parties could otherwise coordinate their strategy. Second, since the governing coalition itself did not have a parliamentary majority it meant that some kind of a compromise would have to be found with some members of the opposition in order to get a coalition candidate elected. Third, precisely because the government was in a minority position the opposition was not at all interested in entering such a compromise; instead in order to put further constraints on an already weak government the opposition parties, led by the People's Party which incidentally also had the most seats in the *Saeima*, sought to have their own candidates advance. In other words, the 1999 presidential election reflected the divided, polarized and fragmented nature of the Latvian parliamentary party system. Just as parties were not able to form a majority government, they also failed to put together a parliamentary majority to support an electable presidential candidate until after all repeated attempts had failed. Four years later, in 2003, the majority coalition government was in office with fifty-five seats under its control. The coalition's unanimous support for the incumbent, Vike-Freiberga, made the outcome of the election predetermined. Therefore, there was no room for the opposition to challenge the candidate who was very popular anyway. In 2007, the coalition once again had a majority and its partners united behind the candidacy of Zatlers. Since there was no incumbent running, thanks to the expiration of Vike-Freiberga's term limit, the opposition ran a candidate whose chances, however, were slim in the face of a united coalition of governing parties.

7.7 CONCLUSION

Indirect presidential elections receive little attention in the literatures on comparative legislatures and coalition politics and the field of post-communist party politics is certainly no exception. Yet, indirectly elected presidencies are extremely important because they can command discretionary powers that might prove of decisive and pivotal value at times of uncertainty. Moreover, indirectly elected presidencies also have immense theoretical and analytical value: the indirect election of a president is a crucial moment that can test the cohesion of the governing coalition and can either reinforce its hold on power or weaken it by producing a divided government. In contrast to directly elected heads of states, no two post-communist states have the same rules to choose an indirectly elected president. As the chapter has shown, presidential election rules that resemble the election of the prime minister, i.e. by way of a majority vote in parliament, make it more likely that the governing coalition will capture the presidency. The more complicated the selection rule, the greater the likelihood that the same coalition of parties that was sufficient to elect a head of government would prove unable to secure the election of a common candidate to the presidency.

The previous chapter argued that purely parliamentary systems lead to more stable governments than systems with a strong directly elected president. In the light of this argument, the finding of the present chapter becomes especially important. By definition, all four states with an indirectly elected head of state belong to the purely parliamentary category, and as such we would expect them to result in stable and durable governing coalitions. In some cases (Hungary, Estonia) this has been the case more often than in others (Latvia, Czech Republic). In any event, this chapter has offered an insight into the inner workings of incumbent coalitions, the difficulties they face and the strategies they choose on one of the most important decisions that their constituents collectively face during their lifespan: to try and secure their own candidate to the office of the head of state. Depending on the rules of the game, some incumbent coalitions are more successful at achieving this than others. In this, the chapter has reminded us that although in general coalition governments may be more durable in parliamentary systems with weaker presidencies, there is still tremendous variation in just exactly how stable they are.

What do these findings tell us about the broader implications of power concentration and power dispersion in a political system? The answer is quite obvious.

The degree of concurrence between the indirect presidential election rules and the selection of the prime minister is consistent with the overall level of institutional power dispersion in three of the four states: Hungary, Latvia, and the Czech Republic. Hungary belongs to the group of states with the highest level of institutional power concentration and its presidential election rules also concentrate decision-making authority in the parliamentary majority, albeit a larger one than what is necessary to elect the head of government. Next in order is Latvia, which belongs to the intermediate category of power dispersion and, indeed, it has a presidential election rule that is less congruent with that for the prime minister. Finally, the Czech Republic has the institutionally most dispersed system of political power, which is further reflected in its presidential election rules. The exception is, of course, Estonia, which scores high on overall power concentration; like Hungary, however, its presidential election rule is as incongruent with that for the prime minister as it is the case in the Czech Republic. Apart from this deviant case, however, we see that the fundamental institutional logic of power concentration is also manifest in the presidential election rules which in turn lead to predictable outcomes in terms of unified or divided control over the executive.

NOTES

1. The remaining thirteen valid votes were cast against Goncz but no in favor of any other candidate.
2. The new coalition was actually three seats short of a parliamentary majority.
3. The combined seat share of the eight parties was seventy-three out of 100; the largest member of the coalition was the DPS with eighteen seats.
4. Under that model, the general public voted for the head of state in a direct popular contest, however, the *Riigikogu* had the ultimate responsibility of selecting the head of state if no candidate succeeded in winning at least 50 percent of the popular vote in a single-round election. In 1992, the only time when the presidency was elected under this rule, none of the four candidates who ran for the office were able to do so. Therefore, the *Riigikogu* had to decide between the top two candidates from the direct election (L. Meri, formerly of Pro Patria, and A. Rüütel, formerly of the Estonia Communist Party). Meri won the parliamentary vote with a fifty-nine to thirty-one margin against Rüütel even though he collected fewer votes in the popular election than his competitor.

8

Conclusion

How do political institutions shape party and coalition government in the new European democracies? I have tried to answer this question by assessing the institutional effects on a series of dependent variables that measure the type of party government at successive stages of the coalition lifecycle: the formation of party coalitions in the electoral contest, the formation of executive party coalitions, the stability of coalition governments, and finally the election of coalition candidates to the presidency where the head of state is not elected directly by the people. At each of these stages, the ECE democracies manifest important patterns of variation. In some states party coalitions start forming at the electoral stage, while in others they are much less frequent, if present at all. In some states elections are followed by the formation of majority coalition government while elsewhere the undersized cabinet solutions are an accepted and recurring norm. The stability of the government that is formed also varies considerably across the ten states. Finally, incumbent party coalitions almost always succeed in securing the election of their candidate to the presidency in some states, while in others same-party control over the head of state and the head of government is a rarity.

Since the central empirical findings are summed up at the end of each chapter, for the purposes of this overall conclusion let me reiterate the main effects that the hard institutional constraints which I surveyed in Chapter Two (the electoral system, the structure and organization of parliament as well as its relative powers vis-à-vis the presidency) have exerted on the different aspects of party coalition behavior. With regard to the *electoral system*, in Chapter Three, I found that two specific electoral system features promoted the formation of electoral coalitions in the ten ECE democracies: relatively small districts and a restrictive electoral formula. In Chapter Four, I further argued that the mixed-member electoral system of Hungary induces political parties to form electoral coalitions that, upon winning the election, actually become the executive coalition government. As such, the electoral system in Hungary constitutes a particularly important part of the overall government formation process. In Chapter Six, I showed that the number of parties has a negative effect on government stability; since electoral systems have a well-known effect on the fragmentation of the party system both in the electoral and the legislative arenas, it stands to reason that electoral systems that promote the proliferation of political parties, i.e. increase the number of parties, would, indirectly, also result in less stable governments.

With regard to the structure and organization of parliament, I have found that (i) bicameralism had a positive effect on the formation of minority governments (Chapter Five) but it had a negative impact on government duration (Chapter Six); and that (ii) positive investiture rules of government formation promoted electoral coalitions (Chapter Three) and government duration (Chapter Six) but they led to less frequent minority governments (Chapter Five). Furthermore, the majority status of the governing coalition had a positive effect on government stability (Chapter Six), which further suggests that positive parliamentarism, which promotes the formation of such coalitions, might have an indirect effect promoting government durability as well. Finally, the nature of the *presidency* appears to have affected both the size and the stability of the government: minority governments were more likely to be formed more frequently in states with a stronger president (Chapter Five) while government duration was found to be negatively affected by a strong presidency (Chapter Six). The effects of the three hard institutional constraints (electoral rules, parliaments, and presidents) on the three principal dependent variables (electoral coalitions, minority governments, and coalition government duration) are summarized in Figure 8.1.

These findings establish that political institutions play a very important role in shaping the patterns of party coalitions in the new democracies of Eastern Europe. However, recognizing and examining the impact of political institutions in an organized analytical fashion is not tantamount to making an argument either for institutional exclusivity or for institutional determinism. In fact, such arguments would be wrong. The world of party politics, just like political life in general, is often messy and made complicated by a variety of factors, both institutional and non-institutional. Social forces and conflicts that emerge from the contested dynamics of the transition to a market economy; ideational norms and cultural values that owe their genesis and development to the specific historical conditions

Institutional constraints	**Electoral coalitions**	**Minority governments**	**Government duration**
Small district magnitude	+	0	0
Small assembly	0	–	0
Bicameralism	0	+	–
Positive investiture	+	–	+
Weak presidency	0	–	+

Note: + indicates a positive effect; – indicates a negative effect; 0 indicates inconsistent or insignificant effect.

FIGURE 8.1 Institutions and their effects on coalition politics in post-communist democracies

that have defined the course of the East Central European political tradition; the impact of Euro–Atlantic integration and the particular impact of the gradually deepening ties with the European Union; important and often colorful and controversial personalities are some of the other additional variables that would have to be included in telling the complete story of party politics in the region. However, telling such a complete story was not the purpose of this book. Instead, my focus was on gaining analytical leverage by concentrating on political institutions, which are well-known to constitute an important source of the incentives that motivate the actions and behavior of political parties, and political actors in general, precisely because in spite of their many historical, sociological and cultural commonalities, the ten post-communist democracies have varied so sharply and markedly in terms of the kinds of political institutions they adopted and sustained after the fall of communism. In other words, an institutionalist perspective should help us understand why patterns of party coalitions in the new democracies of East Central Europe have differed in a patterned fashion even though these societies have had in common so many important social and cultural developments.

At the same time, as I indicated in Chapter Two political institutions never emerge in a historical or sociological vacuum. In fact, the adoption of the new constitutions and electoral laws has been always shaped and informed by, negatively or positively, the historical memory of pre-communist traditions; the immediate legacy of the communist era; the emulation of foreign, i.e. West European, models of government; as well as the more short-term interests and rationality of the actors involved in institutional design. In other words, the choice of specific political institutions, the constitutions and electoral systems that get adopted at any one time, always reflect the dynamically changing nature of the relationship between long-term historical, socially, and culturally defined trends and the shorter-term instrumentally motivated forces. As such, privileged attention to political institutions can never completely abstract away from non-institutional forces and variables since they always reflect and embody them. Indeed, an important reason why political institutions are sticky and immune to frequent radical change is precisely because they reflect the slowly emerging and changing nature of the society that they are designed to govern.

An important question that needs to be addressed at the concluding stage of the book has to do with the relevance and implications of my findings for other parts of the world where new democratic systems of government are being designed and established. In other words, are the findings of this research conditioned by the fact that these new democracies are in Europe and that they have emerged on the ashes of communist, as opposed to other types of, authoritarian political regimes or can we expect them to be universally applicable and replicable? There is no unequivocal answer to this question. On the one hand, since I have focussed singularly on post-communist democracies, my research design does not allow for proper testing and appreciation of the effects of either the temporal or the spatial context of democratic institutionalization. This is the trade-off that one must face when adopting a research design that seeks to tease out reasons for variation among otherwise contextually very similar cases. As such, the findings are, by definition, unique and limited to the post-communist region. On the other hand, if we ask a different question, one that seeks to identify the conditions under we could imagine such or similar findings to be replicated, then the answer is very different. For even though the political institutions that were inherited and adopted at the outset of democratization in the early 1990s had, at least in part, been borrowed from or constituted a reaction against the institutions that had been in place in the immediate communist or the earlier pre-communist eras, are the unique products of specific moments and choices in the national history of each country, I have conceptualized and categorized them as variables precisely to ensure that their effects can be compared with other cases both in space and time. Therefore, we can easily imagine that a new democracy with a parliamentary, or at most a premier-presidential system of government, that adopts a PR or mixed electoral system, with strong bias in favor of the proportional elements, should witness the development of patterns of party and coalition governments that are extremely similar to those in the ten East Central European cases I have covered in this book. However, as we know from the comparative democratization literature the institutional combination of PR and parliamentarism remains a somewhat unique property and characteristic of these new European democracies.

Do any of these arrangements help promote a better system of parliamentary democracy? To the extent that an ideal parliamentary democracy and an ideal party government includes: (i) a combination of elections where meaningful choices are offered to the voters via more or less clearly defined government alternatives; (ii) the formation of governments that command a clear majority in the legislature and thus give full articulation to the principle of majority rule; (iii) the formation of stable governments; and (iv) same party or coalition control over the head of government and the head of state, I maintain that the most desirable institutional mix consists of an electoral system with a relatively small district magnitude using a restrictive electoral formula; a unicameral legislature with positive investiture rules of government formation and an overall weak presidency elected by the legislature using a voting system that enhances the chances of success by the incumbent coalition. These institutions share an important common characteristic: they concentrate rather than disperse or divide political power and in so doing they encourage a clear articulation of majority rule and promote strong party and coalition government.

APPENDIX A

The Development of Post-Communist Electoral Systems

THE STABLE ELECTORAL SYSTEMS OF THE BALTICS

Latvia

Article 6 of the Latvian constitution protects the fundamental PR character of the electoral system, which, similarly to Estonia and Lithuania, had important historical precedents from the inter-war period (Royal Institute of International Affairs 1938: 41).

The electoral system of post-communist Latvia has remained very stable since the transition to democracy and the election of the first democratic *Saeima*. The two main changes that have taken place concern the length of the term of the legislature, which was increased from three to four years in December 1997, and the increase in the nominal threshold for candidate lists from 4 percent to 5 percent in time for the 1995 elections (Rose and Munro 2003: 195–6).

Latvia uses a high magnitude open-list PR system. Candidate lists may be nominated by registered political parties or associations of political parties. Voters can support only one list; however, they can indicate positive or negative preference votes for as many candidates on the list as they like. The final candidate position on the list is decided entirely on the basis of these preference votes (Pettai and Kreuzer 1999: 177). Although an amendment to the electoral law in March 1998 banned electoral coalitions, legally registered association or unions of political parties were able to submit candidate lists (Pettai and Kreuzer 1999: 178). Thus, for example, the coalition of the National Harmony Party and the Economic Rebirth did not qualify for the ballot as a coalition and had to run its candidates as a crypto coalition under the National Harmony label in the election of 1998.

The country is divided into five electoral districts with an average magnitude of twenty seats. However, actual district magnitude varies considerably across the five units given that their magnitude is determined by the distribution of the voting population. For instance, in the election of 2010, the smallest district (Kurzme with thirteen seats) had less than half of the largest districts (Riga with twenty-nine and Vidzeme with twenty-seven seats). Seats are allocated among the qualifying lists, those above the threshold, by using the Saint Lague formula. Seats among candidates on a qualifying list are allocated in a descending order of candidate ranking that takes into account both the negative and the positive preferences indicated by the voters.

Estonia

The principal of PR is enshrined in the current Estonian constitution (Article 60) and it also follows established historical precedent in the country (Royal Institute of International Affairs 1938: 41–51). Elections between 1919 and 1938 were held according to different versions of PR and it was only in 1938 that a majority system was introduced for a very brief period to elect the Chamber of Deputies (National Electoral Committee 2012: 24). The Estonian electoral system is a genuine hybrid of personal and party list votes that allocates parliamentary seats in three tiers. In its essence, the electoral system has not been altered since 1992, however two changes are worth noting: the number of electoral districts was reduced from twelve to eleven in 1995 and then back again to twelve in 2002; and electoral coalitions were banned as of 1999 (Ishiyama 1996; Rose and Munro 2003: 169; National Electoral Committee of Estonia 2012).

In 1990, Estonia was alone among the democratizing communist states to experiment with the single transferable vote (Grofman, Mikkel and Taagepera 1999). However, the results were disappointing and the system was quickly abandoned in favor of a new rule that was unparalleled among the new European democracies in terms of its complexity as well as the perversity of its consequences. The new electoral system established twelve districts with their magnitude ranging from five to thirteen. Voters had to cast their support for one candidate. Candidates received a seat only if they secured a full Hare quota. Of the 101 seats in the *Riigikogu*, these so-called "personally elected" deputies accounted for only seventeen in 1992, fifteen in 1995, eleven in 1999, and fourteen in 2003 (Pettai 2004: 831). Unused remainder votes are pooled by party lists, which could receive additional seats in the districts for each full Hare quota. The number of seast allocated at this second tier has been steadily increasing with every election: twenty-four in 1992, thirty-four in 1995, forty-four in 1999, and sixty in 2003. The third tier of seat allocation takes place among party lists that receive at least 5 percent of the total nationwide vote. These seats are allocated among closed national party lists using a modified d'Hondt formula with its divisors raised to the power of 0.9 (Grofman, Mikkel and Taagepera 1999: 238). Although the number of candidates elected with these compensation mandates was very high in the first two elections (sixty in 1992 and fifty-two in 1995), their numbers have gone down to forty-six in 1999 and twenty-seven in 2003 (Pettai 2004: 831).

An interesting and perverse feature of the Estonian electoral system is that it allows a candidate with very few personal votes to be elected by virtue of being on the same party list as a candidate who receives a much larger number of personal votes. In the Estonian context this phenomenon is called the Toomepuu effect after Juri Toomepuu, a candidate who ran for the Estonian Citizen electoral coalition in the 1992 polls. Toomepuu received the highest number of personal votes of all candidates (16,904) which allowed the coalition both to pick up three district mandates and cross the 5 percent threshold of to get additional compensation mandates. One of the candidates of the Estonian Citizen who clearly benefitted from Toomepuu's popularity was Toivo Uustallo who actually got elected in spite of receiving the fewest personal votes (fifty-two) of all candidates running (National Electoral Committee 2012: 25–6). Understandably, the Toomepuu effect has been among the most criticized features of the Estonian electoral system which has resulted in a couple of changes that aimed to restrict it. In 1994, an amendment was passed to the Riigikogu Election Act to stipulate that a candidate had to secure at least 10 percent of the Hare quota in person votes in order to be eligibel to obtain a district mandate (National Electoral Committee 2012: 29). In 2004 this percentage was lowered to 5 percent; however, the number of mandates that could be won at the district level was increased by giving an extra seat to each party whose remainders were at least 75 percent of the Hare quota (National Electoral Committee 2012: 30).

Apart from limiting the Toomepuu effect, changes to the Estonian electoral system have also focussed on limiting the formation of electoral coalitions. In an apparent attempt to strengthen political parties and help them become the principal actors in the electoral process, the 1994 amendment to the Election Act provided that only political parties could form electoral coalitions; this was followed by another amendment, passed in November 1998 to ban electoral coalitions altogether (National Electoral Committee 2012: 26, 29). In February 1999, the law was further changed to stipulate that each electoral list could only form one parliamentary group. These amendments were supposed to encourage the formation of genuine political parties at the expense of opportunistic alliances and sought to stabilize the parliamentary party system (ODIHR 1999: 4).

Lithuania

Similarly to Hungary, Lithuania has also used a mixed-member electoral system for every post-communist election to the national legislature. In contrast to the Hungarian electoral law, however, the nominal and the PR tiers of the Lithuanian electoral system are parallel; in other words the result of the election in either tier has no impact on the calculation of the result in the other. Although the basic features of the system have been stable, two important changes took place over time: the threshold was increased before the 1996 election and the two-round majority formula was replaced with the first-past-the-post system in the nominal tier in 2000, only to be reversed by 2004.

The electoral system that was introduced for the first post-communist election in 1992 stipulated that nearly half of the 141 seats (seventy-one) in the *Seimas* were elected from single-member constituencies using a two-round majority system, while the other half are elected from party list votes using the Hare quota. In addition to political parties, interest groups and political movements are allowed to nominate lists of candidates, which voters could alter by indicating both their positive and negative preferences. Although parties could technically choose to present closed lists, evidence suggests that they normally refrain from doing so (Clark, Martinatis and Dilba 2008: 323; Pettai and Kreuzer 1999: 177, n. 43).

Furthermore, parties were subject to a nominal 4 percent threshold, while registered ethnic parties had to clear only 2 percent. The conversion of votes to seats in the PR tier was calculated by the Hare quote rule with the proviso that the final ranking of candidates was based on the weighted average of the voters' preference votes and the official party ranking. Moreover, the quota was not applied to the total number of votes cast in the election but only to the total number of votes cast for parties that have exceeded the threshold requirement. This modification in the Hare-based calculation was designed to benefit the largest parties (Pettai and Kreuzer 1999: 173).

Prior to 2000, the election of the winning candidate in the nominal tier was decided in a two-round majority contest subject to a minimum turnout requirement of 40 percent (Krupavicius 1997: 543–5). Four years later a number of changes were effected in the structure of thresholds: the nominal threshold for individual parties was increased to 5 percent, a new threshold of 7 percent was also introduced for electoral coalitions, and the 2 percent threshold for ethnic parties was abolished. At the same time, the position of political parties was strengthened as the electoral law gave them the exclusive right to submit candidate lists in the PR tier (Krupavicius 1997: 545).

A short-term change was implemented before the parliamentary election of 2000 providing for the replacement of the two-round majority rule with first-past-the-post, which was supposed to favour the larger political parties (Fitzmaurice 2003: 162; Martinatis 2012). This electoral change, which was passed in the *Seimas* with the barest majority of a single vote, was replaced with the *status quo ante* by the time of the 2004 elections (Jurkynas 2005: 772). The most recent amendment to the electoral system occurred in 2008 establishing that the final ranking of candidates on the party lists was determined solely on the basis of voters' preference ranking which makes the PR lists effectively into an open one (Jurkynas 2009: 330).

PR SYSTEMS WITH LIMITED CHANGE: CZECH REPUBLIC, POLAND, SLOVAKIA AND SLOVENIA

Czech Republic

The first two elections to the first chamber of parliament in the sovereign post-communist Czech Republic were held under a PR system that divided the territory of the Czech Republic into eight multi-member districts. The magnitude of these districts was variable; each region was entitled to as many seats as its contained whole multiples of the national electoral quota, calculated by the dividing the total number of valid votes cast nationwide by the number of seats in the Chamber, 200. Thus, average district magnitude in the Czech Republic (200/8 = 25) was considerably lower than that in Slovakia (150/4 = 37.5), but still high in comparison with Hungary. Voters had to vote for party lists with the option of casting a maximum of four preferential votes for candidates on the list, a feature that was inherited from the federal Czechoslovak electoral law. In a 1995 amendment the electoral system stipulated that preference votes were taken into account only if at least 10 percent of a list's supporters indicated such preferences and that a candidate who secured at least 10 percent of these preference votes would move to the top position on the party's list in a given district. In 2001, this requirement was lowered to 7 percent (Millard and Popescu (n.d.): 9). To qualify for seats in the 200-member Chamber, political parties had to clear a 5 percent national threshold, while electoral coalitions of two, three, four, or more parties had to receive at least 7 percent, 9 percent, and 11 percent of the vote respectively. In the multi-member districts, parties received as many seats as they had full Hagenbach-Bischoff quota; unallocated seats were distributed among parties that cleared the threshold applying the same quota to parties' remainder votes (Cox 1997: 284–5; Rose and Munro 2003: 136).

After a protracted political battle that involved both chambers of parliament, the president, and the Constitution Court, and lasted for almost four years (Kopecky 2004; Nikolenyi 2011), the Czech electoral system was amended in January 2002 in a number of significant ways. First, the eight multimember districts were replaced with fourteen electoral regions, which reduced the average district magnitude by almost one-half (to 14.3). Second, the new system introduced the d'Hondt method of converting votes to seats, which tends to discriminate in favor of larger parties more than the previous quota-based rule. Finally, the threshold for electoral alliances of two, three, and four or more parties were increased to 10 percent, 15 percent and 20 percent, respectively (Crawford 2001: 55; Birch, Millard, Popescu and Williams 2002: 86; Kopecky 2004: 352).

The origins of this electoral reform package can be traced to the surprising conclusion of the famous Opposition Pact between the Czech Social Democratic Party (CSSD) and the Civic Democratic Party (ODS) after the inconclusive parliamentary election of 1998 (Nikolenyi 2003; Roberts 2003). According to the agreement, the ODS pledged its parliamentary support for the formation of a CSSD minority government in exchange for key parliamentary posts as well as a common bi-partisan commitment to constitutional and electoral reform. With regard to the latter, Article Seven of the agreement specified that the two parties "commit themselves to present within twelve months of signing this agreement a proposal of such amendments of the Constitution of the Czech Republic and other laws that . . . in harmony with the constitutional principles of the Czech Republic strengthen the significance of the outcome of the competition of political parties" (Roberts 2003: 1302). While the article clearly implied that the coalition partners sought to write a new electoral law that would privilege them in the allocation of seats after future elections (Birch, Millard, Popescu and Williams 2002: 80), the call for a constitutional amendment also suggested that the coalition partners considered the wholesale replacement of PR, which at the time enjoyed constitutional entrenchment (Article 18/1). However, the prospects for an outright abolition of PR vanished when the CSSD and the ODS lost their requisite three-fifths majority in Senate by-elections in the spring of 1999.

In the absence of a qualified majority, the CSSD and the ODS proposed such changes to the status quo electoral system that would seemingly not alter its PR character (Crawford 2001). For its part, the ODS proposed to reduce the number of seats in the Assembly from 200 to 162; to increase the number of districts from eight to thirty-five; retaining the 5 percent threshold but replacing the Hagenbach-Bischoff with the Imperiali quota. The CSSD agreed with the drastic increase in the number of districts, however, it proposed to leave the size of the Assembly intact and to replace the Hagenbach-Bischoff quote with the d'Hondt highest average formula. The parties eventually arrived at a compromise and passed legislation on May 26, 2000, to increase the number of electoral districts to thirty-five, leave the size of the Assembly intact but adopt the d'Hondt formula, and increasing the threshold for electoral alliances of two, three, four, or more parties to 10 percent, 15 percent and 20 percent, respectively (Kopecky 2004: 352).

In spite of his earlier support for a single-member majoritarian electoral system, President Havel vetoed the electoral reform bill on the grounds that it violated the constitutional protection of the principle of PR (Birch, Millard, Popescu and Williams 2002: 83). Indeed, it was obvious that the proposed electoral system was PR only in form but majoritarian in its mechanical operation; reports showed that if the proposed electoral system had been used to decide the outcome of the 1998 elections, the CSSD would actually have won a narrow single-party majority in the Chamber of Deputies, while the smaller parties would have lost significantly (Birch, Millard, Popescu and Williams 2002: 82; Roberts 2003: 1289). Although the CSSD–ODS coalition overturned the presidential veto and re-passed the bill, President Havel referred the bill to the Constitutional Court, which struck it down in January 2001 in all but one respect: the Court allowed to leave the new threshold structure in place (Crawford 2001: 55; Kopecky 2004: 352). Upon the initiative of the CSSD, a new bill was passed in both houses of parliament in January 2002 to increase the number of districts moderately from eight to fourteen and adopted the d'Hondt formula. Thus, PR was eventually saved albeit in a modified form at the end of the protracted battle over electoral reform.

Poland

Although Poland has had three different electoral systems in place since 1991, each of them was a variant of a basic open-list PR system. The first electoral system was born out of an intense battle among political parties in the transitional *Sejm* and the Senate, both elected in the partially free elections of 1989, and President Walesa (Birch, Millard, Popescu and Williams 2002: 34–8). Although the president enjoyed considerable advantage over the *Sejm* in terms of legitimacy, due to his direct election to the office as opposed to the partially elected contractual status of the *Sejm*, he could not impose his preferred option, which was a mixed system with a closed-list nationwide PR constituency (Birch, Millard, Popescu and Williams 2002: 36).

The electoral system that was eventually passed by parliament and, after successive failed vetoes by President Walesa, allocated the 460 Sejm seats at two tiers. First, 391 seats were elected and filled in thirty-five open-list PR multimember districts, the magnitude of which ranged from seven to seventeen. There was no threshold percentage of votes that parties had to win in order to qualify for seats in these multimember districts. Voters had to indicate their support for a candidate of their choice on the party list that they supported. The votes cast were converted to seats by using the Hare-Niemayer largest remainder rule. The remaining sixty-nine seats constituted the second tier and these were to be allocated among parties' closed national lists. In order to qualify for a second tier seat, a party had to win at least 5 percent of the national vote. These seats were allocated according to the Saint-Lague method. The electoral system produced a highly fragmented Sejm, in which political parties found themselves incapable of forming durable governing coalitions. Within less than two years of its election, three cabinets succeeded one another eventually paving the way for the premature dissolution of the legislature and the holding of fresh general elections.

A new electoral system that was adopted by the Sejm just in time for the 1993 elections introduced four major changes, each intended to make it increasingly more difficult for smaller parties to win seats:

1) it imposed a threshold of 5 percent on individual parties and 8 percent on coalitions of parties nationwide;
2) it increased the threshold for national lists from 5 percent to 7 percent;

3) it increased the number, from thirty-seven to fifty-two, and slightly decreased the average magnitude of the multimember districts by extending their range from three to seventeen, as opposed to seven to seventeen;
4) it replaced the Hare-Niemayer and Sainte-Lague methods with the d'Hondt rule of seat allocation, which uses highest averages as opposed to the largest remainders (Jasiewicz 1994: 403).

Although the new electoral system clearly remained a variant of PR, it was more restrictive than the rules that governed the 1991 election. The adoption of this more restrictive PR reflected the seat maximizing preferences of political parties at the time: the five largest parties in the Sejm were in favor of the introduction of the d'Hondt rule, smaller districts and higher thresholds while the smaller parties opposed these amendments (Birch, Millard, Popescu and Williams 2002: 40; Benoit and Hayden 2004: 412–4). The key actor in the promulgation of the 1993 electoral system was the Extraordinary Commission of the Sejm, which was formed following the first reading of a bill submitted by the Democratic Union, to introduce a mixed system. The Commission decided to keep the fundamental commitment to PR; retain the national list but increase its threshold to 7 percent; increase threshold for political parties and electoral coalitions to 5 percent and 8 percent, respectively; and introduce the d'Hondt formula. The basic spirit of the amendments was to reduce the fragmentation of the party system to ensure that the kind of divided parliament that was produced in 1991 would not be repeated. Since there was a consensus on this basic commitment among the political parties, the Commission's proposals were adopted by the Sejm with the exception of two provisions: the Sejm voted to keep the party lists open and to increase the national list threshold to 7 percent instead of 8 percent (Birch, Millard, Popescu and Williams 2002: 39–41).

Although the same electoral system remained in place for the 1997 elections it is worth taking note of a constitutional change that had bearing on the electoral system as well as the two concrete attempts that took place trying to change it in favor of a more proportional variant PR. In April 1997 the new Polish constitution was adopted, following several years of uncertainty and negotiations that eventually resulted in a weakening the powers of the presidency in favor of the Sejm and the prime minister. In addition, Article 96/2 of the new constitution enshrined that elections to the Sejm had to be proportional, which would limit the scope of future changes to the fundamental nature of the electoral system. During the 1993–7 parliamentary term there were attempts at amending the electoral system, however neither of them aimed at unmaking its essential PR character. Towards the end of 1996, PSL, which was both the second largest party in the Sejm and the junior partner in the SLD–PSL governing coalition, submitted a bill to replace the d'Hondt formula with the more permissive Saint Lague divisor (Benoit and Hayden 2004: 417). Due to parliamentary recess the bill expired and was not actually voted upon. A few months later, a similar bill was proposed by the small Labor Union seeking to change the d'Hondt rule to a modified Saint Lague divisor.

Thanks to the joint opposition of the largest party in parliament, the SDL, as well as the small right and center-right parties that had already formed the AWS, a new umbrella organization that was expected to and eventually did win a landslide victory in the 1997 election, the bill was defeated. On June 27, 1997, a minor amendment was passed to the electoral system requiring the support of 1,000 voters for the official registration of a political party (Benoit and Hayden 2004: 417).

The most recent major revision of the Polish electoral system was passed by the Sejm in March 2001 following an inter-party debate that lasted for almost two years. The process to revise the electoral rules once again was prompted by the creation of new provinces, which technically implied that the boundaries of electoral districts would have to be redrawn as well (Birch, Millard, Popescu and Williams 2002: 41). Responding to this opportunity, the four largest parliamentary parties (AWS, SLD, UW, and PSL) submitted their separate proposals with two different versions coming from two constituent parties of the AWS. The most modest change was proposed by the largest opposition party, the SLD, which according to the polls was expected to win the next elections under the current system: the party sought a modest increase in district magnitude and wanted national list seats to be allocated to the parties with the most district victories. Initially, the AWS proposals also wanted to keep the d'Hondt system; however the party's two proposals differed with regard to the changes proposed in district magnitude and the national list, which one of them wanted to eliminate altogether. Both smaller parties (UW and PSL) wanted larger districts and some version of the Saint-Lague divisor to replace the d'Hondt system but they differed on whether or not to keep the national lists.

The results and the aftermath of the presidential election of October 2000 led to a change in the AWS's position on electoral reform, which ultimately sealed the outcome in favor of the proposal of the small parties seeking more proportionality. The presidency was won by the incumbent A. Kwasniewski, which, together with polls suggested and SLD victory in the imminent Sejm elections, brought the other parties together in a coalition that sought to limit the electoral gains of the emerging largest party. Indeed, the Sejm vote on the electoral reform bill held on March 7, 2001, was a bipolar division between the SLD and the three non-SLD parties (Birch, Millard, Popescu and Williams 2002: 44–5). The AWS had switched its position in favor of the small party proposals that aimed to eliminate national lists, create higher district magnitudes and re-introduce the Saint-Lague formula (Benoit and Hayden 2004: 422). Therefore, the Polish electoral system was changed once again reversing some of the disproportionalities that had been introduced by the reform of 1993. The 2001 electoral system eliminated the national list and allocated all 460 seats in the Sejm on the basis of electoral results in the local districts. The modified Sainte-Lague formula was re-introduced and M was increased slightly to 11.2 by reducing the number of electoral districts to forty-one.

Slovenia

Slovenia's PR system has changed in two important ways since the transition to democracy. The first electoral reform, in 1992, changed the number and magnitude of electoral districts; the second electoral reform, in 2000, changed the ballot from a closed to an open list. The PR system that was in effect in 1990 featured fourteen multi-member districts, with magnitudes ranging from three to seven, electing a total of seventy-eight deputies, while the PR system that came into effect for the 1992 election provided for eight multi-member districts, each of them with a magnitude of eleven, electing a total of eighty-eight deputies (Rose and Munro 2003: 294–5).[1] This change in the PR system doubled the average district magnitude in Slovenia, moving it from 5.57 in 1990 to eleven in 1992. In addition to district magnitude, the new PR system had one additional important new element. In 1990, political parties received seats for full Hare quotas in the districts with unallocated seats redistributed at the national level on the basis of the d'Hondt rule subject to meeting a threshold of 2.5 percent of the national vote. The new PR system introduced in 1992 replaced this threshold and made the reallocation of unallocated seats subject to parties' receiving at least three seats in two or more of the multi-member districts.

Although the terms of the new electoral system were defined by legislation, the Law on the Electoral System, the constitution specified that changes in the electoral system required a qualified two-thirds majority in the National Assembly. In conjunction with the kind of electoral system that guaranteed a fragmented multi-party parliament, this constitutional provision made future electoral reform via the parliamentary process very difficult (Nikolenyi 2011). Yet, one important electoral reform was effected before the parliamentary elections of 2000. Previously, voters cast their support for one of the competing candidate lists with no possibility to alter the order of candidates. Since 2000, however, voters indicate their support for a single candidate. Seats are allocated among parties in the order of the pooled vote totals of their candidates using the Droop quota (Rose and Munro 2003: 294). As before, lists receive a seat for each full Droop quota contained in their vote totals in the districts with the remainder votes being reallocated among the lists using the d'Hondt rule. Furthermore, the reform of 2000 also changed the threshold of representation from three seats to 4 percent of the total national vote (Toplak 2006: 826).

Similarly to the Czech Republic and Poland (after 1997), Slovenia has also constitutionalized its electoral system. This constitutional entrenchment of PR was the result of an almost four-year long political struggle to replace the electoral system with majoritarian alternatives. The opening for this debate was provided by a Constitutional Court ruling in January 1996 that obliged the National Assembly to amend the electoral law. According to the Court, the status quo electoral system did not comply with the constitutional requirement of *direct* elections to the National Assembly because political parties' lists of candidates were not made available to the voting population in advance of the polls. (Fink-Hafner 2008: 12). In response to the Court' decision, the small opposition Social Democratic Party, which had only won 4.4 percent of the seats in the previous elections, took up the cause of advocating a two-round majority rule in single-member districts. Small parties are usually not in favor of majoritarian electoral systems. In this case, however, the Social Democrats calculated that a run-off electoral system would help it consolidate the Slovenian Spring Alliance, a new partisan bloc that it had formed earlier with the center-right Christian Democratic and the Slovenian Peoples' parties (Fitzmaurice 1997: 405; Matic 2000: 78).

The Slovenian constitution requires a two-thirds parliamentary majority in order to change the electoral law. Since the combined seat share of the three parties that made up the Spring Alliance was very far from this legislative strength, the Social Democratic Party decided in April 1996 to force the issue to be decided by a referendum. In order to do so, the party had to collect the signatures of at least forty thousand voters because Article 90 of the constitution allowed the National Assembly to call a referendum only if one was demanded either by this number of electors or by at least one-third of the deputies. The Social Democrats barely started their signature campaign when a group of thirty-five deputies, also submitted their own demand for a referendum. However, this group wanted the electorate to vote not on the Social Democrats' proposed majoritarian run-off formula but their own modified PR system. Furthermore, almost immediately, the National Council, the second chamber of parliament, also passed its own resolution to call a referendum, which Article Ninety-Seven of the constitution allows, to decide on its own preferred alternative electoral system, a German-style mixed-member rule (Fink-Hafner 2008: 13). As a result of these heresthetic manoeuvres, the Social Democrats' majoritarian run-off proposal lost the center stage in the debate on electoral reform. The public was no longer presented with a binary choice between the status quo PR and the run-off rule. Instead, three alternative reform proposals were launched against the status quo, which increased the likelihood of its stability.

The referendum on the question of alternative electoral reforms eventually took place a month after the general elections, in December 1996. Due to the combination of low electoral turnout (38 percent), a very divisive ballot with three questions on different electoral systems, and lack of clarity on how the results would be interpreted, the referendum failed to change the status quo. Of the three electoral systems that were proposed on the ballot, the majority run-off system sponsored by the Social Democrats received by far the largest number of Yes votes (44 percent), followed by modified PR (26 percent), with the mixed-member proposal trailing at the end (14 percent). However, since majority support was not demonstrated for any of the proposals, the referendum could not alter the status quo. Yet, the issue of electoral reform did not disappear from the political agenda. Two years later, in October 1998, the Constitutional

Court issued a proactive abstract review in which it declared that the winner of the referendum was the proposed majority system that clearly received a plurality support from the electorate (Matic 2000: 79). Accordingly, the Court instructed the Assembly to pass a new electoral law. In the tumultuous landscape of Slovenia's third post-communist parliament, however, no such legislation could be passed. What parties eventually agreed on, in July 2000, was an amendment to the Constitution stating that "deputies . . . are elected according to the principle of proportional representation with a four percent threshold required for election to the National Assembly, with due consideration that voters have a decisive influence on the allocation of seats to the candidates" (Article 80/5).

Slovakia

The fundamental characteristics of Slovakia's electoral system have not changed since the first election in 1994: the country uses high-magnitude PR with the possibility of preferential voting. However, two important changes did take place over time. First, the electoral reform of 1998 created a single nation-wide constituency with higher thresholds imposed on electoral coalitions. Second, the preferential element of the vote was strengthened in 2006.

As in the Czech Republic, Slovakia's initial electoral system was inherited from before the Velvet Divorce (Birch, Millard, Popescu and Williams 2002: 68–72). It featured four large electoral districts with an average district magnitude of 37.5. The actual number of seats per district, however, varied according to the rate of electoral turnout in each. In particular, district magnitude was calculated by dividing the total number of votes cast in the entire country by 150, the number of seats in the parliament, in order to obtain the so-called republican mandate number. In turn, the valid votes cast in each of the four electoral regions were counted and the number was divided by the republican mandate number. The product defined the number of seats that each region was entitled to in that election. In other words, each region had a district magnitude equal to the whole multiples of the republican mandate number contained in its vote total. As a result of this method, there was considerable variation in the actual magnitude of the four districts: the smallest district returned eleven members followed by forty-two, forty-six, and fifty-one in the other three, respectively. In order to qualify for parliamentary representation, parties had to receive at least 5 percent of the vote; the actual vote totals were converted to seats using the Hagenbach-Bishcoff rule. Electoral coalitions were allowed; however, they faced a differentiated threshold structure: coalitions of two or three parties faced a threshold of 7 percent, while coalitions of four or more parties had to clear a 10 percent threshold. The electoral system also provided for four preferential votes per voter, reduced to three by 2002 (Krivy 2003: 75). However, a candidate's position on the party list would change, in the order of the number of preferential votes received, only if at least 10 percent of the voters supporting that list indicated a preference.

The electoral reform of 1998 was initiated by the coalition government of the HZDS, ZRS, and SNS that had come to power after the 1994 elections. At first, the senior coalition partner, the HZDS, preferred the introduction of a single-member majority based electoral system; however, it had to give up this position very quickly when its two junior partners threatened to leave the government in protest (Birch, Millard, Popescu and Williams 2002: 75; Haughton 2005: 67). The actual reform bill that was supported by all three coalition partners and was voted into law just a few months before the next election replaced the four electoral regions with a single nationwide constituency and it changed the way the electoral threshold was applied by stipulating that each member of an electoral coalition must also meet the 5 percent national threshold individually. In essence, this rendered the formation of electoral inter-party cartels and alliances ineffective for the purposes of threshold insurance. Instead, it encouraged smaller political parties that would be unable to meet the threshold on their own to pool their resources, merge and present themselves as a united entity for electoral purposes (Birch, Millard, Popescu and Williams 2002: 77–8).

Although the adoption of the single nationwide constituency was a move towards greater proportionality, the opposition parties, most of them very small at the time the law was passed, protested the de facto abolition of electoral coalitions. Following major international condemnation of the new electoral system that was widely regarded as a move by the Meciar government to keep the opposition perpetually fragmented, as well as an order of the constitutional court in March 1999 which struck down a number of provisions of the new law, the SDK governing coalition that replaced the Meciar government in 1998 elections reversed the changes in the threshold structure and reintroduced the earlier graduated model. Subsequent attempts at further changes to the electoral system failed until a relatively minor piece of legislation was passed in 2006 to reduce the percentage of preference votes needed to alter a party's candidate list from 10 percent to 3 percent (Rybar 2007: 699–700).

LIMITING PROPORTIONALITY: BULGARIA, HUNGARY AND ROMANIA

Hungary

Hungary adopted a rather complex mixed-member electoral system that allocates 386 parliamentary seats at three tiers. The first tier consists of 176 seats, which are filled by the winners of plurality run-off elections in single member districts. The second tier comprises 152 seats that are elected from twenty multimember regional districts. The magnitude of these districts ranges from four to twenty-eight, with an average of 7.6. Regional list seats are awarded only to those parties that cross a 5 percent nationwide threshold (raised from 4 percent after the 1990 election). The threshold is greater for political parties that run common or connected lists. For a joint or connected list of two parties the threshold is 10 percent; for more than two political parties the threshold is 15 percent. Any member of a connected list that fails to cross the 5 percent threshold is omitted from further consideration and may not receive list seats. The same rule applies to connected lists as well.

The allocation of the regional list seats is carried out in two steps by a modified version of the Droop largest remainder rule. First, in each multimember district, the number of total and valid votes cast is divided by M + 1, which yields the quota. Each party receives a seat for every whole multiple of the quota that its district-level vote total contains. Under the pure Droop rule, unawarded seats are allocated to party lists in descending order of their remainders. In Hungary, however, this is modified in that remainders are eligible for seats only if they are above two-thirds of the original quota. Any seat that remains vacant as a result of parties not having large enough remainders to win them under the two-thirds rule is transferred to the final, the national tier of seat allocation.

The last tier of seat allocation takes place at the national level. At least fifty-eight seats plus any more that were left unawarded at the regional level are allocated among national lists submitted by political parties. According to the threshold requirement, only the national lists of those parties are eligible for national list seats that have crossed the threshold. Parties are allowed to submit common national lists or connect their national lists for the purposes of seat allocation. However, in order to submit a national list, a party must have submitted regional lists in at least seven regions. Seats are distributed among the eligible national lists by using the d'Hondt rule. Voters do not directly vote for the national lists; instead, national lists receive seats on the basis of the surplus votes that they had received in the first valid round of elections. More precisely, the vote total of each national list is calculated by adding the number of votes that the party submitting the national list received in the first round of those single member districts where the party's candidate failed to win as well as those regional lists votes which were not awarded seats.

The Hungarian electoral system remained by and large intact until a comprehensive reform was effected by the FIDESZ–KDNP government in the aftermath of their landslide victory in the 2010 elections. Soon after the polls closed, the parliamentary party groups of the two coalition partners submitted an electoral reform bill (T/18) on May 17, 2010. The same day, seven MSZP deputies submitted Bill T/20, which the Socialist Party had already tried to pass in the previous parliament once before. The two bills brought to light the contrasting and conflicting visions of the two main parties, FIDESZ and MSZP, with regard to the type of electoral system that Hungary should have. The only point on which both bills agreed was the size of the assembly, which both bills proposed to reduce to about half of the current number of seats: the FIDESZ–KDNP bill proposed a 198-seat parliament while the MSZP bill recommended 199. Bill T/18 preserved the main features of the mixed electoral system. It sought to give each voter two votes, which could be cast for candidates in individual districts and a closed national party list. The proportion of nominal and list tier seats were to be divided exactly as they were under the status quo system, i.e. 45 percent of the seats (ninety) are allocated to single-member districts, 40 percent (seventy-eight) to party list seats, and 15 percent (thirty) to a compensatory tier. In contrast to the previous system, however, the single member district contrast would be governed by the first-past-the-post rule and territorial party lists would be replaced by a national list. The parties justified the proposed abolition of territorial lists on grounds of proportionality: they claimed that with a smaller parliament the number of votes required to win seats in the territorial multi-member districts would be so high that only the large parties would benefit. As for replacing the two-round system with a single-round first-past-the-post in the single member districts, the Bill cites as its rationale the experience of the most recent parliamentary elections where almost with no exception the winning candidate in the first round ended winning the run-off, which therefore becomes redundant.

The allocation of seats in the compensatory tier follows the same process and method (d'Hondt) that is currently in place with the exception that these seats are given the candidates who were nominated by their parties in the nominal or list tier contest but could not win a seat yet. In other words, unlike under the current rules, parties do not submit separate lists for the compensatory tier. To qualify for seats in the list tier, a party list needs to cross the 5 percent threshold (10 percent for two-party and 15 percent for three-party coalitions or more). The allocation of these seats would continue to follow the Hagenbach-Bischoff rule with the proviso to allow parties with at least two-thirds of the quota to qualify.

The successful reform of the Hungarian mixed system followed a series of earlier failed attempts. For example, shortly after the general elections of 1998 the Hungarian Parliament appointed an ad hoc committee with the mandate to provide recommendations about reforming the electoral system (Kern 2001). The committee was made up of two representatives of each of the six political parties that won parliamentary mandates and it worked on the basis of consensus: for any part of the electoral law to change, the consent of five of the six parties was required. The committee started its deliberations on March 16, 1999, and its report was voted upon by Parliament more than two years later on September 3, 2001. The report was defeated by a wide margin of 192 against eighty-eight in favor; the three parties of the governing coalition (FIDESZ, MDF, FKGP) rejected the committee's report while the three opposition parties (MSZP, SZDSZ, and MIEP) supported it.

The next attempt at reforming the electoral system took place after the 2006 parliamentary elections. In June 2006, J. Petreti, Minister of Justice, submitted an electoral reform bill on behalf of the government which proposed a moderate reduction in the number of seats to 298 and reaffirmed the MSZP's, the senior member of the governing coalition, preference for the introduction of a German style mixed system where list votes would determine the overall share of the seats that parties would obtain in parliament using the d'Hondt rule. The threshold would still be 5 percent, however for a joint list of two and more than two parties it would be 10 percent and 15 percent respectively. The list tier of the proposed mixed system was to be made up of closed national lists with the entire country serving as a single large multi-member district. According to the rationale for the bill, the government's central objective was to produce a smaller and cheaper parliament. This objective, however, could not be realized within the framework of the existing electoral system without further increasing the tendency towards disproportionality. While the government gave credit to the status quo electoral law system for producing stable governments in the critical years after the transition to democracy, the bill also stressed that the territorial list component had to be abolished as it unduly limited the proportionality of the system. Moreover, the bill also stressed that the adoption of a one round first-past-the-post system in the nominal tier and the provision that the overall allocation of seats would be driven by parties' list votes would remove the incentive to create pre-electoral coalitions, alliances and would thus prevent the formation of partisan blocs. The bill failed to secure the required two-thirds majority in parliament: with the three opposition parties (FIDESZ, MDF, KDNP) voting against, it only received a simple majority of 192:154 on July 24, 2006, which was not sufficient for passage.

Towards the end of the legislative cycle, the MSZP–SZDSZ government submitted yet another electoral reform bill. Although the electoral system envisioned in the bill was fundamentally different from what had been proposed in 2006, it was based on arguments that had been floated by MSZP politicians before. Bill T/9081 provided for a pure PR system and a significantly reduced parliament of 199 deputies. Indeed, during the parliamentary debates of Bill T/235 in 2006, the electoral reform expert of the MSZP, G. Wiener, argued that the party could imagine supporting a pure PR system as long the size of the assembly was reduced to near 200 or 220 deputies. However, Wiener could not accept the combination of a mixed system with such a drastically reduced parliament, which the opposition parties had supported. The new bill allocated 176 seats among territorial party lists using the existing Hagenbach-Bischoff method and left twenty-three seats to the national compensatory tier where seats would be distributed according to the d'Hondt rule. As in the current system, parties with more than 5 percent of the national vote could qualify for territorial list seats if they received at least two-thirds of the Hagenbach-Bischoff quota of the district. Unallocated seats would be transferred to the compensatory tier. The bill also sought to tighten the rule on electoral coalitions by requiring parties that form a joint list to do so in a uniform fashion in every district. Concurrently with the government bill, four deputies, two from each of the MDF and the SZDSZ, also submitted an alternative electoral reform bill (T/9057) in March 2009. The bill was unusual in that it proposed three alternative electoral systems based on the argument that any of them would satisfy the three objectives that its authors sought to attain simultaneously: to reduce the size of parliament; to achieve greater proportionality between the voters' choice and the composition of parliament; and to make the electoral campaign shorter and cheaper. In order to achieve these objectives, the bill prosed a new mixed system (Version A) and two different PR list systems (Version B/1 and B/2). All three versions set the number of parliamentary seats at 200, proposed a single electoral round, and gave one vote for each voter.

Version A proposed that half of the seats (100) would be filled by the winning candidates from the single member districts using the first-past the-post rule. The second half of the seats was to be allocated among the lists of parties whose candidate received at least 5 percent of the total nationwide vote. The number of list seats that each party would be accorded was calculated by (i) establishing the exact proportion of seats every qualifying party would be entitled to based on their vote total, and (ii) subtracting from this number the seats that a party has already won in the nominal tier. Version B/1 called for the establishment of a single nation-wide electoral district and the allocation of seats among parties with more than 5 percent of the vote using the d'Hondt rule. Version B/2 also proposed a list PR system with the d'Hondt rule; however, it suggested the creation of seven large multi-member districts, with their magnitude ranging from nineteen to fifty-seven, following the boundaries of Hungary's recently created territorial regions. During the committee stage of the legislative process, Versions B/1 and B2 were removed from the bill, however regional boundaries were still used in order to determine the allocation and distribution of single member districts in the country. Eventually, both of these electoral reform bills (T/9057 and T/9081) were defeated on the floor due to the combined opposition of FIDESZ and the KDNP, whose support would have been necessary in order to secure the required two-thirds majority support. Bill T/9081 failed by a margin of 200 in favor to 144 against while T/9057 received 199 votes in favor and 149 abstentions.

Romania

Romania's PR system has undergone frequent changes since the transition to democracy. Although these point to a gradual weakening in the permissiveness of the electoral system, its fundamentally PR character has remained (Pilet and de Waele 2007). Between the first and second post-communist elections to the Chamber of Deputies, the first chamber of parliament, average district magnitude decreased slightly from 9.66 to 7.81, the formula was changed from the Hare quota to the more restrictive d'Hondt divisor, and the nominal threshold increased. The latter continued to increase in 2000 when an executive decree set the minimum share of the vote for parliamentary representation at 5 percent for individual parties, 8 percent for two-party electoral coalitions, and adding an additional 1 percent for each additional party joining the coalition up to a maximum threshold of 10 percent. Overall, these changes point to a gradual weakening in the proportionality of the electoral system; however, with no direct change in its underlying fundamental principle. In addition to the Chamber, the constitution also provides for a president, directly elected in majority run-off system, and a second parliamentary chamber, the Senate, elected in multi-member PR. In 2003, the term of the Romanian presidency was increased to five years, which effectively de-linked elections to the executive and legislative branches of government. Previously, elections to both chambers of parliament and to the presidency were held concurrently.

The most drastic change in the electoral system took place in 2007 and 2008 following an intense fight between Parliament and President Basescu (Nikolenyi 2011). The eventual compromise solution divided the country into 315 single member districts for purposes of elections to the Chamber, and 137 for the purposes of electing the Senate. Voters no longer vote for closed party lists but, instead, for individual candidates who can win the district upon securing a majority of the votes cast. Districts where no majority winner obtained are re-allocated among parties using the d'Hondt formula and subject to a 5 percent threshold. Parties allocate the seats that they qualify for among their candidates in a descending order of their electoral performance in the district where they ran (Coman 2012).

The origins of Romania's electoral reform can be traced to the outcome of the 2004 parliamentary and presidential elections, which was the first to produce a divided executive. Previous elections (1992, 1996, and 2000) always resulted in the same political party capturing both the presidency and the prime ministership. However, in 2004, the presidential race was won by the candidate of the National Liberal Party (PNL), former Mayor of Bucharest T. Basescu, while the prime ministership went to C. P. Tariceanu, the leader of the Democratic Party (PD) that contested the election in alliance with the PNL. As part of his strategy to combat corruption in state institutions and Romanian politics in general, President Basescu advocated the idea of adopting the majority run-off voting system in national elections that were already used at the local level. In doing so, the president drew on his party's earlier support for a candidate-centered *uni-nominal* electoral system that it had proposed in 2000. An interesting feature of this proposal was its populist overtone: the PNL expressed its support for a *uni-nominal* candidate-centered voting system that would increase the power of the electorate at the expense of party leaders by making deputies directly accountable to their constituents. (Birch, Millard, Popescu and Williams 2002: 102–3; Pilet and de Waele 2007: 7).

On March 1, 2007, the parliament defeated the president's request to hold a referendum on the question of electoral reform (*Southeast European Times* March 2, 2007). Souring relations between the president and the prime minister, which were only made worse by the conflict over electoral reform, led to the latter's dismissal of all PNL ministers from the cabinet thus terminating the PNL–PD coalition on April 1. Two weeks later, the parliament voted to suspend the president on grounds of alleged unconstitutional interference with the prime minister's position, which, however, the Constitutional Court did not uphold. Nonetheless, a referendum now had to be held, according to Article Ninety-Five of the constitution, to decide whether the president's impeachment would stay in effect or not. The questions of electoral reform took central stage at this juncture.

Basescu claimed that if winning the referendum he would press ahead with electoral reform and call yet another referendum for November 2007 on the introduction of a *uni-nominal* electoral system and a 20 percent reduction in the size of parliament. Indeed, the President won the impeachment referendum (*Southeast European Times*, May 21, 2007). To counter the president's agenda, the government proposed an electoral reform bill that proposed an electoral system combining a candidate-centered *uni-nominal* vote with compensatory seats to be distributed among national party lists. The president vetoed the bill and referred it to the Constitutional Court on the grounds that its provision for national party lists that were not directly voted for by the electorate violated the principle of popular sovereignty, which was enshrined in the constitution.

The referendum on electoral reform was held concurrently with Romania's first elections to the European Parliament. Although an overwhelming majority of voters supported the presidential initiative, low turnout at 26 percent rendered the referendum inconclusive (*Southeast European Times*, November 27, 2007). Thus, the issue of electoral reform returned to parliament where a compromise was hammered out meeting with the approval of the president and all parliamentary parties with the exception of the extreme-right Greater Romania Party (*International Herald Tribune*, March 4, 2008).

Bulgaria

Post-communist Bulgaria has witnessed two major changes in her electoral system. The Grand National Assembly, which acted as the Constituent Assembly after the fall of communism, was elected in 1990 using a mixed-member electoral system. Half of the 400 deputies were elected from single-member districts under a two-round majority rule, while the other half were elected from thirty-one multimember districts using the d'Hondt rules. Parties presented closed lists of candidates and were subject to a 4 percent threshold. The magnitude of the electoral district varied between three and fourteen (Rose and Munro 2003: 103–4). This electoral system was in effect only for one election and was replaced by the PR tier as of the next legislative election that was held in 1991. As mentioned in the previous chapter, the number of seats in the National Assembly was also reduced from 400 to 240.

Although the closed-list PR system remained in place for the next five elections (Crampton 1997, 1995; Harper 2003; Spirova 2006) it is worth noting that in 1997 there was a failed attempt to lower the threshold to 3 percent and that in 2005 a number of changes were made to the electoral law to subject political parties, coalitions and even Independent candidates to more stringent registration requirements and financial deposits (Spirova 2006: 617). Shortly before the 2009 election a mixed-member system was introduced with the creation of one single-member district in each of the thirty-one multi-member districts using the first-past-the-post rule. The overall number of parliamentary seats remained unchanged, which meant a reduction in the number of PR seats to 209. Although the proposed amendment to the electoral law also stipulated an increase in the threshold for electoral coalitions to 8 percent, the Constitutional Court did not allow it (Spirova 2010: 276). It is important to note that the introduction of the single-member districts did not weaken the central position of political parties in the electoral process for at least two reasons. First, the overwhelming majority of parliamentary deputies were still elected by closed-list PR. Second, the new electoral law also stated that if an elected candidate became a cabinet minister, a position that is incompatible with holding a legislative seat, he/she is replaced by the candidate next in line on the party list. However, nominal seats that are vacated otherwise are replaced through by-elections.

NOTE

1. There are two additional deputies in the National Assembly who represent the Italian and Hungarian minorities of Slovenia. These deputies are elected by members of the two respective communities using the Borda count method.

APPENDIX B

Government Formation Rules in Post-Communist Democracies[1]

VARIATIONS OF POSITIVE PARLIAMENTARISM

Bulgaria

Although the Bulgarian constitution provides the directly elected president with the power of appointing the prime minister (Article 99/1) it also imposes significant constraints on presidential authority. First, the constitution stipulates that the president must appoint as prime minister that person who is nominated by the party that won the plurality of seats in the National Assembly. Should this candidate fail to form a government within a short period of seven days, the president must invite the nominee of the second largest party in parliament who also has seven days to form a council of ministers (99/2). In case of yet another failed attempt at government formation, the president is free to invite a candidate put forward by one of the smaller parties (99/3). Only when a candidate for prime minister succeeds in forming a government does the president of Bulgaria ask the National Assembly to formally elect the person as head of government together with the other ministers (99/4, 84/7). In case all three rounds of government formation prove unsuccessful, the president can appoint a caretaker government and call for fresh parliamentary elections.

Once elected, the prime minister becomes the head of government; however, the Assembly also retains a considerable degree of authority over the cabinet. The hiring and firing of deputy ministers remains the sole prerogative of the head of government (108/2) and the National Assembly can elect and dismiss ministers only upon his/her recommendation (84/6). Moreover, while the Assembly has the legislative power to create new ministries or terminate existing ones, it can only do so upon the proposal of the head of government (84/7). At the same time, the constitution does not allow the inclusion of ministers without portfolio in the council of ministers unless it has passed a resolution to this effect (108/3). A further important limitation on prime ministerial authority is the absence of a constructive no-confidence clause in the constitution. The National Assembly can dismiss the government by passing an ordinary no confidence vote; however, it cannot censure individual ministers. Furthermore, it is only the council of ministers as a collective group, as opposed to the prime minister alone that can rescind an act issued by an individual minister (107).

The constitution makes explicit reference to the scope of the ministerial "selectorate" by providing for the so-called "sleeping mandate," according to which an elected member of the assembly can become a minister; however, during his/her service in government a substitute deputy would have to be provided for (68).

Estonia

The selection of the prime minister and the formation of the government are given detailed description in Article 89 of the constitution. The president of the Republic has two successive opportunities to nominate a person for the position of prime minister. Within fourteen days of such a nomination, the candidate has to present to Parliament the bases on which he/she would proceed to form a government, which is followed by an immediate parliamentary vote to authorize the candidate to proceed. If the vote fails, or if the vote passes but the government formation process fails within seven days, then the entire process is repeated one more time. If the candidate succeeds in forming a government then its members are immediately appointed by the president without further parliamentary input in the process. If, however, no government is formed after the first two attempts, then the right to nominate the prime minister is transferred to parliament. Failure to produce a government on this third trial results in new elections (89/6).

The Estonian prime minister does not command complete authority over his council of ministers. Although changes to the composition in the ministerial team can be effected only upon his proposal to the president (90), parliament can also censure individual ministers by passing a vote of no confidence (97/1). The head of government is also constrained in his ability to re-organize ministries, which can only be created and altered by legislation. However, the prime minister can appoint ministers without portfolio to his cabinet (94/4).

Hungary

The constitution of post-communist Hungary establishes the rules on government formation in its Article 33/3, which states that the prime minister is elected by a majority of the members of parliament upon the recommendation of the president. It is further stated that both the person of the prime minister and the program of the new government are voted upon simultaneously by the legislature. Upon successful passage of this vote, the prime minister recommends ministers to the new government who are in turn appointed by the president (Article 33/4) without any further parliamentary consultation. It is important to stress that the investiture vote calls for a majority of all the 386 members of the newly elected parliament to express a positive consent to the person of the head of government and program that he proposes.

The constitution is also very clear about the consequences of a failed investiture vote. According to Article 28/3b, if parliament does not elect the prime minister who was nominated by the president within forty days after the president made his first such nomination, the head of state can dissolve the legislature and call for new elections. This constitutional provision has not had to be invoked on any single occasion so far, not even in those instances when coalition talks between the formateur and proposed coalition partners appeared to be more protracted than usual. The forty-day period officially starts after the president has made the first formal nomination for prime minister after the election, which means that in cases of apparent deadlock of difficult negotiations, the head of state can wait to offer parties more time to hammer out the details of their coalition bargain. At the same time, the Constitution also allows the president to put pressure on parties, if necessary, for once he has made his recommendation about who the new head of government should be, parties have up to forty days only to arrive at forming a coalition capable of winning the investiture vote or else risk new elections.

The Hungarian constitution is often noted for having created a German style chancellor democracy early on after the transition to democracy. Indeed, the constitution does provide for a very wide scope and range of prime ministerial authority and powers. As mentioned above, ministers are appointed and dismissed by the president on the recommendation of the head of government who is also free to appoint ministers without portfolio. Parliament can pass only a constructive vote of no-confidence (39/A), which further buttress the position of the prime minister. Moreover, since the creation and re-organization of ministries is outside the list of powers reserved for parliament, the prime minister enjoys considerable discretion to re-organize and re-shuffle his cabinet. The constitution does not render the role of the parliamentary deputy incompatible with that of a minister.

Poland

Of the ten post-communist states, Poland has gone through the most extensive constitutional changes with direct effect on the institutional sources of the selection and de-selection of ministers. Articles 57–62 of Small Constitution of 1992 provided for multiple rounds of voting for prime minister involving the president and the Sejm. The first move of the process was given to the head of state who could appoint, as opposed to merely nominating, the prime minister and, on the latter's motion, the members of the new government within fourteen days after the first sitting of the Sejm. The newly appointed government, however, had only another fourteen days to submit its program to the Sejm and receive from it a positive investiture vote. Failure to do so would result in the Sejm receiving the second opportunity to nominate a prime minister and vote him/her as well as member of the new government into office within twenty-one days. Successful passage of this vote obliged the president to appoint the new government into office (Article 58), while a failed investiture vote resulted in the repetition of the entire process. In other words, the president would have one more opportunity to select a prime minister and, in case of a failed parliamentary vote, the Sejm would also have one more chance to select a new head of government within the same time frames as before. In the case of yet another failed vote, the president could either immediately dissolve the Sejm and call for new parliamentary elections or he could appoint a new government which would either have to receive a vote of confidence from the Sejm or survive a no-confidence vote within six months or the chamber would be automatically dissolved (Article 62).

The so-called Small Constitution, which was largely limited to regulating the relationship between the different branches, and levels, of government, was replaced by the new constitution of 1997, which was narrowly passed by a popular referendum in May of that year. The new constitution changed the investiture process in three significant ways. First, it reduced the time frame available to the two major players, i.e. the president and the Sejm, to arrive at an agreement on the new government. While the president still had fourteen days to appoint a new prime minister after the first sitting of the Sejm, the latter would also have the same fourteen-day period, as opposed to twenty-one days under the Small Constitution, to make a counter-nomination in case the president's choice cannot win the investiture vote. Second, the new constitution also limited the Sejm to making only one such counter-nomination, in contrast to two attempts under the Small Constitution. Third, presidential powers were also curtailed by removing the president's discretionary authority to appoint a government, in case of a deadlocked investiture game, which would have to prove its parliamentary support within six months. The new constitution also increases the political costs of deadlock by making it obligatory to dissolve the Sejm immediately and hold new parliamentary elections.

The 1997 constitution significantly increased the authority of the prime minister over his cabinet vis-à-vis the politically powerful presidency in a number of ways. First, while the president was able to appoint three important members of the council of ministers under the Small Constitution (the three presidential portfolios were defence, foreign, and home affairs), the new constitution gave the prime minister the unequivocal right to make changes in his ministerial team, although it still needs the consent of the president. The new constitution also established a constructive no-confidence mechanism; however, the *Sejm* may still censure individual ministers by a regular no confidence vote (159).

The constitution provides a detailed list of offices that are incompatible with that of a parliamentary deputy; however, it explicitly mentions that deputies can be appointed to government (103). Ministers can either be at the head of individual ministries or may perform particular functions assigned by the prime minister (149). The right to appoint such ministers with special tasks, without heading and executive portfolio, further increases the power of the prime minister within the cabinet. Finally, the 1997 constitution also gave the government the right to control its own internal organization, as opposed to making it dependent on legislative authorization (146).

Romania

The directly elected president can designate a candidate for head of government after he has consulted with the majority party in parliament or, absent such a party, with all other parliamentary party groups (Article 103) The prime ministerial candidate has ten days to present his new government and its program for a vote of investiture to both houses of the Romanian parliament that have to vote in a joint session. If two such attempts at investing a prime minister fail or if parliament has not passed a vote of confidence within sixty days after the first nomination was made, the head of state can dissolve the legislature and call for new elections (89/1).

The prime minister enjoys a considerable degree of authority over his government. Although ministries and state institutions can only be created and changed by the legislature (72/3d, h), the head of government can make personal changes in his government without seeking parliamentary approval (85.2). The two houses of parliament can pass a vote of no-confidence only against the government as a whole but not against its individual members (112). Government ministers can be members of either house of parliament; however, they cannot occupy any other public office (104/1). Article 106 reaffirms the authority of the prime minister by stating that he "shall direct Government actions and co-ordinate activities of its members" (106/1).

Slovenia

The constitution of Slovenia provides for a multi-round process of choosing and selecting the prime minister that involves both the president, who is elected directly by the voting population, and the lower house of parliament, the National Assembly (111). The president has the right to nominate to the National Assembly, after he has consulted with political parties represented in parliament, a candidate for prime minister whose appointment is subject to a parliamentary vote of investiture. If this vote fails, then the president can nominate another candidate, who can be the same person, within fourteen days. Should this nomination also prove unsuccessful, parliamentary party groups with at least ten deputies can also put forward their nominees who are voted upon in the order of their nomination. However, if the president wishes to nominate yet another candidate of his or her own choosing then this candidate will be voted upon first by the Assembly. The president can dissolve the Assembly and call for fresh elections in case this third attempt also fails. However, the Assembly can counter the order of dissolution by passing a vote in favor of yet another round of balloting. Failure to choose a head of government on this fourth ballot, however, automatically triggers fresh elections.

Although the Assembly has to vote only upon the person of the prime minister, individual ministers are formally appointed, and dismissed, by the Assembly upon the recommendation of the head of government (112). The Assembly, however, cannot directly dismiss a minister by passing a vote of no-confidence; in fact, the Assembly can only remove the prime minister by passing a constructive vote of confidence against him or her (116). The National Assembly has the power to alter the number and the competency of the various ministries (113). The constitution is silent about the incompatibility of ministerial office with other positions, which leaves the ministerial "selectorate" potentially very wide in its scope.

VARIATIONS OF NEGATIVE PARLIAMENTARISM

Czech Republic

Article 68/2 of the Czech constitution allows the president to appoint the prime minister, and other members of the government upon the latter's motion, without specifying any time limit within which the appointment has to take place. However, once the appointment has been made, the new government has to get a vote of confidence from the Chamber of Deputies within 30 days. In case the government fails to win a confidence vote, the president will appoint yet another government, which would have another thirty days to prove that it enjoyed the confidence of the Chamber. In contrast to Poland, the Chamber, therefore, does not have to power to counter-nominate a prime minister. However, it is important to note that a second failed appointment allows the Chairman of the Chamber (the speaker) to recommend the next candidate for prime minister who in turn is appointed by the President. Should this government also fail to win a confidence vote, the President may dissolve the Chamber of Deputies (Article 35).

The Czech constitution allows the lower house of parliament to pass a vote of no confidence only in the government as a whole but not in its individual ministers (Article 71). While the prime minister must submit his resignation directly to the president, other members of the cabinet have to do so through the prime minister (Article 73). The Chamber of Deputies, however, is entirely removed from the process of effecting or confirming changes in the ministerial composition of the government, which, *ceteris paribus*, strengthens prime ministerial authority. However, the constitution limits the powers of the head of government by stressing that the government resolutions must be passed with the support of an absolute majority of its members (Article 76/2), and that ministries and state agencies can be created only by law duly passed by parliament (Article 79/1).

The constitution allows cabinet ministers to be drawn from the legislature, however it also provides a carefully constructed list of the positions that parliamentary deputy who is also a member of the government cannot occupy. These positions are the chair- and vice-chairmanship of both houses of the Czech parliament, any parliamentary committee or commissions of inquiry (Article 32).

Latvia

The Latvian constitution is the most laconic of all ten constitutions considered. With regard to government formation, it simply states that the person invited by the president should form a government (Article 56). Although parliament (*Saeima*) does not need to pass an investiture vote in the newly appointed government, it can pass a vote of no-confidence in either the entire council of ministers or in its individual members (Article 59). Barring this vote of no-confidence in ministers, the power of the prime minister over his ministers' careers is virtually unconstrained since the constitution is completely silent about other possible ways in which changes can be made to the personnel composition of the government. Parliamentary authority over the government is buttressed by the provision that requires the passage of legislation in order to change either the number of ministries or the scope of their activity and authority (Article 57). Although the constitution does not mention explicitly the incompatibilities that members of the government face, it does make it clear in Article 63, regarding ministerial initiatives, that ministers can but do not have to be members of the legislature.

Lithuania

The selection and appointment of the Lithuanian prime minister is at the discretion of the president. However, the new head of government, whose authority to nominate and choose his ministers is limited only by the provision that members of the government must be members of parliament (Article 60/2), must present to the *Seimas* the program of the government within fifteen days of his appointment (Article 92). If parliament fails to vote on this program within thirty days or if it rejects the program twice within a sixty-day period, then the president of the Republic may call for fresh parliament elections (Article 58/2/1).

The constitution imposes several checks on prime ministerial authority over the government. First, it stipulates that ministers must head individual ministries, which effectively prevents the prime minister from appointing loyal political allies to the government as ministers without portfolio (Article 98). Second, the constitution also requires legislation for changing and establishing ministries, although these can only be done upon the recommendation of the government (Article 67/8). Third, although the prime minister is free to dismiss members of his government, via recommending it to the president, his government must receive a new vote of confidence from the legislature if more than half of the original members of the government have changed (Article 101). Finally, parliament can pass a vote of no-confidence not only in the government as a collective but also in the individual ministers (Article 67/9).

Slovakia

The Slovak constitution is similar to its Czech counterpart in two important ways: the president does not have a specific time limit during which he must appoint the new government, and, second, once appointed the new government must win a confidence vote from the National Council within thirty days (Article 113). In contrast to the Czech case, however, an unsuccessful formation attempt in Slovakia is neither linked to the possibility of dissolving the legislature nor can it be followed by an alternative recommendation coming from the Council. Although it might be worth noting that the inability of the National Council to act on a confidence motion in general does allow the president to dissolve it (Article 102/1b).

Duly elected members of the Slovak National Council are eligible to be appointed as government ministers; however, they cannot exercise their mandate while they hold executive office (Article 77/2). The National Council has significant powers over both the organization and the ministerial composition of the government. First, the establishment of ministries and other state institutions is tied to the passage of relevant legislation (Article 86/f) and, second, the Council can pass votes of no confidence in both the government as a whole as well as in its individual members (Article 86/g). The authority of the prime minister is checked by the provision that allows individual ministers to submit their resignation directly to the president of the Republic rather than to the head of government (Article 116/2).

NOTE

1. Adopted from Fettelschoss and Nikolenyi (2009: 205–12).

APPENDIX C

Electoral Coalitions in Post-Communist Elections

BULGARIA

Electoral coalitions have played an important role in each of Bulgaria's post-communist elections. In 1991, the plurality winner of the election was the Union of Democratic Forces (SDS), a coalition of seventeen constituent parties and organziations opposed to the continued influence of the ex-communist Bulgarian Socialist Party (BSP). The SDS won a near-majority of the seats (45.8 percent) for 34.4 percent of the votes. In 1994, in addition to the SDS another electoral coalition also made a successful entry to the National Assembly; the Popular Union (NS), which was formed by the Democratic Party, two Agrarian factions that had split off from the SDS, the Radical Democratic Party and the United Democratic Center (Crampton, 1995: 239). The two coalitions won 28.7 percent and 7.5 percent of the votes, respectively. Their combined seat share in the new parliament was 36.25 percent.

The 1997 elections were almost entirely dominated by electoral coalitions: of the five formations that crossed the threshold of representation four were electoral coalitions winning a combined total of over 90 percent of both votes and seats. The winner of the election was the ODS, a coalition that was formed the year before the election by the SDS, the BSDP and the NS. Although the DPS initially participated in setting up this coalition, it eventually left it and contested the election leading another alliance, called the National Salvation. Prior to the election, in February 1997, the SDS resolved to transform itself into a political party (Crampton 1997: 561). The ODS won 52.3 percent of the vote and 137 out of the 240 seats. The largest member of the coalition was the SDS followed by the NS which resolved to form its own parliamentary group after the election with fourteen deputies. The outgoing governing party, the BSP, formed an electoral coalition, called the Democratic Left (DL) with its earlier ally, the Ekoglasnost. The third electoral coalition, the Euro-Left Coalition (KE), was formed by a former BSP ally, the BZNS-AS, the Civic Union of the Republic and the Movement for Social Humanism (Crampton, 1997: 562). Finally, the fourth electoral coalition was the National Salvation (ONS) that was spearheaded by the DPS and included also the Green Party, a faction of the Agrarian Union, and the Kingdom of Bulgaria Confederation (Rose and Munro 2003: 107).

The continued dominance of electoral coalitions in the 2001 elections was indicated by the fact that all four formations that entered parliament were such. The near-majority winner of the election was the National Movement Simeon II (NDSV), which contested the race with the Party of Bulgarian Women and the Movement for National Revival. The NDSV, a party that had been founded shortly before the polls by the former monarch returning from exile, was denied registration as an individual political party. However, it could enter the election as a member of a broader coalition, which eventually managed to win 42.7 percent of the vote and exactly 50 percent of the parliamentary seats (Harper 2003: 337). The second largest electoral coalition in the National Assembly was the ODS, which comprised the same three parties as it had in 1997 (the SDS, the BSDP, and the NS) and won 18.2 percent of the votes and 21.25 percent of the seats. The BSP had formed the Coalition for Bulgaria with a number of smaller leftist organziations and parties and grabbed 17.2 percent of the votes and 20 percent of the seats. The remaining seats in the Assembly (8.75 percent) went to a fourth electoral coalition formed by the DPS, the Liberal Union and Euroroma (Harper 2003: 336–8). There were other electoral coalitions running in the election, such as the one formed by the Internal Macedonian Revolutionary Organization and the St. George's Day Movement, however none succeeded in crossing the threshold of representation.

In 2005, two newly formed electoral coalitions entered the race and won seats in the Assembly in addition to the ODS and the Coalition for Bulgaria. The first of these was the coalition "National Union Attack" which brought together three extreme right-wing parties: the National Movement for the Salvation of the Fatherland, the Bulgarian National Patriotic Party, and the Union of Patriotic Forces and Militaries of the Reserve Defence. Similarly to the NDSV four years before, the Attack was denied registration as a political party in time for the elections, which made it necessary to formalize the electoral coalition among the constituent parties. Attack received 8.1 percent and 8.1 percent of the votes and seats, respectively. The second new coalition in the Assembly was the Bulgarian National Union (BNS) formed by BANU, VMRO, and the Union of Free Democrats. The performance of this coalition was more modest as it won only 5.2 percent of the votes and 5.7 percent of the seats (Spirova 2006: 618).

Electoral coalitions scored their weakest performance in the 2009 election as only two smaller formations made it to the Assembly: the Coalition for Bulgaria, winning 16.7 percent of the seats and the newly formed Blue Coalition formed by the SDS, the Democrats for Strong Bulgaria (SDS) and two smaller parties with 6.3 percent of the seats (Spirova 2010: 277).

CZECH REPUBLIC

Political parties formed only one electoral coalition in elections to the Chamber of Deputies, in 2002, and once in elections to the Senate, in 2000. The typical form of electoral coordination has been to form crypto-coalitions whereby political parties would accommodate other parties' candidates on their own lists. In the 2000 Senate election four centrist political parties formed an electoral coalition: the Freedom Union (US), the Christian Democrats (KDU), the Civic Democratic Alliance (ODA), and the Democratic Union (DU). The coalition swept the polls and won seventeen of the twenty-seven seats that were contested. Two years later, following mergers among the four parties, only two parties remained, the KDU and US and these two formed an electoral coalition for the purposes of the Chamber elections in which they secured thirty-one of the 200 seats, eight fewer than what the two parties had been able to win in the 1998 election running separately.

ESTONIA

The institutional restriction of PECs found its most extreme manifestation in the small Baltic state of Estonia. Following in the footsteps of adopting similar legislation for local elections, the *Riigikogu* passed a law on November 17, 1998, banning electoral alliances and coalitions in future national elections (Bugajski: 52; Lagerspetz and Vogt 2004: 64). As a result, political parties were not able to form PECs after the first two post-communist elections, in 1992 and 1995, even though, as we shall see, they did so extensively in both polls. The 1992 election was held under the newly adopted electoral system that replaced the STV system in place for the last communist-era election in 1990 (Grofman, Mikkei and Taagepera 1999). Under the new system, PECs strongly dominated the electoral competition: in 1992, their vote and seat shares stood at 76 percent and 89.1 percent, respectively. Three years later, however, both their vote and seat share dropped to 63.7 percent and 65.3 percent.

Out of the nine formations that won seats in the 1992 election only two were individual political parties, the Estonian National Independence Party (ERSP) and the Estonian Entrepreneurs' Party (EEK), while the others were all coalitions. The largest PEC, in terms vote and seat shares, was Pro Patria (*Isaama*), which consisted of six nationalist and conservative parties.[1] After the national elections, the alliance was transformed into a united political party; however, it never managed to repeat its strong electoral performance in the first election. For the March 1995 elections, the Pro Patria formed a coalition with ERSP, which won 7.9

percent of the votes and only eight seats. Later that year the two parties merged and became the Pro Patria Union (*Isamaalit*).

The next largest PECs in the 1992 polls was the Secure Home (KK) alliance formed by the Coalition Party (EK), the Rural Union (EM), and the Democratic Justice Union (EDO). In 1995, the EK and the EM formed a PEC once more and won forty-one out of the 101 seats in the legislature.[2] The senior party in the both of these coalitions was the EK, which advocated the adoption of liberal market reforms and the cause of European integration. The KK supported the candidacy of Arnold Rüütel in the presidential election of 1992.

The third largest PEC in the 1992 election was the Estonian Popular Front (*Rahvarinne*), a successor to the umbrella organization that had united the various reform oriented groups in the last years of communism (Lagerspetz and Vogt 2004: 61). In 1992, the Front consisted of four parties, the largest of them being the Estonian Center Party (ERK), which remained one of the largest political parties even after the ban on electoral alliances was introduced.[3] Similarly to the outcome of the legislative elections, the Front's presidential candidate, political scientist Rein Taagepera, also finished third place. The fourth PEC that contested both the 1992 and the 1995 elections was the alliance between the Estonian Social Democratic Party (ESDR) and the Rural Center Party (EMK) under the Moderates label. This center-left oriented coalition lost half of the seats between the two elections (from twelve to six). Eventually, these two parties were also joined by the People's Party (PP) in a merger that created the People's Party Moderates (RM).

There were three other smaller PECs represented in the first *Riigikogu*. These were the Independent Royalists (SK)[4], the Estonian Citizens (EK)[5], and the Greens (R)[6] (Lagerspetz and Vogt 2004: 86). Another small PEC that ran in the elections but failed to win a single seat was the Left Alternative (VV) that included the Independent Communist Party. In the 1995 election one small new PEC, the Our Home is Estonia (MKE), which brought together three political parties representing Estonia's Russian-speaking community, was able to win seats in parliament. There were also three other electoral coalitions running in this election; however, none of them succeeded to cross the threshold of representation.[7]

HUNGARY

A detailed account of electoral coalitions in Hungary is given in Chapter Four.

LATVIA

Similarly to Estonia, Latvian legislation has also restricted the participation of electoral coalitions in national parliamentary elections since 1998. However, while the Estonian law banned coalitions outright, the amendment to the Latvian electoral law allowed coalitions to submit joint candidate lists as long as the association was legally registered (Bugajski 2001: 104). Nonetheless the impact of the law was still clear and present as the number of electoral coalitions that have entered the *Saeima* since 1998 has clearly dropped. In the first two elections, 1993 and 1995, three electoral coalitions succeeded to have their candidates elected to the parliaments: the alliance of the National Harmony Party and Economic Rebirth, winning 12 percent of the votes and 13 percent of seats in 1993; the United List that combined the Farmers' Union, the Christian Democratic Union, and a splinter of the Democratic Party, which won 6 percent of the votes and 8 percent of the seats in 1995; and the coalition of the Latvian National Conservative and the Green Parties, which won together 6.3 percent of the vote and also 8 percent of the seats in 1995. Following the next three parliamentary elections (1998, 2002, and 2006), the number of electoral coalitions in the *Saeima* has essentially remained the same: one in 1998 (the Latvian Social Democratic Alliance brought together the Latvian Social Democratic Workers Party and the Latvian Democratic Labor Party and winning 14 percent of the seats for 13 percent of the votes); one in 2002 (the union of the Green Party and Latvian farmers' Union wining 12 percent of the seats for 9.5 percent of the votes); and two in 2006 (the same coalition of the Green Party and the Farmer Union that won 17 percent of the vote and 18 percent of the seats; and the coalition of the Latvia First and the Latvia's Way that won 10 percent of the seats for 9 percent of the votes).

In addition to these relevant coalitions, there were other alliances that did not make it to parliament such as three-party coalition of the Latvian Christian Democrats, the Green Party and the Labor Party in 1998 or the Labor and Justice coalition in 1995. Pettai and Kreuzer (1999: 163) find that there were a total of ten electoral coalitions in the 1993 and 1995 elections including a total of nineteen different parties.

LITHUANIA

The significance of electoral coalitions has varied considerably in Lithuania's post-communist elections. After the first two elections, in 1992 and 1996, in which they did not play a major role, electoral coalitions became the central contenders in the parliamentary polls of 2000 and 2004. In 2008, however, only one electoral coalition ran and crossed the threshold of representation in the *Seimas*.

Three coalitions participated and won seats in the parliamentary elections of 1992. The most successful of them was the three-party alliance of the Lithuanian Christian Democratic Party, the Lithuanian Democratic Party, and the Lithuanian Union of Political Prisoners and Deportees was able to cross the threshold of representation. The coalitions won 14.1 percent of the seats in the PR tier and 11.2 percent of the seats in the nominal tier of the electoral contest. The other two coalitions were able to win seats only in the nominal tier of the competition. The two-party coalition of the Lithuanian Nationalist Union (LTS) and the (NP) won four seats (three and one by the two parties respectively), while the coalition of the (LKDS) and the (LTJS) won a single seat only, which went to the former. Four years later the LTS formed a new coalition with the (LDP), however, the electoral performance of the coalition was exactly the same as before, i.e. the coalition won a single seat from the nominal tier of the contest.

Electoral coalitions became central players in the elections of 2000 and 2004. In the former, the electoral coalition of four parties on the Left, united behind the leadership of former President Algirdas Brazauskas, won the largest number of votes and seats, 31.08 percent and 40 percent, respectively in the PR tier and 32.4 percent in the nominal tier. The four constituent parties of the coalition were the Lithuanian Democratic Labor Party, the Lithuanian Social Democratic Party, the New Democracy Party, and the Union of the Russians of Lithuania. The formation of the Social Democratic coalition was prompted by the rise of a new centrist force in the Lithuanian party system, the New Policy Bloc, which disturbed the bipolar structure of competition between the Conservatives on the Right and the Social Democrats on the Left that had developed since the transition to democracy. The New Policy Bloc was an alliance of four parties (the New Union, the Lithuanian Liberal Union, the Lithuanian Center Union, and the Modern Christian Democratic Union), however they contested the election independently (Fitzmaurice, 2003: 162–3). The New Policy bloc won a near majority of seats in the election (46.8 percent) and proceeded to form a government. However, the government did not last long and was soon replaced in office by the Social Democrats and the New Union, which had split away from the alliance.

The 2004 elections were in close proximity to the presidential polls for the first time due to the premature termination of President Paksas' term, who had assumed that office in 2000, via impeachment (Jurkynas, 2005: 770). Supporters of the disgraced president, the Liberal Democratic Party which Paksas had founded in 2001, and the Lithuanian People's Union formed the Coalition for Rolandas Paksas "For Order and Justice." On the Left, the Lithuanian Social Democratic Party and New Union ran together as the Coalition of Algirdas Brazauskas and Arturas Paulauskas. The plurality of seats (27.7 percent) in the election was won by a new formation, the Labor Party, however the Brazauskas–Paulauskas coaliton won the second largest number of both votes and seats and as such it assumed a prominent position in the new government, holding not only the prime ministership, in the person of Brazauskas, but also five ministerial portfolios (Jurkynas 2005: 775). In the 2008 elections, electoral coalitions returned to their earlier peripheral role. Of the sixteen candidate lists there was only one submitted by a coalition, the Labor Party and Youth, which received 7.1 percent of the seats in the newly elected *Seimas* (Jurkynas 2009).

POLAND

An important anchor of stability in the otherwise fast changing landscape of the Polish electoral system was the electoral coalition of leftist parties called the Democratic Left Alliance (SLD). At the center of the coalition was the reformed ex-communist party, the Social Democrats of Poland (SdRP), which brought together a number of leftist formations in support of the candidacy of its presidential nominee, W. Cimoszewicz, in the 1990 presidential polls (Curry 2003: 28). Prior to the parliamentary elections held in October 1991, the SdRP formally launched the SDL, which would contest all parliamentary and presidential elections until it was eventually transformed into a single political party in April 1999 (Curry 2003: 44). An important part of the reason for this transformation had to do with the need to comply with the rule which stated that trade unions could no longer run in elections and that organizations could not formally belong to political parties (Millard 2003: 70). Given that the second most important member of the SLD was a trade union, the All Poland Trade Union Coalition (OPZZ), the transformation was necessary (Curry 2003: 51). The dominance of the coalition by the SdRP was indicated by the prevalence of the party's candidates on the coalition's candidate lists as well as among its successfully elected deputies. In the 1991 elections thirty-nine of the SLD's sixty-one deputies in the Sejm were SdRP candidates followed by eighty-six out of 173 in 1993 (Markowski, 2002: 58). Very little is recorded about the other members of the electoral coalition, which "were of a much more mercurial nature" (Zubek, 1995: 291).

The first post-communist election in Poland resulted in the most fragmented of all parliaments in the region since 1990. Among the twenty-nine formations that entered the fractured Sejm in that election, five were electoral coalitions: the SLD, which won the plurality of both votes and seats; the Catholic Electoral Action (WAK) centered around the Christian National Union (ZChN); the Peasant Party–Programmatic Alliance which brought together the Polish Peasant Party (PSL) with the Union of Rural Youth; the Peasant Accord comprising the Polish Peasant Party Solidarity, the Solidarity of Private Farmers, and the Polish Peasant Party–Wilkanow (Jasiewicz 1992: 498); the Christian Democracy, a coalition headed by the Christian Democratic Labor Party (Millard 1992: 844). In addition to these coalitions, the Confederation of Independent Poland (KPN) linked its lists for vote counting and seat allocation purposes with two small formations, the Polish Western Union, and the Alliance of Women Against Hardships. After the elections, these parties formed one united parliamentary faction (Jasiewicz 1992: 498). The combined vote and seat shares of the five electoral coalitions were 37.2 percent and 41.3 percent.

In the early elections of 1993, only two formally registered electoral coalitions participated: the SLD and the Catholic Election Committee "Fatherland." The latter was formed by four parties: the Christian National Union (ZChN), the Conservative Party, the Party of Christian Democracy (PChD), and the Christian-Peasant Party (SLCh). While the SLD not only crossed the mandatory 8 percent threshold for coalitions but it actually won a plurality of both votes and seats in the Sejm, the Fatherland coalition received only 6.4 percent of the votes and, therefore, was not represented in parliament (Millard 1994: 491). It is worth noting, however, that the coalition would have qualified for parliamentary seats if it had run in the election as a single political party. A similar miscalculation prevented another electoral coalition on the Right, the AWSP, from entering parliament in 2001, as we shall see.

The 1997 election was a bipolar contest dominated by two electoral coalitions: the SLD and the Solidarity Electoral Action (AWS), which was formed on June 8, 1996, by the Solidarity Trade Union and twenty-one other right-wing parties and groups with the avowed goal of "creating an electoral bloc, capable of winning the next parliamentary elections" (Wenzel 1998: 144). By the time of the election the membership of the AWS coalition had grown to include thirty-five parties and groups (Szcerbiak 2004: 62; 1999: 84; Rose and Munro 2003: 234). The combined vote and shares of two electoral coalitions were 60.9 percent and 79.4 percent, respectively. The AWS won the plurality of both votes and seats (33.8 percent and 43.7 percent) and proceeded to form Poland's next government in coalition with the Freedom Union (UW).

In the 2001 elections, fifteen lists competed for seats in the Sejm. Of these only two were submitted by formal electoral coalitions: the first by the SLD and the UP, and the second by remnants of the outgoing governing coalition, renamed as the Solidarity Electoral Action of the Right (AWSP) including the RS AWS, ZChN, and the PPChD (Millard 2003; Szczerbiak, 2002: 49). According to the revised electoral law, coalitions had to meet an 8 percent national threshold in order to qualify for seats. The SLD-UP coalition had no difficulty meeting this requirement; winning 41.04 percent of the vote the coalition swept the elections and collected 47 percent of the seats in the Sejm. In stark contrast, the AWS electoral coalition secured a mere 5.6 percent of the total national vote and, therefore, did not qualify for seats. Other parties, such as Law and Justice or the League of Polish Families formed hidden coalitions but they contested the election as individual single parties. In retrospect, had the AWSP done so it would have qualified for seats in the newly elected parliament. However, by registering for the electoral competition as a coalition the AWSP scored a major "own goal" (Szczerbiak 2004: 68).

In the 2005 Polish election twenty-two candidate lists were submitted, all of them by individual political parties and other associations permitted by Polish electoral law. Two years later, in 2007, there were only ten competing candidate lists and one of them was submitted by a registered electoral coalition of parties: the Coalition of Left and Democracy consisting of the SLD, SDPL, PD, and UP. The coalition ran a total of 889 candidates, close to the maximum 920, and was represented in each of the country's forty-one districts. Although the coalition formally consisted of four political parties its lists also accommodated candidates that either belonged to other parties or had no explicit partisan affiliation. As a matter of fact, non-partisan candidates accounted for 15 percent of all coalition candidates, second only to the SLD, which ran 55 percent thereof. Of the remaining three parties, the SDPL ran 13.3 percent of the candidates, followed by PD's 10.1 percent and the UP's 4.2 percent. The overall electoral performance of the coalition was weak as it received only 13.15 percent of the total national vote and secured only 11.52 percent of the seats (fifty-three out of 460) in the Sejm. The majority of these seats (thirty-seven) were won by the SLD, the largest member of the coalition, followed by the SDPL with ten seats and the PD with a single seat. The remaining five seats were secured by non-partisan candidates.

ROMANIA

The 1992 parliamentary election featured one relevant electoral coalition: the Democratic Convention of Romania. The genesis of the Convention lay in the formation of a parliamentary alliance among the opposition parties in 1991 leading to the creation of an electoral coalition under the label of the National Convention for the Installation of Democracy. At its foundation, the Convention brought together six political parties, however, its membership quickly swelled to double that number (International Republican Institute 1992: 15). The Convention successfully contested the municipal elections that were held in February 1992 by winning five of the mayoral races including the capital city Bucharest. Prior to the parliamentary elections held later on in the Fall of 1992 one of its founding parties, the National Liberals, left the Convention. The exit of the Liberals not only forced the Convention to change its name, adopting the Democratic Convention of Romania label, but it also meant that the Convention became dominated by the National Peasant Party–Christian Democrats (PNT–CD). Indeed, PNT–CD candidates filled almost a majority of the spots on the coalition's candidate lists and it was also the party's nominee, Emil Constantinescu, who represented the Convention in the presidential race (International Republican Institute 1992: 32–3).[8] Of the eighty-two seats that the Convention won in the Chamber the

PNT-CD held forty-two, while in the Senate the party held twenty-one of the Convention's thirty-four seats (Stan 2005a: 188). Although the Convention lost both the parliamentary and the presidential elections, it won only 10 percent fewer parliamentary seats than the largest party, the Democratic National Salvation Front. In contrast, the largest party in 1990, the National Salvation Front won 59 percent and 66 percent more seats than the second largest party in the Chamber and the Senate, respectively.

In 1996, two of the three electoral coalitions that entered the electoral race were able to win seats in the national legislature. The most successful coalitions were the Democratic Convention of Romania, which won not only the plurality of seats in both chambers of parliament as well as captured the presidency, and the Social Democratic Union, which ended up with the third largest number of seats in both the Chamber and the Senate. Six political parties ran together and won parliamentary representation on the Democratic Convention list: the National Peasant Party–Christian Democrats, the National Liberal Party, the National Liberal Party–Democratic Convention, the Alternative Romania Party, the Ecologist Party of Romania, and the Romanian Ecologist Federation. The balance of gains among the coalition partners was very uneven with the National Peasant Party winning almost 68 percent of the 122 seats that the coalition won in the Chamber and 51 percent of the coalition's fifty-three seats in the Senate. The Social Democratic Union was a coalition of the Democratic Party, formed and led by the Romania's first post-communist prime minister, Petre Roman, and the Social Democratic Party. Similarly to the Convention, the partners in this coalition also made very uneven gains with the Democratic Party bagging 81 percent of the coalition's fifty-three seats in the Chamber and 96 percent of the twenty-three coalition seats in the Senate. The third electoral coalition that contested the polls was the National Liberal Alliance of the Civic Alliance Party and Liberal Party 93. However, this coalition did not win a single seat in either chamber of parliament.

Four years later, in the general election of 2000, the National Liberals once again left the Democratic Convention and contested the election on their own. The strategy worked; while the Liberals were able to cross the threshold of parliamentary representation, the truncated CDR-2000 secured only 5 percent of the national vote, which was not sufficient for an electoral coalition. At the same time, the electoral coalition of the Left, bringing together the Social Democracy Party of Romania (PDSR), the Social Democratic Party (PSDR) and the Humanist Party (PUR) under the name of the Democratic Social Pole of Romania, won a near-majority of seats in both the Chamber (44.9 percent) and the Senate (46.4 percent) as well as the presidential race (Popescu 2003: 331).

The 2004 election was a straightforward contest between two large electoral coalitions: the National Union Alliance, formed by the Social Democrats, an amalgamation of the PDSR and the PSDR, and the Humanist Party on the Left, and the Justice and Truth alliance, formed by the Liberal and the Democratic Parties, on the Right. As in 2000, the electoral coalition of the Left was clearly dominated by one party, the Social Democrats, which won 86 percent of the coalition's 132 seats in the Chamber, whereas the Justice and Truth alliance was much more balanced: the Liberals won sixty-four against the Democrat's forty-eight seats. According to the pre-electoral agreement between the latter two parties, the coalition initially nominated Theodor Stolojan, of the Liberal Party, as its presidential candidate and Traian Basescu, of the Democratic Party, to the post of prime minister. Shortly before the elections, however, Stolojan had to withdraw from the race leaving Basescu as the coalition's presidential candidate and Calin Popescu-Tariceanu, a founding member of the Liberal Party and co-chair of the Justice and Truth Alliance, as the coalition's prime ministerial nominee. The election produced a most unusual outcome: although the PSD–PUR coalition won more seats than the PNL–PDL, the latter was invited to form a government by the newly elected president, Basescu, who had led the junior partner in that coalition (Stan 2005b; Downs 2006). Four years later, in 2008, the PSD renewed its coalition with the Conservative Party, which was the renamed Humanist Party, while the Justice and Truth alliance had fallen apart (Downs, 2009; Stan, 2009; Marian, 2010).

SLOVAKIA

The importance of electoral coalitions has steadily declined over time in Slovakia's parliamentary elections. In 1994, the first election to the parliament of independent Slovakia, the three largest contenders were electoral coalitions while the fourth largest party was a crypto-coalition. The former included the coalitions of the HZDS and the RSS, which won the election by securing 40.6 percent of the seats; the Common Choice (SV) coalition of four parties, the SDL, SDSS, ZRS, and the HP; and a coalition of three Hungarian ethnic parties, the Coexistence Party, the MOS, and the MKDH. The only crypto-coalition that ran in the election and won seats in the National Council was the list of the KDH which accommodated one successful candidate of the DS. (International Republic Institute, 1999: 35–6).

In response to the new regulations that the 1998 electoral reform imposed on electoral coalitions, all of the contenders that submitted candidate lists for the 1998 parliamentary elections did so on their own, formally. Similarly, electoral coalitions were not formed in the subsequent elections of 2002 and 2006 either even though the graduated threshold for electoral coalitions was re-introduced in 1999 (Malova and Ucen, 2007: 1101; Rybar, 2007: 700). Although crypto coalitions were banned under the terms of the electoral change of 1998, the coalition partners of the outgoing government (HZDS and SNS) did accommodate candidates from other parties on their lists.[9] The three Hungarian parties merged to form a single political party, the SMK, while two former members of Common Choice, the SDSS and the ZRS, formed a new electoral party, the Slovak Democratic Coalition (SDK), together with the DU, DS and the KDH. For our purposes, it is appropriate to consider the SDK an electoral coalition because its five constituent members retained their own internal platforms in contrast to the SMK (Meseznikov, 2003: 43).

After the 1998 election, the restrictive regulations on electoral coalitions were reversed. As a result political parties engaged in a series of attempts to form coalitions before the polls in 2002. However, none of these attempts succeeded. The PSNS and the SNS were unable to agree on whether to form a real electoral coalition, which was the PSNS' preference, or a hidden coalition that would have accommodated PSNS candidates on the SNS list (Meseznikov 2003: 44). Similarly, the movement to create a broad electoral coalition of all non-leftist parties, proposed and advocated by the recently formed Alliance of the New Citizen (ANO), was not acceptable to all prospective members. In an interesting development, the DS formed a hidden coalition with the DU by accommodating the latter's candidates on its list, however, it subsequently withdrew from the election according to a pact it made with the SDKU (Meseznikov 2003: 44). The SDL tried to form an electoral coalition of the leftist parties, however, the efforts result only in a hidden coalition where the SDL included candidates from the SDSS and the SOP (Fitzmaurice, 2004: 161; Ucen, 2003: 1071). Although none of them came to fruition, there were several additional attempts at forming electoral coalitions prior to the 2002 elections.

SLOVENIA

Electoral coalitions have not played a major role in Slovenian elections. Although political parties clustered into two distinct blocs in each of the country's post-communist elections, they submitted individual candidate lists for the most part. Indeed, among all the contenders that have won seats in the country's five post-communist elections, I found only two electoral coalitions. The first was the United List of Social Democrats (ZLDS), which started in 1992 as an electoral coalition of the Party of Democratic Reform, the Social Democratic Union, and the Democratic Party of Pensioners of Slovenia. However, the coalition was transformed into a political party in 1993 and contested the subsequent elections as such (Rose and Munro 2003: 298). In the 1992 election the ZLSD won the third highest percentage of votes (13.6 percent) and seats (15.6 percent). The second electoral coalition was formed only much later in 2008 between the Slovenian People's Party (SLS) and the Youth Party of Slovenia (SMS). The coalition secured 5.21 percent of the vote and won five seats all of which went to SLS candidates (Fink-Hafner, 2009: 1112).

NOTES

1. Lagerspatz and Vogt (2004: 86) list the following parties and constituents of the Pro Patria PEC: the Christian Democratic Party (EKDE), the Christian Democratic Union (EKDL), the Liberal Democratic Union (ELL), the Estonian Liberal Democratic Party (ELP), the Conservative Peoples' Party (EKR), and the Republican Coalition Party (EVK). According to Bugajski, however, the Pro Patria was "a coalition of four national conservative parties" (72).
2. In 1995, the two parties were also joined by the Country People's Party, the Pensioners' and Families' Union, and the Farmers' Assembly in the electoral coalition. (Lagerspetz and Vogt 2004: 87).
3. In 1992, the Front comprised the Popular Front of Estonia (ER), the ERK, the Assembly of Nations in Estonia (ERU), and the Women's Union (EN). Running alone, the Center Party won a plurality of the seats in both 1999 and 2003. In the latter it finished neck-to-neck with the brand new Res Publica, each winning twenty-eight seats.
4. The SK comprised the Royalist Party (ERP) and the Royalist Association Free Toome (RuVT).
5. The EK included the Party of the Republic of Estonia (EVP), the Association of Legal Real Estate Owners in Tartu (TOOU), and the Association of Healthy Life in Noarootsi (NTES).
6. The Greens list consisted of the Green Movement (ERL), the Green Party (EER), the European Youth Forest Action in Estonia (KENME), the Maardu Green League (URM), and the Green Regiment (RR).
7. These PECs were Justice, the Better Estonia, and the Fourth Force.
8. According to the International Republican Institute report, the breakdown of candidates among the coalition partners was as follows: PNT–CD 45 percent, Civic Alliance Party 18 percent, the PNL–CD and the PNL–AT, two splinters of the PNL, 14 percent, and the PDSR 9 percent.
9. The HZDS list included candidates of the New Agrarian Party and the Party of Businessmen and Entrepreneurs, while the SNS list included candidates form the Slovak Green Alliance and the Christian Social Union (International Republican Institute 1999: 9).

APPENDIX D

Government Coalitions in Post-Communist Democracies[1]

BULGARIA

Since the first post-transition elections in 1991, Bulgaria had eight governments, three of which were caretaker administrations (Berov, Indzhova, and Sofiyanski). The five regular cabinets were formed by four different kinds of party coalitions: one of them was a single-party minority government (Dimitrov); two were single-party majority governments (Videnov, Kostov); one was a minimum winning coalition (Sax-Coburg-Gota), and one was an oversize majority coalition (Stanishev). Overall, there has been a strong tendency in Bulgaria towards the formation of majority governments.

The history of government formation during the first decade of the country's post-transition period (1991 to 2001) reflected the domination of the party system by two major formations: the ex-communist BSP and the SDS/ODS. Over the first three electoral cycles (1991, 1994, 1997), the two parties alternated as electoral winners and whichever won a plurality or a majority of the seats proceed to form a government. In 1991 the SDS formed a minority government relying on the negotiated support of the DPS, while the 1994 and 1997 elections resulted in single-party majority government first by the BSP and then by the ODS.

The 2001election marked the end of the two-party era in the Bulgarian party system. The plurality winner of the election was the NDSV, which contested the polls and entered the National Assembly for the first time. Although the party won exactly 50 percent of the seats, which could plausibly have allowed it to form a single-party minority government, the NDSV started coalition talks with each of the other three parties that won parliamentary seats (BSP, ODS and DPS). In the end, a minimum winning coalition was formed with the DPS, the smallest of the four parliamentary parties.

In contrast to this narrow coalition, the 2005 election resulted in the first oversized majority coalition in the country. The 2005 Bulgarian election resulted in a significant jump in parliamentary fragmentation to 4.8 (from 2.9 in the previous polls!) while also bringing a number of new parties to the legislature. Although the BSP won a plurality of the seats and thus received the mandate to form a government it failed to forge a majority solution thus letting the next largest party, the NDSV, to lead the next attempt. However, the NDSV also failed. Eventually, fifty-one days after the election, a new Bulgarian government was formed under the leadership of Prime Minister S. Stanishev of the BSP. The coalition included the three largest parties in parliament, the BSP, the NDSV, and the DPS (Spirova 2006: 620).

CZECH REPUBLIC

The Czech Republic has had eight governments in the four Chambers of Deputies elected since the inception of the new sovereign state. Two of these (Tosovsky and Fischer) were caretaker administrations, while the remaining six were split between minority governments (Klaus, Zeman, and Topolanek) and minimum winning coalitions (Spidla, Gross, Paroubek). These six governments were formed by five distinct coalitions. Therefore, even though there has been regular alternation in office between Left and Right coalitions, there was considerable fluctuation in their composition. At the same time, it speaks to the relative stability of the Czech party system that every general election resulted in the same two parties (ODS and CSSD) winning the most seats and the one with the plurality forming the government.

Two general elections were followed by the formation of Right (Klaus, Topolanek) and Left coalition governments (Zeman, Spidla) respectively. Interestingly, the collapse of both Right coalitions was followed by the induction of caretaker cabinets, whereas the disintegration of Spidla's government was followed by the formation of a new cabinet supported by the same coalition partners. In contrast to some of the other countries, such as Hungary or Slovakia, where the alternating governing coalitions had no overlapping members, the Czech Republic's centrist KDU participated in coalition government of both the Left and the Right.

The 1996 election produced a six-party legislature with the center-right ODS and the center-left CSSD winning the largest number of seats. The new government was formed by the same three conservative parties (ODS, KDU and ODA) that had formed the outgoing executive. With a combined seat share of ninety-nine out of 200 seats the coalition partners came within a hair's breadth of a parliamentary majority. The largest opposition party, the CSSD, found it impossible to propose an alternative majority coalition because neither of the other two opposition parties proved to be realistic partners. The KSCM was generally considered an "untouchable" by all other parties because of its association with the ousted communist regime. Similarly, the SPR was too extreme and radical at the other end, the far-right, of the political spectrum, which made it an impossible partner in any coalition.

The premature collapse of the government led to the early elections of 1998, which produced a CSSD plurality. President Havel invited four of the five parliamentary parties to participate in the government formation process while explicitly excluding the KSCM. The exclusion of the Communist Party did not create much of a discontent as it was justified and broadly accepted on grounds of the party's lack of democratic credentials. However, the unavailability of the communists as a potential coalition partner exerted considerable constraint on the government formation talks by reducing the number of feasible combinations. Essentially, President Havel's decision meant that the two smaller parties, the KDU and the US, would have a veto on the formation of a majority coalition led by either of the two large parties.

In the end, the two parties were unable to overcome their coordination dilemma and thus paved the way to the formation of a single-party CSSD cabinet supported from the outside by the leading opposition party, the ODS (Nikolenyi 2030). The terms of cooperation between the two large parties were defined in a pact, known as the Opposition Agreement, that included provisions for the allocation of parliamentary and state offices, coordination between the CSSD and ODS on policy initiatives with special attention to constitutional reform, a commitment to not forming a coalition with a third party (Roberts 2003: 1301–3). The commitment to constitutional change targeted the electoral system, which the two large parties wanted to amend in order to reduce the influence of the smaller parties in the party system (Crawford 2001; Nikolenyi 2011). Whereas the ODS pledged neither to participate in the initial vote of confidence that the incoming government must receive nor to "raise a vote of no-confidence in the government nor to utilize constitutional channels leading to the dissolution of the Chamber of Deputies," the two parties reserved their right to vote freely on any other pieces of legislation without coordinating with one another (Roberts 2003: 1032).

Although the cooperative arrangement between the CSSD and the ODS soon broke down, the government was able to remain in office for a full term. Moreover, the CSSD even succeed to win a plurality of seats in the subsequent elections of 2002 and form a bare majority minimum winning coalition government with the KDU and the US. This coalition formed three successive cabinets (Spidla, Gross, and Paroubek) during the term of the 2002–6 Chamber of Deputies.

The 2006 election resulted in the most difficult and protracted government formation process ever not only in the Czech Republic but in all of post-communist East Central Europe. Following the elections, it took 219 days for the new cabinet to be sworn-in. Although the ODS won the most seats, the freshly elected Chamber was divided equally between the two parties of the two parties of the Left (KSCM and the CSSD) and the three parties of Right and Center (ODS, SZ, and KDU). Following a failed attempt by the ODS to form a single-party minority government, a Center-Right minority coalition was formed by the aforementioned three parties. Although the coalition controlled only 50 percent of the seats, the new government led by M. Topolanek won its investiture vote of confidence thanks to the abstention of two dissenting CSSD deputies (Linek 2008: 947–9).

ESTONIA

In the four legislatures that have completed their term in post-communist Estonia by 2009 political parties formed eight regular and one caretaker (Tarand) governments. Except for the latter, all other governments consisted of a distinct party coalition which indicates the unsettled and volatile character of the Estonian party system. The first two elections (1992, 1995) were followed by the formation of a government headed by the plurality party (Isaama and KMU respectively). In contrast, the party that won the most seats in the 1999 polls (EK) did not find its way to the cabinet until almost three years after the election. In 2003, two parties, the EK and the newly formed RP, tied for first place with each winning 28 percent of the seats and eventually both of them entered the governing coalition. Yet, even though the EK won the most seats in two elections (1999 and 2003), it was never able to lead a government and supply the prime minister. The history of post-communist governments shows a marked bias towards majorities as all but two of the eight governments were minimum winning coalitions. It is important to note that neither of the two minority governments (Siimann and Kallas) were immediate post-election cabinets. Similarly to Latvia, none of Estonia's governments were formed by a Left coalition of parties.

Although the first post-communist election resulted in a fragmented *Riigikogu*, the largest party, Isaama, assumed a dominant position thanks to winning nearly 30 percent of the seats while the second and third largest parties, KK and ER, were able to capture only half of that. Upon being invited to form a government, the party reached a minimum winning coalition deal with the ERSP and the M, each having won twelve out of the 101 seats. Although this coalition of the Right-of-Center survived until the next election, Prime Minister M. Laar was replaced by A. Tarand for the last six months in a caretaker capacity after the former had been voted out of office.

The 1995 election brought the KMU to victory with 40 percent of the seats. As before, the second largest party (ER) once again captured only half of the seats grabbed by the plurality winner of the election. Although the second post-communist *Riigikogu* saw somewhat more turbulence in its executive politics as two prime ministers and three different coalitions succeeded one another, some semblance of stability was provided by the fact that each of these governments was formed and led by the plurality party. Following the election, the KMU formed a short-lived minimum winning coalition with the EK. After seven months in office Prime Minster Vahi was forced to step down. Although the coalition was dissolved, the prime minister was able to re-negotiate his way back to power by getting the ER, the second largest party, to form a larger minimum winning coalition with his own KMU. This coalition lasted a little longer than its predecessor but the last two years of the *Riigikogu's* term were completed under a single-party KMU government led by Prime Minister Siimann.

The third post-communist election resulted in a small reduction in the gap between the first and second largest parties' seat shares. The relative weakening of the plurality party (EK) was also reflected in its inability to control the government formation processes during the ensuing four years. After the election, a minimum winning coalition government was formed by the I, R, and M, which were the second, third, and fourth largest parties in the *Riigikogu* respectively (actually, the I and R had the same number of seats, eighteen each). This government stayed in office under Prime Minister Laar for nearly three years after which it was replaced a nearly winning minority coalition of the EK and the ER. Although the plurality part had more cabinet seats in this government, the ER supplied the new prime minister in the person of S. Kallas.

The election of 2003 produced a tie between the two largest parties; the newly formed RP and the EK won twenty-eight seats each. Eventually, both of these parties found their way in a governing coalition during the term of the fourth post-communist *Riigikogu* which saw the formation of two minimum winning governing coalitions. The post-election government of Prime Minister J. Parts was headed by the RP and it included the ER and R as junior coalition partners. After almost exactly two years in office, the government collapsed following the prime minister's resignation. The two smaller partners formed a new coalition with the EK, although the prime minister, A. Ansip, was supplied by the ER.

HUNGARY

A detailed account about government formation in Hungary is given in Chapter Four.

LATVIA

Independent Latvia's first post-communist legislature saw the formation of two minority coalition governments in relatively quick succession. Both governments were headed by the LC, the plurality winner of the 1993 election, although by different prime ministers. The LC's coalition partner in the Birkavs government was the LZS; the two parties controlled a near majority of 48 percent of the seats. After a year in power, the LZS left the coalition. Although President Ulamis urged the formation of a conservative majority coalition between the LC and LNNK, eventually the new government was formed by the LC and the tiny

TPA, a splinter from the TSP, under the leadership of M. Gailes (Müller-Rommel and Norgaard 2001: 33).

In contrast to the first post-communist *Saeima*, majority coalitions dominated Latvia's second post-communist legislature. The post-election government formed after the 1995 polls was a broadly based oversized coalition that included six (DPS, LC, TB, LNNK, LVP, and the united list of the LZS, LKDS and the LLDP) of the nine parliamentary parties with a combined share of 73 percent of the seats. The excluded parties were the pro-Russian LSP and TSP as well s the ultra-nationalist TKL-ZP, a splinter from the LNNK. Prime Minister A. Skele resigned after a little more than a year in office but was appointed by President Ulmanis to form the new government, which included all previous members of the coalition with the exception of the LVP. Six months later Prime Minister Skele resigned but the same coalition of parties re-formed the new government under Prime Minister G. Krasts, whose own LNNK had recently merged with the TB. Although DPS left the coalition in April 1998, a move that deprived the government of its legislative majority, Krasts's government remained in power until the next election in October 1998.

The third post-communist *Saeima* saw the formation of three distinct coalition governments among four political parties. As in previous cases, the party that represented the country's Russian-speaking minority, TSP, was excluded from these coalitions. The election was followed by the formation of a minority coalition of the Right-of-Center (LC, LNNK + TB, and the recently created JS) that resolved to support the candidacy of V. Kristopans to the post of head of government. In order to buttress their legislative support base, the coalition partners tried to attract Prime Minister A. Skele's newly founded TP, which actually won the most seats in the election, into cabinet. When the talks broke down over the allocation of specific portfolios (EECR 7:4), the coalition turned to the LSDA. Although the party did not formally join the conservative coalition, it agreed to sending one minister, P. Salkazanovs to occupy the portfolios of Agriculture, upon successful completion of an accord with Prime Minister Kristopans in February 1999 (EECR 8:1). Technically, this accord transformed the minority status of the governing coalition into a minimum winning one.

Securing continued cooperation among the coalition partners proved to be an uneasy task. Although the government survived an early confrontation between the LNNK + TB and the JS over ministerial appointments as well as the splintering of the three-party coalition during the presidential balloting in the summer of 1999, the prime minister eventually resigned on July 5, 1999, when the opposition TP and the LNNK + TB signed an agreement of cooperation. Within two weeks, A. Skele was sworn in as prime minister of a minimum winning coalition government comprising the TP, the LC, and the LNNK + TB, the three largest parties in the *Saeima* (EECR 8:4). In the following May, the government underwent yet another change both in the person of the prime minister (A. Berzins) and in its party composition. The last government that was formed in this *Saeima* included all four parties that had formed the previous two cabinets, i.e. TP, LC, LNNK + TB, and JS. Thus, the last government of the third post-communist *Saeima* was extremely broadly based as it included four of the six parliamentary parties controlling 70 percent of the seats.

The fourth parliament continued the same pattern as three governments succeeded each other within a span of four years. Also repeating the previous pattern, each of these governments consistently excluded the party that represented the Russian-speaking minority, this time the PCVTL, which meant that the three government coalitions were formed by different combinations of the five Latvian parties that won seats in the parliament. The post-election coalition was a four-party minimum winning majority led by the largest party, the JL under Prime Minister E. Repse. The plurality party had only a single seat advantage over the second largest party, the PCTVL, and formed a narrow majority that was but five seats over the majority threshold. The coalition included the JL, the TB + LNNK, ZZS and the LPP. When the prime minister's party pulled out of the coalition, a minority government was sworn in headed by I. Emsis of the ZZS that also included the LPP and the TP. The third government was formed in December 2004 following the failure of the Emsis government to have its budget accepted by the *Saeima*. Although the incoming prime minister, A. Kalvitis of the TP, was at first able to put together heading an oversized majority coalition, with the cooperation of the LPP, ZZS, and the JL, the latter withdrew from the coalition in April 2006 letting the Kalvitis government finish the reminder of its term in a minority status.

LITHUANIA

The history of government coalitions in post-communist Lithuania is unique among the post-communist democracies in that political parties have formed every main type of coalition with almost the same frequency. Altogether fourteen governments were formed in the four completed post-communist parliaments, five of which were caretaker administrations (Lubys, Degutiene-I, II, Gentvilas, and Balcytis). The nine actual governments were formed by six distinct coalitions, which indicates that a number of these coalitions suffered with internal instability. In particular, coalitions of the single-party majority and the over-sized majority type changed several prime ministers and cabinets during their term in office, while minority coalitions and minimum winning majorities were always terminated when the government that they supported changed. The temporal sequence in which the different types of coalitions were formed is indicative of the gradual fragmentation of the Lithuanian party system. In the first two post-communist elections, the largest party was able to win either an actual parliamentary majority

(1992) or near majority (1996). In the former, the majority party (LDDP) formed single-party majority governments, while in the latter (the TS) it opted for oversized coalitions. In the subsequent two elections (2000 and 2004), the plurality party no longer enjoyed the same kind of numerical advantage as it won only 36 percent and 27 percent of the mandates, respectively. It was in these later *Seimases* that minority and minimum winning coalitions succeeded each other. Except for one instance (Paksas 2000), governments and governing coalitions were always led by the plurality, or majority, party, which also supplied the prime minister.

The first post-communist election to the *Seimas* of newly independent Lithuania produced a majority winner in the LDDP, the communist successor party. Despite its extremely strong electoral mandate, the LDDP tried to form a broadly based coalition government with Sajudis, its principal opposition, which won only twenty-eight seats against the LDDP's seventy-three (Rommel and Hansen 2001: 42). Eventually, the efforts failed and the LDDP had to assume alone the responsibility of government. Even so, the new prime minister, B. Lubys, agreed to take office on a caretaker basis until the presidential elections that were due in early 1993. The LDDP's candidate, A. Brazauskas, swept the presidential polls and in March 1993 the party formed an actual working government under the leadership of A. Slezevicus. After three years in office, he lost a vote of confidence and thus the LLDP government finished its last year of its term under Prime Minister L. Stankevicius.

The electoral pendulum shifted markedly in 1996 when the principal party of the re-organized Right, TS (LK), won one seat short of a majority in the country's second post-communist parliamentary election. The plurality winner formed an oversized coalition government that included the second largest party, the LKDP, and the LCS. Although the TS-led coalition government lasted a full term, it was headed by three different prime ministers in the short span of four years: G. Vagnorius, R. Paksas, and A. Kubilius.

The third and fourth elections produced considerably more fragmented *Seimases* where, for the first time, different party coalitions replaced one another in government during the same inter-election period. After the 2000 election, the second and third largest parties, the LLS and NS formed a minority coalition government led by R. Paksas. This government, however, was replaced by a minimum winning coalition government formed by the NS and the LSDP, the party that won the most seats at the polls, after less than a year in office. The new prime minister, A. Brazauskas, served until the next elections of 2004, and then again in the new parliament until the summer of 2006 at the head of a four-party minimum winning coalition comprising the LSDP, the newly formed DP, which was also the largest party in the Seimas, the SLP, and the New Union. In the aftermath of Brazauskas' resignation, two alternative party blocs attempted to form a new government. On the Left, the coalition of the LSDP, the Peasant People's Union and the CDP, a splinter from the disintegrating DP, put forward Z.

Balcyts as their candidate for prime minister with the support of the Liberal and Center Union. On the Right, a coalition of the HU, the Liberal Movement and the New Union nominated former Prime Minister A. Kubilius as head of government. For his part, the president tried to broker an agreement between the LSDP and the HU to form a broadly based coalition government by the two larger parties of the respective blocs.

Once the president's attempt failed, he appointed Balcytis to stand for a vote of confidence in the *Seimas*. Although this vote failed, a slightly re-organized coalition of the Left, including the LSDP, LCU, CDP, and the LPPU succeeded to secure the investiture of G. Kirkilas of the LSDP, who proceed to form a minority coalition government consisting of ministers from these four parties. In January 2008, the coalition became broader when the SLU decided to join the government formally.

POLAND

Polish political parties formed ten governments in the country's five complete post-communist legislatures. Four of these (Olszweski, Suchocka, Belka, and Marcinkiewicz) were undersized minority cabinets while the other six were minimum winning coalitions (Pawlak, Oleksy, Cimoszewicz, Buzek, Miller, and Kaczynsky). However, the tendency toward minority governments is even more acutely demonstrated when considering that three of these minimum winning coalitions (Buzek, Miller, and Kaczinsky) actually turned into minority governments as a result of the break-up in the coalition arrangement that supported them in the first place. Yet, most of the post-election cabinets that were formed after the general elections were majority coalitions (Pawlak, Buzek, and Miller).

Polish governments regularly alternated between Left and Right although the ten governments were formed by seven different coalitions. Similarly to Hungary, there was considerable stability and continuity in the composition of the coalitions that formed the governments of the Left and four of them (Pawlak, Oleksy, Cimoszewicz, and Miller) were formed by the same two parties; the reformed communist SLD and the PSL. While there was one other Left government formed by the SLD by itself (Belka), all five governments of the Right were formed by a different coalition, which points to the more general state of instability on that part of the ideological and political spectrum.

The Polish party system underwent major changes during the first two post-communist decades as it moved from being the most fragmented to having one of the least fractionalized systems of party competition in the region. Thanks to an extremely permissive and proportional electoral system, the first post-communist Sejm had eleven effective parliamentary parties with the largest controlling no more than 13.5 percent of the seats. Two Right-of-Center governments were formed in this Sejm (Olszewski, Suchocka) in quick succession each of consisting of a minority coalition of four and seven parties respectively. While Olszewski's cabinet barely controlled more than a quarter of all seats, Suchocka's came closer to the majority threshold with a combined strength of 40.9 percent. Eventually the Sejm dissolved itself after only two years but passed a new electoral law that would significantly reduce the number of parties in the new parliament to be elected in 1993.

Although neither minority governments in the outgoing *Sejm* included the plurality party, the SLD, the formation of all subsequent governments would be headed by the party with the most seats. In the 1993 *Sejm*, the plurality party was the SLD, with 37.2 percent of the seats, and it formed three successive governments with the same coalition partner, the PSL, which was also the second largest party in the *Sejm* with 28.7 percent of the seats. In the immediate post-election government, the prime ministerial berth went to the junior partner, which was more a reflection of the high degree of presidential interference in the internal politics of the cabinet than the genuine outcome of bargaining between the coalition partners. Avowedly anti-communist, President Walesza insisted to appoint W. Pawlak as the prime minister of the incoming Left coalition government as well as dictate the appointment of his preferred candidate to the three presidential portfolios in the cabinet.

The general election of 1997 resulted in the victory of the AWS, an electoral coalition of right and center-right formations, which proceeded to form a minimum winning and ideologically connected coalition with the UW. In contrast to the previous SLD–PS coalition, the difference in the parliamentary weight of the coalition's partners was much more substantial with the AWS having 43.7 percent and the UW only 13 percent of the seats. Also, the margin by which the AWS–UD controlled the legislatures was significantly smaller. Whereas the SLD–PSL coalition had controlled more than two-thirds of the seats in the Sejm, the AWS–UD coalition commanded only 56.7 percent of the seats. The 2001 election produced yet another SLD plurality, with 47 percent of the seats, and a coalition government with the PSL. However, this time the overall the size of the coalition (56.1 percent) and the size of the junior partner (9.1 percent) were much smaller than was the case in the 1993–7 period.

Although the Sejm that was elected in 2005 was very short-lived, it saw the formation of two governments, both headed by the plurality party, the PiS. Throughout the election campaign the two leading parties of the re-organized Polish Right, the PiS and PO, promised the electorate that they would form a coalition government should they win the elections. However, for the first time ever in Poland's post-communist electoral history, the presidential elections and the parliamentary polls were held in very close temporal proximity. Although the two parties did win a landslide in the parliamentary elections, their cooperation gave way to conflict and competition as their respective candidates (L. Kaczynsky of the PiS and D. Tusk of the PO) also came to dominate the presidential race. Thus, the PiS proceeded to form a minority government, with the support of the smaller and ideologically more extreme SRP and LPR, headed by K. Marczinkiewicz. After only half a year, this informal arrangement was replaced by a formal coalition government of the three parties led by J. Kaczynszky, the twin brother of the winner of the presidential race.

ROMANIA

Romania had nine governments in the four parliaments that completed their term by 2009. It is indicative of the volatile state of party politics in the country that three of these governments were temporary caretaker administrations (Dejeu, Athanasiu, and Bejinariu) and that each of the six regular cabinets were supported by a different party coalition. At the same time, Romania displayed a pattern of regular alternation in executive between Left and Right, each pole forming governments after two elections respectively; the Left after 1992 and 2000, and the Right after 1996 and 2004. Similarly to Poland and the Czech Republic, minority governments abounded in Romania (Vacariou, Nastase, and Tariceanu), although none of the majority coalitions were of a minimum winning size. Thus, Romania defies the regional pattern in that the type of government that is formed the most frequently in the region, i.e. minimum winning majority coalitions, never obtained there. Another important characteristic of the history of Romanian governments pertains to the role of the president. Since parliamentary and presidential elections are always held at the same time and given the powerful nature of the Romanian presidency, plurality parties could form a government in Romania only if their candidates also won the presidential race. In other words, winning the presidency has been a better predictor of who forms the government than winning a plurality in the election.

The 1992 election was followed by the formation of single-party government by the FSDN under Prime Minister Vacariou, himself a non-partisan candidate. Although the FSDN was dissolved as an organization during the term of Vacariou's government, its successor, the PDSR, continued to support the government coalition with the PUNR and then again by itself when the PUNR withdrew from the coalition four months before the 1996 elections. In spite of the changes that took place both in the partisan composition of the coalition and the organizational identity of the party that formed Romania's first post-communist government, Vacariou remained in office for a full term.

The next parliament elected in 1996 produced five prime ministers including the three caretaker heads of government, none of which was undersized. The election was won by the Right, whose main protagonist, the CDR, controlled not only a plurality of seats in both chambers of parliaments but also the Presidency. Yet, instead of going it alone, the CDR opted to form oversized coalitions with the UDMR and alternating between the USD (Ciorbea, Isarescu) and PDSR (Vasile).

The 2000 elections returned to power the Romanian Left, headed by the PDSR, both in parliament and the presidency. With 44.9 percent of the seats in the lower house, the PDSR won the largest plurality in any Romanian election before and since. Of the four other parties that won parliamentary representation, only the extreme right PRM was excluded from the ensuing coalition formation talks. In the end, the PDSR could only secure a "non-aggression pact" with the UDMR and the PNL as opposed to their full participation in a coalition cabinet. Thus, Romania was once again governed by a single-party minority cabinet (Nastase) for a four-year period.

The 2004 elections produced a split outcome: the Presidency was won in an extremely tight and narrow contest by the T. Basescu, the candidate of the opposition PNL-PD alliance, while the incumbent PSD, in coalition with the small PUR, won a plurality of seats in the legislative polls. The newly elected President gave the mandate of government formation to his own PNL-PD, which proceeded to form a minority coalition upon securing the participation of the UDMR and, surprisingly, the PUR. Thus, for the first time ever since the inception of Romania's post-communist democracy, a "coalition of losers" (Popescu 2004: 232) assumed government of the country. This was all the more perplexing because for the first time the Romanian electorate returned the incumbents with a legislative plurality.

SLOVAKIA

Slovakia's pattern of government formation is unique among the post-communist democracies for a number of reasons. First, of all ten states Slovakia has had the fewest governments per legislature. In each of the four parliaments there was only one government formed, and with minor changes in their composition, they all lasted for a full four-year term. Although there was considerable stability in the composition of the governments that the two main partisan blocs formed respectively, none of these coalitions was exactly the same. Second, Slovakia is also the only state in the region where political parties never formed a minority government; instead all but one of the coalitions was minimally winning. The exception to this pattern was the Dzurinda-I government, which included two smaller parties (MK and SOP) even though either of them would have given the two larger members of the coalition (SDK and SDL) a parliamentary majority. Third, while plurality parties formed most of the governments most of the time in the other East Central European democracies, this was not the rule in Slovakia. Even thought the

HZDS won the most seats in each of the first three elections (1994, 1998, 2002), it could lead a winning coalition only once, in 1994.

Following its electoral victory in 1994, the HZDS formed a majority coalition with the SNS and the ZRS. The HZDS and the SNS would find themselves in the same coalition once again after the 2006 election as junior partners in the Smer-led government. In contrast to these three-party coalitions of the Left, both the 1998 and the 2002 elections resulted in the formation of four-party Right-of-Center coalitions led by the SDK, and its successor, the SDKU, respectively. While the ethnic Hungarian SMK was a member of both of these coalitions, the other two members changed: in 1998 the SDL and the SOP, in 2002 the KDH and ANO supplied ministers in the new government.

SLOVENIA

Slovenia's record of government formation stands out from among those of the new post-communist democracies because of the pivotal position played by one political party, the LDS, in nearly every Slovenian cabinet coalition during the period examined. The LDS won a plurality of seats in three of the four elections (1992, 1996, 2000) and headed four of the country's six governments (Drnovsek-I, II, III, and Rop), three of which were led by the same prime minister. Each and every Slovenian government was formed by a multi-party coalition, two of which were undersized (Drnovsek-II, Bajuk), three were oversized (Drnovsek-I, Drnovsek-III, Rop), and one was minimally winning (Jansa). The composition of the party coalitions that formed and supported these governments was unique in every case except for the Rop government that continued the same coalition line-up as the previous cabinet when its prime minister, J. Drnovsek, had to step down upon winning the 2002 election to the Slovenian presidency. Otherwise, the LDS changed its coalition partners during both the Drnovsek-I and -II governments.

The first government in Slovenia's new post-communist legislature was formed by a grand coalition of four political parties. The plurality party, the LDS, which had also headed the last government in the outgoing transitional parliament, formed a new government with the second and third largest parties, the SKD and the ZLSD respectively, as well as the smallest parliamentary party, the SDS. Although Prime Minister J. Drnovsek remained in office for a full term until the next elections, the grand coalition changed its composition during the parliamentary cycle as both the ZLSD and the SDS eventually departed from its ranks. Nonetheless, changes in the composition of the coalition did not bring about the need to form and choose a new government.

The second post-communist parliament, elected in 1996, witnessed the formation of two governments (Drnovsek-II and Bajuk). The LDS was once again returned with a plurality of seats in the Assembly but this time it formed a minimum winning majority coalition government that included the second largest party, the SLS, and the second smallest party, DESUS. Although the two largest parties controlled a near majority of the seats, forty-four out of the ninety, they did not proceed with the formation of a minority government. The decision by the SLS to join the LDS-led coalition government was puzzling in the light of the fact that the party had contested the election as part of a three-party Right-of-Center Slovenian Spring Alliance, including the SKD and the SDS, which actually won exactly half of the parliamentary seats. Moreover, the SLS did not even support Drnovsek's election to the post of prime minister, which he secured due to the support of the LDS, ZLSD, DESUS, SNS, the two minority representatives in the Assembly as well as a single defector from the SDK (Müller-Rommel and Gaber 2001: 99).

After a little more than three years in office, the Drnovsek-II government collapsed upon losing a no-confidence vote prompted by the departure of the SLS from the coalition. The new government was formed by a minority coalition of parties, called Coalition Slovenia, consisting of the now merged SLS + SKD and the SDS. In other words, the Center-Right coalition that contested the election as a bloc eventually assumed power under Prime Minister A. Bajuk.

The third post-communist election once again produced an LDS plurality and the return of J. Drnovsek to the prime ministership. Exploiting its centrist pivotal position the LDS successfully proposed and formed a four-party surplus majority coalition that included two parties from the Left-of-center, DESUS and ZLSD, and one from the Right-of-Center, SLS-SKD. The same coalition remained in office when Drnovsek was elected to the presidency in 2002 and was replaced by A. Rop as the head of government.

The fourth post-communist election was the first in which Slovenian voters denied the LDS a legislative plurality. As in all previous elections the parliamentary balance between the two main blocs was extremely tight. Although the SDS won the most seats in the Assembly, the three-party Right-of-Center electoral alliance that it had formed with the NiS and the SLS won exactly 50 percent of the seats. In a surprise move, DESUS, a partner of the LDS in several previous coalition governments, cast its support behind and joined the SDS-led coalition (Toplak 2006: 829).

NOTE

1. In addition to the sources indicated, this section also draws on the Parliament and Government Composition Database (at: http://www.parlgov.org/).

Bibliography

Agh, A. (1997). Parliaments and policy-making bodies in East Central Europe: The case of Hungary. *International Political Science Review* 18 (4): 417–32.

Andrews, J. T. and Jackman, R. (2005). Strategic fools: electoral rule choice under extreme uncertainty. *Electoral Studies* 24: 65–84.

Axelrod, R. (1970). *Conflict of Interest.* Chicago: Markham.

Bale, T. and Bergman, T. (2006). A taste of honey is worse than none at all? Coping with the generic challenges of support party status in Sweden and New Zealand. *Party Politics* 12 (2): 189–209.

Baylis, T. A. (1996). Presidents versus prime ministers: shaping executive authority in Eastern Europe. *World Politics* 48 (3): 297–323.

Beliaev, M. V. (2006). Presidential powers and consolidation of new postcommunist democracies. *Comparative Political Studies* 39 (3): 375–98.

Benoit, K. (2004). Models of electoral system change. *Electoral Studies* 23: 363–89.

Benoit, K. and Hayden, J. (2004). Institutional change and persistence: the evolution of Poland's electoral system. *Journal of Politics* 66 (2): 396–427.

Benoit, K. and Schiemann, J. W. (2001). Institutional choice in new democracies: bargaining over Hungary's 1989 electoral law. *Journal of Theoretical Politics* 13 (2): 159–88.

Bergman, T. (1993). Formation rules and minority governments. *European Journal of Political Research* 23 (1): 55–66.

Biezen, I. van. (2003). *Political Parties in New Democracies*. Palgrave Macmillan.

Birch, S. (2003). *Electoral Systems and Political Transformation in Post-Communist Europe.* Houndmills: Palgrave Macmillan.

Birch, S., Millard, F., Popescu, M. and Williams, K. (2002). *Embodying Democracy: Electoral system Design in Post-Communist Europe.* Houndmills: Palgrave MacMillan.

Black, D. (1958). *The Theory of Committees and Elections.* Cambridge: Cambridge University Press.

Blais, A., Aldrich, J. H., Indridason, I. H., and Levine, R. (2006). Do voters vote for government coalitions? *Party Politics* 12 (6): 691–705.

Blais, A. and Indridason, I. H. (2007). Making candidates count: the logic of electoral alliances in two round legislative elections. *Journal of Politics* 69 (1): 193–205.

Blondel, J. (1968). Party systems and patterns of government in western democracies. *Canadian Journal of Political Science* 1: 180–203.

Blondel, J. and Cotta, M. (1996). *Party and Government: An Inquiry into the Relationship between Government and Supporting Parties in Liberal Democracies*. Palgrave MacMillan.

Blondel, J. and Müller-Rommel, F. (eds.) (2001). *Cabinets in Eastern Europe.* Houndmills: Palgrave.

Bocian, M. (2008). Government coalition breaks up in Hungary. *CES Commentary* 5: 1–4.

Bozóki, A. (1992). A magyar partok 1991-ben [Hungarian parties in 1991]. In S. Kurtán, P. Sandor and L. Vass (eds.), *Magyarország Politikai Évkönyve 1992* [Hungary's Political Yearbook 1992]. Budapest: Demokracia Kutatasok Kozpontja, 123–31.

Brokl, L. and Mansfeldova, Z. (1999). Czech republic. *European Journal of Political Research* 36: 349–69.

Browne, E. C. (1986). The process of cabinet dissolution: an exponential model of duration and stability in western democracies." *American Journal of Political Science* 30*:* 628–50.

Browne, E. C. (1988). Contending models of cabinet stability. *American Political Science Review* 82: 930–41.

Budge, I. and Keman, H. (1990). *Parties and Democracy: Coalition Formation and Government Functioning in Twenty States.* Oxford: Oxford University Press.

Budge, I. and Laver, M. J. (1986). Office seeking and policy pursuit in coalition theory. *Legislative Studies Quarterly* 11: 485–506.

Bugajski, J. (2001). *Political Parties of Eastern Europe: A Guide to Politics in the Post-Communist Era*. London: M.E. Sharpe.

Cameron, R. (2008). Constitutional crisis looms as MPs, senators argue over secret ballot. *Czech Radio* http://www.radio.cz/en/article/100494. Last accessed: May 27, 2014.

Carey, J., Formanek, F. and Karpowicz, E. (2002). Legislative autonomy in new regimes: the Czech and Polish cases. In G. Loewenberg, P. Squire and R. Kiewiet (eds.), *Legislatures: Comparative Perspectives on Representative Assemblies*. Ann Arbor: University of Michigan Press, 352–86.

Carey, J. and Shugart, M. S. (1995). Incentives to cultivate a personal vote. *Electoral Studies* 14 (4): 417–39.

Carroll, R. and Cox, G. W. (2007). The logic of Gamson's law: pre-election coalitions and portfolios allocations. *American Journal of Political Science* 51 (2): 300–13.

Carstairs, A. M. (1980). *A Short History of Electoral Systems in Western Europe*. London; Boston: Allen and Unwin.

Cheibub, J. A. (2002). Minority governments, deadlock situations, and the survival of presidential democracies. *Comparative Political Studies* 35 (3): 284–312.

Cheibub, J. A., Przeworski, A. and Saiegh, S. M. (2002). Government coalitions under presidentialist and parliamentarist democracies. *Dados* 45 (2): 187–218.

Cheibub, J. A., Przeworski, A. and Saiegh, S. M. (2004). Government coalitions and legislative success under presidentialism and parliamentarism. *British Journal of Political Science* 34 (4): 565–87.

Chirot, D. (ed.) (1991). *The Origins of Backwardness in Eastern Europe: Economics and Politics from the Middle Ages to the Early Twentieth Century.* University of California Press.

Chiva, C. (2007). The institutionalization of post-communist parliaments: Hungary and Romania in comparative perspective. *Parliamentary Affairs* 60 (2): 187–211.

Christensen, J. G. (2006). Ministers and mandarins under Danish parliamentarism. *International Journal of Public Administration* 29 (12): 997–1019.

Clark, T. D. (2005). Presidentialism and the effect of electoral law in postcommunist systems. *Comparative Political Studies* 38 (2): 171–88.

Clark, T., Martinatis, Z. and Dilba, R. (2008). Electoral mandate and party cohesion: does it matter in Lithuania? *Journal of Communist Studies and Transition Politics* 24 (3): 317–37.

Clark, T. D., Verseckaite, E. and Lukosaitis, A. (2006). The role of committee systems in post-communist legislatures: a case study of the Lithuanian Seimas. *Europe-Asia Studies* 58 (5): 731–50.

Colomer, J. (2001). *Political Institutions: Democracy and Social Choice*. Oxford: Oxford University Press.

Colomer, J. (ed.) (2004). *Handbook of Electoral System Choice*. Houndmills: Palgrave Macmillan.

Coman, E. E. (2008). Legislative behavior in Romania: the effect of the 2008 Romanian electoral reform. *Legislative Studies Quarterly* 37 (2): 199–224.

Cox, G. W. (1997). *Making Votes Count: Strategic Coordination in the World's Electoral Systems*. Cambridge: Cambridge University Press.

Crampton, R. (1995). The Bulgarian elections of December 1994. *Electoral Studies* 14 (2): 236–40.

Crampton, R. (1997). The Bulgarian elections of 19 April 1997. *Electoral Studies* 16 (4): 560–3.

Crawford, K. (2001). A system of disproportional representation. *Representation* 38 (1): 46–58.

Crombez, C. (1996). Minority governments, minimum winning coalitions and surplus majorities in parliamentary systems. *European Journal of Political Research* 29: 1–29.

Csizmadia, Ervin. (2006). "Egy új jelölési modell: A 2006. évi köztársaságelnök választás [A new nomination model: the 2006 presidential election]." In P. Sando, L. Vass and A. Tolnai. (eds.), *Magyarország Politikai Évkönyve 2005* [Hungarian Political Yearbook 2005]. Budapest: Demokracia Kutatasok Magyar Kozpontja Kozhasznu Alapitvany, pp. 150–9.

Curry, J. L. (2003). Poland's ex-communists: from pariahs to establishment players. In J. L. Curry (ed.), *The Left Transformed in Post-communist Societies*. Lanham: Rowman and Littlefield, 19–60.

Davies, P. J. Ozolins, A. V. (2001). The 1998 parliamentary elections in Latvia. *Electoral Studies* 20: 135–41.

De Dios, M. S. (2006). Output of the Spanish Cortes (1979–2000): a case of adaptation to party government. *European Journal of Political Research* 45 (4): 551–79.

Deemen, A. van. (1989). Dominant players and minimum size coalitions. *European Journal of Political Research* 17: 313–32.

Deemen, A. van. (1991). Coalition formation and centralized policy games. *Journal of Theoretical Politics* 3: 139–62.

Deutsch, T. and Gyarmati, L. (1999). A jövő választása: A Fidesz—Magyar Polgári Párt 1998-as országgyűlési választási kampányáról [The election of the future: about the 1998 election campaign of the Fidesz—Hungarian Civic Party]. In S. Kurtán, P. Sándor and L. Vass (eds.), *Magyarország Politikai Évkönyve 1998* [Hungary's Political Yearbook 1998]. (Budapest: Demokracia Kutatako Kozpontja): 88–93.

Diermeier, D. (2006). Coalition government. In B. Weingast and D. Wittman (eds.), *Oxford Handbook of Political Economy,* Oxford: Oxford University Press, 162–79.

Diermeier, D., Eraslan, H. and Merlo, A. (2003). A structural model of government formation. *Econometrica,* 71: 27–70.

Diermeier, D., Eraslan, H. and Merlo, A. (2007). Bicameralism and government formation. *Quarterly Journal of Political Science* 2: 227–52.

Diermeier, D. and Krehbiel, K. (2003). Institutionalism as a methodology. *Journal of Theoretical Politics* 15: 123–44.

Diermeier, D. and Myerson, R. B. (1999). Bicameralism and its consequences for the internal organization of legislatures. *American Economic Review* 89: 1182–96.

Dimitrov, V., Goetz, K. H. and Wollman, H. (2006). *Governing After Communism*. London: Rowman and Littlefield.

Dodd, L. (1974). Party coalitions in multiparty parliaments: a game theoretic analysis. *American Political Science Review* 68: 1093–117.

Dodd, L. (1976). *Coalitions in Parliamentary Government*. Princeton: Princeton University Press.

Downs, A. (1957). *An Economic Theory of Democracy*. New York: Harper & Row.

Downs, W. (2009). The 2008 parliamentary elections in Romania. *Electoral Studies* 28, 510–13.

Downs, W. and Miller, R. V. (2006). The 2004 presidential and parliamentary elections in Romania. *Electoral Studies* 25: 409–15.

Druckman, J. N. and Roberts, A. (2005). Context and coalition bargaining: comparing portfolio allocation in Eastern and Western Europe. *Party Politics* 11: 535–55.

Druckman, J. N. and Roberts, A. (2008). Measuring portfolio salience in Eastern European parliamentary democracies. *European Journal of Political Research* 47: 101–34.

Druckman, J. N. and Roberts, A. (2007). Communist successor parties and coalition formation in Eastern Europe. *Legislative Studies Quarterly* 32 (1): 5–31.

Druckman, J. N. and Thies, M. F. (2002). The importance of concurrence: the Impact of bicameralism on government formation and duration. *American Journal of Political Science* 46 (4): 760–71.

Duverger, M. (1954). *Political Parties*. New York: Wiley.

Edin, P. and Ohlsson, H. (1991). Political Determinants of budget deficits: coalition effects versus minority effects. *European Economic Review* 35 (8): 1597–603.

EECR (East European Constitutional Review). Various years. http://www1.law.nyu.edu/eecr/

Elgie, R. (ed.) (1999). *Semi-presidentialism in Europe*. Oxford: Oxford University Press.

Elster, J. (1993). Rebuilding the boat in the open sea: constitution-making in Eastern Europe. *Public Administration* 71: 169–217.

Elster, J, Offe, C. and Preusse, U. K. (eds.) (1998). *Institutional Design in Post-Communist Societies: Rebuilding the Ship at Sea*. Cambridge: Cambridge University Press.

Epperly, B. (2011). Institutions and legacies: electoral volatility in the postcommunist world. *Comparative Political Studies* 44 (7): 829–53.

Evans, G. (2006). The social bases of political division in post-communist Eastern Europe. *Annual Review of Sociology* 32: 245–70.

Evans, G. A. and Whitefield, S. (1993). Identifying the bases of party competition in Eastern Europe. *British Journal of Political Science* 23 (4): 521–48.

Evans, G. A. and Whitefield, S. (2000). Explaining the formation of social cleavages in post-communist democracies. In H. D. Klingemann, E. Mochmann and K. Newton (eds.), *Elections in Central and Eastern Europe: The First Wave*. Berlin: Stigma, 36–70.

Farrell, D. (2011). *Electoral Systems: A Comparative Introduction*. Palgrave Macmillan. 2nd edition.

Ferrara, F. and Herron, E. S. (2005). Going it alone? Strategic entry under mixed electoral rules. *American Journal of Political Science* 49 (1): 16–31.

Fettelschoss, K. and Nikolenyi, Cs. (2009). The selection and de-selection of cabinet ministers in post-communist democracies. In K. Dowding and P. Dumont (eds.), *The Selection of Ministers in Europe: Hiring and Firing*. Routledge, 204–27.

Fink-Hafner, D. (2008). Much ado about nothing: electoral reform in Slovenia. Unpublished typescript.

Fink-Hafner, D. (2009). Slovenia. *European Journal of Political Research* 48 (7–8): 1106–13.

Fiorina, M. (1987). Party government in the United States. In R. Katz (ed.), *Party Governments: European and American Experiences*. Berlin: Walter de Gruyter, 270–300.

Fitzmaurice, J. (1997). The Slovenian parliamentary elections of 10 November 1996. *Electoral Studies* 16 (3): 403–7.

Fitzmaurice, J. (2003). Parliamentary elections in Lithuania, October 2000. *Electoral Studies* 22 (2003): 161–5.

Fitzmaurice, J. (2004). The parliamentary election in Slovakia, September 2002. *European Journal of Political Research* 23: 160–6.

Frendreis, J. P. (1986). The study of cabinet dissolutions in parliamentary democracies. *Legislative Studies Quarterly* 11: 619–28.

Frye, T. (1997). A politics of institutional choice: post-communist presidencies. *Comparative Political Studies* 30 (5): 523–52.

Gamson, W. G. (1961). Theory of coalition formation. *American Sociological Review* 26: 373–8.

Gallagher, M. and Mitchell, P. (2005). *The Politics of Electoral Systems*. Oxford: Oxford University Press.

Galligan, Y. and Clavero, S. (2008). Prospects for women's legislative representation in postsocialist Europe: the view of female politicians. *Gender and Society* 22 (2): 149–71.

Geddes, B. (1995). A comparative perspective on the Leninist legacy in Eastern Europe. *Comparative Political Studies* 28 (2): 239–74.

Geddes, B. (1996). Initiation of new democratic institutions in Eastern Europe and Latin America. In A. Lijphart and C. H. Waisman (eds.), *Institutional Design in New Democracies: Eastern Europe and Latin America*. Boulder: Westview Press, 14–52.

Golder, S. N. (2005). Pre-electoral coalitions in comparative perspective: a test of existing hypotheses. *Electoral Studies* 24: 643–63.

Golder, S. N. (2006a). *The Logic of Pre-electoral Coalition Formation*. Columbus: Ohio State University Press.

Golder, S. N. (2006b). Pre-electoral coalition formation in parliamentary democracies. *British Journal of Political Science* 36 (2): 193–212.

Gschwend, T. and Hooghe, M. (2008). Should I stay or should I go? An experimental study on voter responses to pre-electoral coalitions. *European Journal of Political Research* 47: 556–77.

Gschwend, T. and Leuffen, D. (2005). Divided we stand—unified we govern? The issue of cohabitation in the French elections of 2002. *British Journal of Political Science* 35 (4): 691–712.

Green-Pedersen, C. and Thomsen, L. H. (2005). Bloc politics vs. broad cooperation? The functioning of Danish minority parliamentarism. *The Journal of Legislative Studies* 11 (2): 153–69.

Grofman, B. (1989). The comparative analysis of coalition formation and duration: distinguishing between-country and within-country effects. *British Journal of Political Science* 19: 291–302.

Grofman, B., Mikkel, E. and Taagepera, R. (1999). Electoral system change in Estonia, 1989–1993. *Journal of Baltic Studies* 30 (3): 227–49.

Grofman, B., Straffin, P. and Noviello, N. (1996). The sequential dynamics of cabinet formation, stochastic error, and a test of competing models. In N. Schofield (ed.) *Collective Decision-Making: Social Choice and Political Economy.* Boston: Kluwer Academic Publishers, 281–93.

Grofman, B. and van Roozendaal, P. (1997). Modelling cabinet durability and termination. *British Journal of Political Science* 27 (3): 419–51.

Grofman, B. A. (1994). Toward a theoretical explanation of premature cabinet termination with application to post-war cabinets in the Netherlands. *European Journal of Political Research* 26: 155–70.

Grzymala-Busse, A. M. (2001). Coalition formation and the regime divide in new democracies: East Central Europe. *Comparative Politics* 34 (1): 85–104.

Grzymala-Busse, A. M. (2002). *Redeeming the Communist Past: The Regeneration of the Communist Successor Parties in East Central Europe.* Cambridge: Cambridge University Press.

Grzymala-Busse, A. M. (2007). *Rebuilding Leviathan: Party Competition and State Exploitation in Post-Communist Democracies.* Cambridge: Cambridge University Press.

Han, B. (2007). Institutional determinants of party policy change in advanced democracies: a preliminary test of party behavioral theory. *Journal of International and Area Studies* 14 (1): 95–109.

Hanson, S. E. (1995). The Leninist legacy and institutional change. *Comparative Political Studies* 28: 306–24.

Harfst, P. (2000). Government stability in Central and Eastern Europe: the impact of parliaments and parties. *ECPR Joint Session of Workshops.* Copenhagen.

Harper, M. A. G. (2003). The 2001 parliamentary and presidential elections in Bulgaria. *Electoral Studies* 22 (2): 335–44.

Haughton, T. (2005). *Constraints and Opportunities of Leadership in Post-Communist Europe.* Aldershot: Ashgate.

Hazan, R. (2003). Does cohesion equal discipline? Toward a conceptual delineation. *Journal of Legislative Studies* 9 (4): 1–11.

Heidar, K. and R. Koole (eds.) (2000). *Parliamentary Party Groups in European Democracies.* London: Routledge.

Heller, W. B. and Mershon, C. (eds.) (2009). *Political Parties and Legislative Party Switching.* New York: Palgrave Macmillan.

Hellmann, J. (1996). Constitutions and economic reform in the postcommunist transitions. *East European Constitutional Review* 5, 46–53.

Herman, V. and Pope, J. (1973). Minority governments in Western democracies. *British Journal of Political Science* 3: 191–212.

Hibbing, J. R. and Patterson, S. (1992). A Democratic Legislature in the Making: The Historic Hungarian Elections of 1990. *Comparative Political Studies* 24(4): 430–54.

Holzhacker, R. (2005). The power of opposition parliamentary party groups in European scrutiny. *The Journal of Legislative Studies* 11 (3–4): 428–45.

Huang, M. (1999). The Amber Coast: a new president for Latvia. *Central Europe Review* 39, June 21, 1999. http://www.ce-review.org/authorarchives/amber_archive/amber39old1.html

Huber, J. and Bingham Powell, G. (1994). Congruence between citizens and policymakers. *World Politics* 46 (3): 291–326.

Ikstens, J. (2003). Latvia. *European Journal of Political Research* 42: 1003–9.

Ikstens, J. (2004). Latvia. *European Journal of Political Research* 43: 1054–8.

Ilonszki, G. (2000). Parties and parliamentary party groups in the making: Hungary 1989–1997. In K. Heidar and R. Koole (eds.), *Parliamentary Party Groups in European Democracies: Political Parties behind Closed Doors*. London: Routledge, 214–30.

Ilonszki, G. (2007). From minimal to subordinate: a final verdict? The Hungarian parliament, 1990–2002. *Journal of Legislative Studies* 13 (1): 38–58.

Ilonszki, G. and Edinger, M. (2007). MPs in post-communist and post-Soviet nations: a parliamentary elite in the making. *Journal of Legislative Studies* 13 (1): 142–63.

Ilonszki, G. and Kurtán, S. (1994). Hungary. *European Journal of Political Research* 26: 319–25.

Ilonszki, G. and Kurtán, S. (2005). Hungary. *European Journal of Political Research* 44: 1033–40.

Ilonszki, G. and Kurtán, S. (2006). Hungary. *European Journal of Political Research* 45: 1120–7.

International Republican Institute. (1992). Election observation report: Romania's 1992 presidential and parliamentary elections. Available at: http://www.iri.org/sites/default/files/Romania%27s%201992%20Presidential%20and%20Parliamentary%20Elections.pdf Accessed on June 1, 2014.

International Republican Institute. (1999). *Final Report and Recommendations 1998 Parliamentary Elections in Slovakia*. Washington, DC: International Republican Institute.

Ishiyama, J. and Bozóki, A. (2002). *The Communist Successor Parties of Central and Eastern Europe*. London: M. E. Sharpe.

Ishiyama, J. (1996). Electoral system experimentation in the new Eastern Europe: the single transferable vote and the additional member system in Estonia and Hungary. *East European Quarterly* 29 (4): 487–507.

Jasiewicz, K. (1992). Poland. *European Journal of Political Research* 22 (4): 489–504.

Jasiewicz, K. (1994). Poland. *European Journal of Political Research* 26 (3–4): 397–408.

Jowitt, K. (1992). The Leninist legacy. In I. Banac (ed.), *East Europe in Revolution*. Ithaca: Cornell University Press, 207–24.

Juberias, C. F. (2004). Eastern Europe: general overview. In J. Colomer (ed.), *Handbook of Electoral System Choice*. London: Palgrave-Macmillan, 309–31.

Jurkynas, M. (2005). The 2004 presidential and parliamentary elections in Lithuania. *Electoral Studies* 24: 770–7.

Jurkynas, M. (2009). The parliamentary election in Lithuania, October 2008. *Electoral Studies* 28: 329–33.

Kaminski, M. (2001). Coalitional stability of multi-party systems: evidence from Poland. *American Journal of Political Science* 45 (2): 294–312.

Kaminski, M. (2002). Do parties benefit from electoral manipulation? Electoral laws and heresthetics in Poland, 1989–93. *Journal of Theoretical Politics* 14 (3): 325–58.

Katz, R. (1986). Party government: a rationalistic conception. In Francis G. Castles and Rudolf Wildenmann (eds.), *Visions and Realities of Party Government*. Berlin: Walter de Gruyter.

Katz, R. (1987). Party government and its alternatives. In Richard Katz (ed.), *Party Governments: European and American Experiences*. Berlin: Walter de Gruyter, 1–26.

Kern, T. (2001). Választójogi reform Magyarországon. [Electoral Reform in Hungary]. Unpublished typescript. Available at: http://www.doksi.hu/get.php?lid=3172 Accessed on June 1, 2014.

King, G. J. (1990). A unified model of cabinet dissolution in parliamentary democracies. *American Journal of Political Science* 34: 846–761.

Kitschelt, H. (1995). Formation of party cleavages in post-communist democracies: theoretical propositions. *Party Politics* 1 (4): 447–72.

Kitschelt, H., Mansfeldova, Z., Markowski, R. G. Toka, G. (1999). *Post-Communist Party Systems: Competition, Representation, and Inter-Party Cooperation.* Cambridge: Cambridge University Press.

Kluonis, M. (2003). Factors causing government (in)stability: the case of Central and Eastern Europe. In A. Jankauskas (ed.), *Lithuanian Political Science Yearbook.* Vilnius: Vilnius University, 99–115.

Kohno, M. (1997). *Japan's Postwar Party Politics.* Princeton: Princeton University Press.

Kopecky, P. (2000). The limits of whips and watchdogs: parliamentary parties in the Czech Republic. In K. Heidar and R. Koole (eds.), *Parliamentary Party Groups in European Democracies: Political Parties Behind Closed Doors.* London: Routledge, 177–94.

Kopecky, P. (2004). The Czech Republic: entrenching proportional representation. In J. Colomer (ed.), *Handbook of Electoral System Choice.* Houndsmills: Palgrave MacMillan, 347–58.

Kopecky, P. (2006). Political parties and the state in post-communist Europe. *Journal of Communist Studies and Transition Politics* 22 (3): 251–73.

Korosenyi, A. (1993). Bal es jobb. Az europai es a magyar politikai paletta [Left and Right: The European and the Hungarian political spectrum]. *Politikatudomanyi Szemle* 3: 94–114.

Kostadinova, T. (2003). Voter turnout dynamics in post-communist Europe. *European Journal of Political Research* 42 (6): 741–59.

Kreuzer, M. and Pettai, V. (2003). Patterns of political instability: affiliation patterns of politicians and voters in post-communist Estonia, Latvia, and Lithuania. *Studies in Comparative International Development* 38: 76–98.

Kreuzer, M. and Pettai, V. (2009). Party switching, party systems, and political representation. In W. B. Heller and C. Mershon (eds.), *Political Parties and Legislative Party Switching.* New York: Palgrave Macmillan, 265–86.

Krouwel, A. (2003). Measuring presidentialism and parliamentarism: an application to Central and East European countries. *Acta Politica* 38 (4): 333–64.

Krivy, V. (2003). Election results and trends. In G. Meseznikov, O. Gyarfasova, M. Kollar and T. Nicholson (eds.), *Slovak Elections 2002.* Bratislava: Institute for Public Affairs, 63–112.

Krupavicius, A. (1997). The Lithuanian parliamentary elections of 1996. *Electoral Studies* 16 (4): 541–9.

Kunicova, J. and Remington, T. F. (2008). Mandates, parties and dissent: effect of electoral rules on parliamentary party cohesion in the Russian State Duma, 1994–2003. *Party Politics* 14: 555–74.

Laakso, M., Taagepera, R. (1979). Effective number of parties: a measure with application to Western Europe. *Comparative Political Studies* 12: 3–27.

Lagerspetz, M. and Vogt, H. (2004). Estonia. In Sten Berglund, Joakim Ekman and Frank H. Aarebrot (eds.), *The Handbook of Political Change in Eastern Europe.* 2nd Edition. Cheltenham: Edward Edgar Publishing.

Laver, M. (1974). Dynamic factors in government coalition formation. *European Journal of Political Research* 2: 259–70.

Laver, M. (1998). Events, equilibria and government survival. *American Journal of Political Science* 42: 28–54.

Laver, M. and Budge, I. (1992). *Party Policy and Government Coalitions.* London: St. Martin's Press.

Laver, M. and Schofield, N. (1990). *Multiparty Government: The Politics of Coalition in Europe*. Oxford: Oxford University Press.

Lawson, K., Rommele, A. and Karasimeonov, G. (1999). *Cleavages, Parties and Voters: Studies from Bulgaria, the Czech Republic, Poland and Romania*. London: Prager.

Lazarova, D. (2007). Will Jiri Cunek's political ambitions bring down the government? *Czech Radio*. http://www.radio.cz/en/article/98390 Last accessed: May 27, 2014.

Lazarova, D. (2008a). The Prime minister gives the president full backing ahead of the February presidential elections. *Czech Radio*. http://www.radio.cz/en/article/99238 Last accessed: May 27, 2014.

Lazarova, D. (2008b). Controversy at the eleventh hour: some deputies propose electing president by acclamation. *Czech Radio.* http://www.radio.cz/en/article/100106 Last accessed: May 27, 2014.

Leiserson, M. (1966). Coalitions in politics. Yale University (PhD Thesis).

Leiserson, M. (1968). Factions and coalitions in one-party Japan: an interpretation based on the theory of games. *The American Political Science Review* 62 (3): 770–87.

Lewis, P. (1996). *Party Structure and Organization in East Central Europe*. London: Edward Elgar Publishing.

Lewis, P. (2006). Party systems in post-communist Central Europe: patterns of stability and consolidation. *Democratization* 13 (4): 562–83.

Lijphart, A. (1984a). *Democracies: Patterns of Majoritarian and Consensus Government in Twenty-One Countries*. New Haven: Yale University Press.

Lijphart, A. (1984b). Measures of cabinet durability: a conceptual and empirical evaluation. *Comparative Political Studies* 17 (2): 265–79.

Lijphart, A. (1992). Democratization and constitutional choices in Czecho-Slovakia, Hungary and Poland 1989–91. *Journal of Theoretical Politics* 4 (2): 207–23.

Lijphart, A. (1994). *Electoral Systems and Party Systems: A Study of Twenty-Seven Democracies, 1945–1990.* Oxford: Oxford University Press.

Linek, L. (2003). Czech Republic. *European Journal of Political Research* 42: 916–30.

Linek, L. (2008). Czech Republic. *European Journal of Political Research* 47: 947–51.

Linek, L. (2009). Czech Republic. *European Journal of Political Research* 48: 939–44.

Linek, L. and Mansfeldova, Z. (2004). Czech Republic. *European Journal of Political Research* 43: 980–8.

Linek, L. and Mansfeldova, Z. (2007). The parliament of the Czech Republic, 1993–2004. *Journal of Legislative Studies* 13 (1): 12–37.

Lipset, S. M. and Rokkan, S. (1967). Cleavage structures, party systems and voter alignments. In S. M. Lipset and S. Rokkan (eds.), *Party Systems and Voter Alignments*. Toronto: Canada Free Press, 1–64.

Lowell, L. A. (1896). *Government and Parties in Continental Europe*. Cambridge, MA: Harvard University Press.

Lucky, C. (1993). Tables of presidential power. *East European Constitutional Review*, 2 (4), 3 (1): 81–94.

Lupia, A. and Strom, K. (1995). Coalition termination and the strategic timing of parliamentary elections. *American Political Science Review* 89: 648–65.

Lundberg, T. C. (2009). Post-communism and the abandonment of mixed-member electoral systems. *Representation* 45 (1): 15–27.

Maeda, K. and Nishikawa, M. (2006). Duration of party control in parliamentary and presidential governments: a study of 65 democracies, 1950 to 1998. *Comparative Political Studies* 39 (3): 352–74.

Mainwaring, S. (1993). Presidentialism, multipartism and democracy: the difficult combination. *Comparative Political Studies* 26: 198–228.

Malova, D. and Krause, K. D. (2000). Parliamentary party groups in Slovakia. In K. Heidar and R. Koole (eds.), *Parliamentary Party Groups in European Democracies: Political Parties behind Closed Doors*. London: Routledge, 195–213.

Malova, D. and Ucen, P. (2007). Slovakia. *European Journal of Political Research* 46, 1096–106.

Marian, C. G. (2010). Plus ça change: electoral law reform and the 2008 Romanian parliamentary election. *Communist and Post-Communist Studies* 43: 7–18.

Markowski, R. (2002). The Polish SLD in the 1990s. In A. Bozóki and J. T. Ishiyama (eds.), *The Communist Successor Parties of Central and Eastern Europe*. Armonk: M. E. Sharpe, 51–88.

Martinatis, Z. (2012). Explaining electoral reforms in Lithuania. *Journal of Baltic Studies* 43 (3): 389–400.

Matic, A. A. (2000). Electoral reform as a constitutional dilemma. *East European Constitutional Review* 9 (3): 77–81.

Maxfield, E. (2009). Romania's parliamentary elections, 30 November 2008. *Representation* 45 (4): 485–94.

McFaul, M. (1999). Institutional design, uncertainty, and path dependency during transitions: cases from Russia. *Constitutional Political Economy* 10: 27–52.

McGregor, J. (1994). The presidency in East Central Europe. *RFE/RL Research Report* 3 (2): 23–31.

Meseznikov, G. (2003). Parliamentary elections in 2002 and the development of the political party system. In G. O. Meseznikov (ed.), *Slovak Elections 2002: Results, Implications, Context*. Bratislava: Institute for Public Affairs, 35–48.

Metcalf, L. K. (2000). Measuring presidential power. *Comparative Political Studies* 33: 661–85.

Millard, F. (1992). The Polish parliamentary elections of October 1991. *Soviet Studies* 44 (5): 837–55.

Millard, F. (1994). The shaping of the Polish party system. *East European Politics and Societies* 8 (3): 467–94.

Millard, F. (2003). Elections in Poland 2001: electoral manipulation and party upheaval. *Communist and Post-Communist Studies* 36: 69–86.

Millard, F. and Popescu, M. (n.d.). Preference voting in post-communist Europe. Unpublished manuscript. Available at: http://www.policy.hu/popescu/PREFERENCEVOTING1.pdf Accessed on June 1, 2014.

Montgomery, K. (1999). Electoral effects of party behavior and development evidence from the Hungarian national assembly. *Party Politics* 5: 507–23.

Moraski, B. and Loewenberg, G. (1999). The effect of legal thresholds on the revival of former communist parties in East-Central Europe. *Journal of Politics* 61 (1): 151–70.

MPE (*Magyarország Politikai Évkönyve*) (Hungarian Political Yearbook). (Various years) Budapest: Demokrácia Kutatások Magyar Központja Alapítvány [Foundation for Hungarian Center of Democracy Reserach].

Mukherjee, B. and Leblang, D. (2006). Minority governments and exchange rate regimes: examining evidence from 21 OECD countries, 1975–1999. *European Union Politics* 7 (4): 450–76.

Müller-Rommel, F. K. (2004). Party government in Central Eastern European democracies: a data collection (1990–2003). *European Journal of Political Research* 43: 869–93.

Müller-Rommel, F. and Gaber, S. (2001). Slovenia. In J. Blondel and F. Müller-Rommel (eds.), *Cabinets in Eastern Europe*. Houndmills: Palgrave, 95–105.

Müller-Rommel, F. and Hersted, O. (2001). Lithuania. In J. Blondel and F. Müller-Rommel (eds.), *Cabinets in Eastern Europe*. Houndmills: Palgrave, 40–9.

Müller-Rommel, W. and Strom, K. (eds.) (1999). *Policy, Office, Votes: How Political Parties in Western Europe Make Hard Decisions*. Cambridge: Cambridge University Press.

Müller-Rommel, W. and Strom, K. (eds.) (2000). *Coalition Government in Western Europe*. Oxford: Oxford University Press.

Müller-Rommel, F. and Norgaard, O. (2001). Latvia. In J. Blondel and F. Müller-Rommel (eds), *Cabinets in Eastern Europe*. Houndmills: Palgrave, 29–39.

Müller-Rommel, F. K., Fettelschoss, K., and Harfst, P. (2004). Party Government in Central Eastern European Democracies: A Data Collection (1990–2003). *European Journal of Political Research* 43: 869–93.

Müller-Rommel, F. and Gaber, S. (2001b). "Slovenia." In J. Blondel and F. Muller-Rommel (eds.), *Cabinets in Eastern Europe*. Houndmills: Palgrave, 95–105.

Müller-Rommel, F. and Hersted, O. (2001a). "Lithuania." In J. Blondel and F. Muller-Rommel (eds.), *Cabinets in Eastern Europe*. Houndmills: Palgrave, 40–9.

Narud, H. M. (1995). Coalition termination in Norway: models and cases. *Scandinavian Political Studies* 18: 1–29.

National Electoral Committee of Estonia. (2012). *Elections in Estonia, 1992–2011*. Tallin. Available at: http://issuu.com/vabariigi_valimiskomisjon/docs/elections_in_estonia_1992-2011_eng/25?e=0 Accessed on 1 June 2014.

Neto, O. A. (2006). The presidential calculus: executive policy making and cabinet formation in the Americas. *Comparative Political Studies* 39 (4): 415–40.

Neto, O. A. and Borsani, H. (2004). Presidents and cabinets: the political determinants of fiscal behavior in Latin America. *Studies in Comparative International Development* 39 (1): 3–27.

Nikolenyi, Cs. (2003). Coordination problem and grand coalition: the puzzle of the government formation game in the Czech Republic, 1998. *Communist and Post-Communist Studies* 36 (3): 325–44.

Nikolenyi, Cs. (2004a). Strategic coordination in the 2002 Hungarian elections. *Europe-Asia Studies* 56 (7): 1042–58.

Nikolenyi, Cs. (2004b). Cabinet stability in post-communist Central Europe. *Party Politics* 10 (2): 123–50.

Nikolenyi, Cs. (2004c). The impact of the electoral system on government formation: the case of post-communist Hungary. *Japanese Journal of Political Science* 5 (1): 159–78.

Nikolenyi, Cs. (2005). Cabinet stability in post-communist democratic legislatures. In Z. Mansfeldova, D. Olson and P. Rakusanova (eds.), *Central European Parliaments: First Decade of Democratic Experience*. Prague: Institute of Sociology, Academy of Sciences of the Czech Republic.

Nikolenyi, Cs. (2011). When electoral reform fails: the stability of proportional representation in post-communist democracies. *West European Politics* 34 (3): 607–25.

Nikolenyi, Cs. and Shenhav, S. (2011). In search of party unity: explaining the adoption of anti-defection legislation in Israel and India. Unpublished typescript.

Norton, P. (2004). How many bicameral legislatures are there? *The Journal of Legislative Studies* 10 (4): 1–9.

Norton, P. and Olson, D. M. (2007). Post-communist and post-Soviet legislatures: beyond transition. *Journal of Legislative Studies* 13 (1): 1–11.

ODIHR (Office for Democratic Institutions and Human Rights). 1999. *Republic of Estonia Parliamentary Elections, 7 March 1999*. Warsaw: Organization for Security and Cooperation in Europe.

Olson, D. M. (1998). Party formation and party system consolidation in the democracies of Central Europe. In R. Hofferbert (ed.), *Parties and Democracy*. Oxford: Blackwell, 10–42.

Olson, D. M. (1999). From electoral symbol to legislative puzzle: the Polish Senat. In S. Patterson and A. Mughan (eds.), *Senates: Bicameralism in the Contemporary World*. Columbus: Ohio State University Press, 301–32.

Olson, D. and Crowther, W. E. (2002). *Committees in Post-Communist Democratic Parliaments: Comparative Institutionalization*. Columbus: Ohio State University Press.

Olson, D. M. and Ilonszki, G. (2012). *Post-Communist Parliaments: Change and Stability in the Second Decade*. London: Routledge.

Olson, D. M. and Norton, P. (2007). Post-communist and post-soviet parliaments: divergent paths from transition. *Journal of Legislative Studies* 13 (1): 164–96.

Ostrow, J. M. (2000). *Comparing Post-Soviet Legislatures: A Theory of Institutional Design and Political Conflict*. Columbus: Ohio State University Press.

Patterson, S. and Mughan, A. (eds.) (1999). *Senates: Bicameralism in the Contemporary World*. Columbus: Ohio State University Press.

Pech, G. (2004). Coalition governments versus minority governments: bargaining power, cohesion and budgeting outcomes. *Public Choice* 121 (1–2): 1–24.

Pettai, V. (2002). Estonia. *European Journal of Political Research* 41: 947–51.

Pettai, V. (2004). The parliamentary elections in Estonia, March 2003. *Electoral Studies,* 23: 828–34.

Pettai, V. (2007). Estonia. *European Journal of Political Research* 46: 943–8.

Pettai, V. and Kreuzer, M. (1999). Party politics in the Baltic States: social bases and institutional context. *East European Politics and Society* 13 (1): 148–89.

Pető, I. (1995). Az MSZP- SZDSZ kormánykoalíció. In *Magyarország Politikai Évkönyve 1995*. [The governing coalition of the MSZP and the SZDSZÍ in Hungary's Political Yearbook 1995]. Budapest: Demokracia Kutatasok Kozpontja, 168–86, at 176.

Pilet, J. B. and de Waele, J. M. (2007). Electoral reforms in Romania: towards a majoritarian electoral system? *European Electoral Studies* 2 (1): 63–79.

Polonsky, A. (1972). *Politics in Independent Poland: The Crisis of Constitutional Government*. Oxford: Clarendon Press.

Popescu, M. (2003). The parliamentary and presidential elections in Romania, November 2000. *Electoral Studies* 22: 325–35.

Powell, B. G. (2000). *Elections as Instruments of Democracy*. New Haven: Yale University Press.

Proksch, S. and Slapin, J. B. (2006). Institutions and coalition formation: the German election of 2005. *West European Politics* 29 (3): 540–59.

Protsyk, O. (2005). Prime ministers' identity in semi-presidential regimes: constitutional norms and cabinet formation outcomes. *European Journal of Political Research* 44 (5): 721–48.

Protsyk, O. (2006). Intra-executive competition between president and prime minister: patterns of institutional conflict and cooperation under semi-presidentialism. *Political Studies* 54: 219–44.

Rae, D. (1967). *The Political Consequences of Electoral Laws*. New Haven: Yale University Press.

Reif, K. (1987). Party government in the Fifth French Republic. In R. Katz (ed.), *Party Governments: European and American Experiences*. Berlin: Walter de Gruyter, 78–117.

Remington, T. F. (1994). *Parliaments in Transition: The New Legislative Politics in the Former USSR and Eastern Europe*. Boulder: Westview Press.

Remington, T. F. and Smith, S. (1996). Political goals, institutional context, and the choice of an electoral system: the Russian parliamentary election law. *American Journal of Political Science* 40 (4): 1253–79.

RFE/RL (Radio Free Europe/Radio Liberty) Archives. http://www.rferl.org/info/archive/1854.html Accessed on June 8, 2014.

Richter, J. (2008a). Presidential campaign heats up. *Czech Radio*. http://www.radio.cz/en/article/100369 Last accessed: May 27, 2014.

Richter, J. (2008b). Communists nominate Jana Bobosikova as their candidate for president. *Czech Radio*. http://www.radio.cz/en/article/100796 Last accessed: May 27, 2014.

Riker, W. (1962). *Theory of Political Coalitions*. New Haven: Yale University Press.

Roberts, A. (2003). Demythologizing the Czech opposition agreement. *Europe-Asia Studies* 55 (8): 1273–303.

Roberts, A. (2006). What kind of democracy is emerging in Eastern Europe? *Post- Soviet Affairs* 22 (1): 37–64.

Robertson, J. D. (1983). The political economy and the durability of european coalition cabinets: new variations on a game theoretic perspective. *Journal of Politics* 45: 932–57.

Rohrschneider, R. and Whitefield, S. (2009). Understanding cleavages in party systems: issue position and issue salience in 13 post-communist democracies. *Comparative Political Studies* 42 (2): 280–313.

Rose, R. (1995). Mobilizing demobilized voters in post-communist societies. *Party Politics* 1 (4): 549–63.

Rose, R. and Munro, N. (2003). *Elections and Parties in New European Democracies*. Washington, D.C.: CQ Press.

Roozendaal, P. van. (1992a). The effect of dominant and central parties on cabinet composition and durability. *Legislative Studies Quarterly* 17: 5–35.

Roozendaal, P. van. (1992b). *Cabinets in Multi-Party Democracies: The Effect of Dominant and Central Parties on Cabinet Composition and Durability*. Amsterdam: Thesis Publishers.

Roozendaal, P. van. (1998). Coalition predictions with ordinal policy position data. *British Journal of Political Science* 24 (1): 132–8.

Rotschild, J. and Wingfield, N. M. (2008). *Return to Diversity: A Political History of East Central Europe Since World War II*, 4th edition. New York: Oxford University Press.

Royal Institute of International Affairs (1938 [1970]). *The Baltic States: A Survey of the Political and Economic Structure and the Foreign Relations of Estonia, Latvia, and Lithuania*. Reprinted by Westport, Conn.: Greenwood Press.

Rueschmeyer, M. and Wolchik, S. L. (2009). *Women in Power in Post-Communist Parliaments*. Indiana: Indiana University Press.

Rybar, M. (2007). The parliamentary election in Slovakia, June 2006. *Electoral Studies* 26: 699–703.

Sakamoto, T. (2001). Effects of government characteristics on fiscal deficits in 18 OECD countries, 1961–1994. *Comparative Political Studies* 34 (5): 527–54.

Sakamoto, T. (2005). Economic performance of 'weak' governments and their interaction with central banks and labour: deficits, economic growth, unemployment and inflation, 1961–1998. *European Journal of Political Research* 44 (6): 801–36.

Samuels, D. and Shugart, M. S. (2010). *Presidents, Parties, and Prime Ministers: How the Separation of Power Affects Party Organization and Behavior*. Cambridge: Cambridge University Press.

Sanders, D. and Herman, V. (1977). The stability and survival of governments in western democracies. *Acta Politica* 12: 346–77.

Sartori, G. (1976). *Parties and Party Systems: A Framework for Analysis*. Cambridge: Cambridge University Press.

Schleiter, P. and Morgan-Jones, E. (2009a). Party government in Europe? Parliamentary and semi-presidential democracies compared. *European Journal of Political Research* 48 (5): 665–93.

Schleiter, P. and Morgan-Jones, E. (2009b). Constitutional power and competing risks: monarchs, presidents, prime ministers, and the termination of East and West European cabinets. *American Political Science Review* 103 (3): 496–512.

Schleiter, P. and Morgan-Jones, E. (2009c). Review article: citizens, presidents, and assemblies. The study of semi-presidentialism beyond Duverger and Linz. *British Journal of Political Science* 39 (4): 871–92.

Schleiter, P. and Morgan-Jones, E. (2009d). Party control over European cabinets? *European Journal of Political Research* 48 (5): 665–93.

Schleiter, P. and Morgan-Jones, E. (2010). Who's in charge? Presidents, assemblies and the political control of semi-presidential cabinets. *Comparative Political Studies* 43 (11): 1415–41.

Schofield, N. (2007). Political equilibria with electoral uncertainty. *Social Choice and Welfare* 28 (3): 461–90.

Schopflin, G. (1993). *Politics in Eastern Europe*. Oxford: Blackwell.

Shabad, G. and Slomczynski, K. M. (2004). Inter-party mobility among parliamentary candidates in postcommunist East Central Europe. *Party Politics* 10: 151–76.

Shepsle, K. A. and Laver, M. (1996). *Making and Breaking Governments: Cabinets and Legislatures in Parliamentary Democracies*. Cambridge: Cambridge University Press.

Shugart, M. S. (1998). The inverse relationship between party strength and executive strength. *British Journal of Political Science* 28: 1–29.

Shugart, M. S. and Carey, J. M. (1992). *Presidents and Assemblies: Constitutional Design and Electoral Dynamics*. Cambridge: Cambridge University Press.

Shugart, M. S. and Wattenberg, M. P. (eds.) (2001). *Mixed-Member Electoral Systems*. Oxford: Oxford University Press.

Siaroff, A. (2003a). Comparative presidencies: the inadequacy of the presidential, semi-presidential and parliamentary distinction. *European Journal of Political Research* 42: 287–312.

Siaroff, A. (2003b). Varieties of parliamentarism in the advanced industrial democracies. *International Political Science Review* 24 (4): 445–64.

Spirova, M. (2006). The parliamentary elections in Bulgaria, June 2005. *Electoral Studies* 25 (3): 616–21.

Spirova, M. (2010). The 2009 parliamentary elections in Bulgaria. *Electoral Studies* 29 (2): 276–8.

Staar, R. F. (1962). *Poland 1944–1962: The Sovietization of a Captive People*. Louisiana: Louisiana State University Press.

Stan, L. (2005). From riches to rags: the Romanian Christian Democrat Peasant Party. *East European Quarterly* 39 (2): 179–227.

Stan, L. (2005). The opposition takes charge: the Romanian general elections of 2004. *Problems of Post-Communism* 52 (3): 3–15.

Stan, L. (2009). Old wine in new bottles: the Romanian elections of 2008. *Problems of Post-Communism* 56 (5): 47–61.

Strom, K. (1984a). Minority governments in parliamentary democracies: the rationality of nonwinning cabinet solutions. *Comparative Political Studies* 17 (2): 199–227.

Strom, K. (1985). Party goals and government performance in parliamentary democracies. *American Political Science Review* 79 (3): 738–54.

Strom, K. (1990). *Minority Government and Majority Rule.* New York: Cambridge University Press.

Strom, K., Browne, E. C., Frendreis, J. P. and Glieber, D. W. (1988). Contending models of cabinet stability. *American Political Science Review* 82: 930–41.

Strom, K., Budge, I. and Laver, M. (1994). Constraints on cabinet formation in parliamentary democracies. *American Journal of Political Science* 38: 303–35.

Strom, K., Müller-Rommel, W. C. and Bergman, T. (eds.) (2003). *Delegation and Accountability in Parliamentary Democracies.* Oxford: Oxford University Press.

Strom, K., Müller-Rommel, W. C. and Bergman, T. (eds.) (2010). *Cabinets and Coalition Bargaining: the Democratic Life Cycle in Western Europe.* Oxford: Oxford University Press.

Swaan, A. de. (1973). *Coalition Theory and Cabinet Formation: A Study of Formal Theories of Coalition Formation Applied to Nine European Parliaments After 1981.* Amsterdam: Elsevier Scientific Publishing Company.

Szczerbiak, A. (1999). The impact of the 1998 local elections on the emerging Polish Party system. *Journal of Communist Studies and Transition Politics* 15 (3): 80–100.

Szczerbiak, A. (2002). Poland's unexpected political earthquake: the September 2001 parliamentary election. *Journal of Communist Studies and Transition Politics* 18 (3): 41–76.

Szcerbiak, A. (2004). The Polish centre-right's (last?) best hope: the rise and fall of solidarity electoral action. *Journal of Communist Studies and Transition Politics* 20 (3): 55–79.

Taras, R. (ed.) (1997). *Postcommunist Presidents.* Cambridge: Cambridge University Press, 1997.

Tavits, M. (2005). The development of stable party support: electoral dynamics in post-communist Europe. *American Journal of Political Science* 49: 283–98.

Tavits, M. (2009). *President with Prime Ministers*. Oxford: Oxford University Press.

Taylor, M. and Hermann, V. M. (1971). Party systems and government stability. *American Political Science Review* 65: 28–37.

Taylor, M. and Michael, L. (1973). Government coalitions in western Europe. *European Journal of Political Research* 1: 205–48.

Toka, G. (1996). Parties and electoral choices in East Central Europe. In G. Pridham and P. Lewis (eds.), *Stabilizing Fragile Democracies: New Party Systems and Southern and Eastern Europe*. London: Routledge, 100–24.

Toka, G. (1997). *Political parties and democratic consolidation in East Central Europe*. Glasgow: Centre for the Study of Public Policy.

Toplak, J. (2006). The parliamentary election in Slovenia, October 2004. *Electoral Studies* 25: 825–31.

Tsebelis, G. (1988a). When do allies become rivals? *Comparative Politics* 20 (2): 233–40.

Tsebelis, G. (1988b). Nested games: the cohesion of French electoral coalitions. *British Journal of Political Science* 18 (2): 145–70.

Tsebelis, G. (1990). *Nested Games: Rational Choice in Comparative Politics*. Berkeley: The University of California Press.

Tsebelis, G. (1995). Decision making in political systems: veto players in presidentialism, parliamentarism, multicameralism and multipartyism. *British Journal of Political Science* 25 (3): 289–325.

Tsebelis, G. (2000). Veto players and institutional analysis. *Governance* 13 (4): 441–74.

Tsebelis, G. (2002). *Veto Players: How Political Institutions Work*. Princeton: Princeton University Press.

Tucker, J. (2006). *Regional Economic Voting: Russia, Poland, Hungary, Slovakia, and the Czech Republic*. Cambridge: Cambridge University Press.

Tworzecki, H. (2004). *Learning to Choose: Electoral Politics in East-Central Europe*. Stanford: Stanford University Press.

Ucen, P. (2003). Slovakia. *European Journal of Political Research* 42, 1067–77.

Velinger, J. (2008a). Christian Democrat leadership recommends lawmakers vote for Klaus. *Czech Radio*. http://www.radio.cz/en/article/99628 Last accessed: May 27, 2014.

Velinger, J. (2008b). Klaus and Svejnar to face off in presidential debate. *Czech Radio*. http://www.radio.cz/en/article/99857 Last accessed: May 27, 2014.

Virgilio, A. D. (1998). Electoral alliances: party identities and coalition games. *European Journal of Political Research* 34: 5–33.

Webb, P. and White, S. (2007). *Party Politics in New Democracies*. Oxford: Oxford University Press.

Wenzel, M. (1998). Solidarity and Akcja Wyborcza "Solidarnosc": an attempt at reviving the legend. *Communist and Post-Communist Studies* 31 (2): 139–56.

White, S. and MacAllister, I. (1995). *How Russia Votes*. Chatham: Chatham House.

Whitefield, S. (2002). Political cleavages and postcommunist politics. *Annual Review of Political Science* 5: 181–200.

Wiatr, J. (ed.) (1997). Special issue on "elections and parliaments in post-communist East Central Europe." *International Political Science Review* 18 (4).

Williams, K. (2003). Proportional representation in post-communist Eastern Europe: the first decade. *Representation* 40 (1): 44–54.

Willoughby, I. (2008a). Svejnar hoping to win over public but really needs to win more backing in parliament. *Czech Radio.* http://www.radio.cz/en/article/99375 Last accessed: May 27, 2014.

Willoughby, I. (2008b). Third round of voting in presidential election inconclusive. *Czech Radio.* http://www.radio.cz/en/article/100650 Last accessed: May 27, 2014.

Willoughby, I. and Johnston, R. (2008). First day of voting in presidential elections inconclusive. *Czech Radio.* http://www.radio.cz/en/article/100620 Last accessed: May 27, 2014.

Willoughby, I. and Richter, J. (2008). President and challenger appear in front of social democrat senators and the TV cameras. *Czech Radio.* http://www.radio.cz/en/article/100155 Last accessed: May 27, 2014.

Woldendorp, J. H. (1998). Party government in 20 democracies: an update (1990–1995). *European Journal of Political Research* 33: 125–64.

Woldendorp, J. H. (2000). *Party government in 48 democracies (1945–1998)*. London: Kluwer.

Zajc, D. (2007). Slovenia's national assembly 1992–2004." *Journal of Legislative Studies* 13 (1): 83–98.

Zielinski, J. (2002). Translating social cleavages into party systems: the significance of new democracies. *World Politics* 54 (2): 184–211.

Zubek, V. (1995). The phoenix out of the ashes: the rise to power of Poland's post-communist SdRP. *Communist and Post-Communist Studies* 28 (3): 275–306.

Index